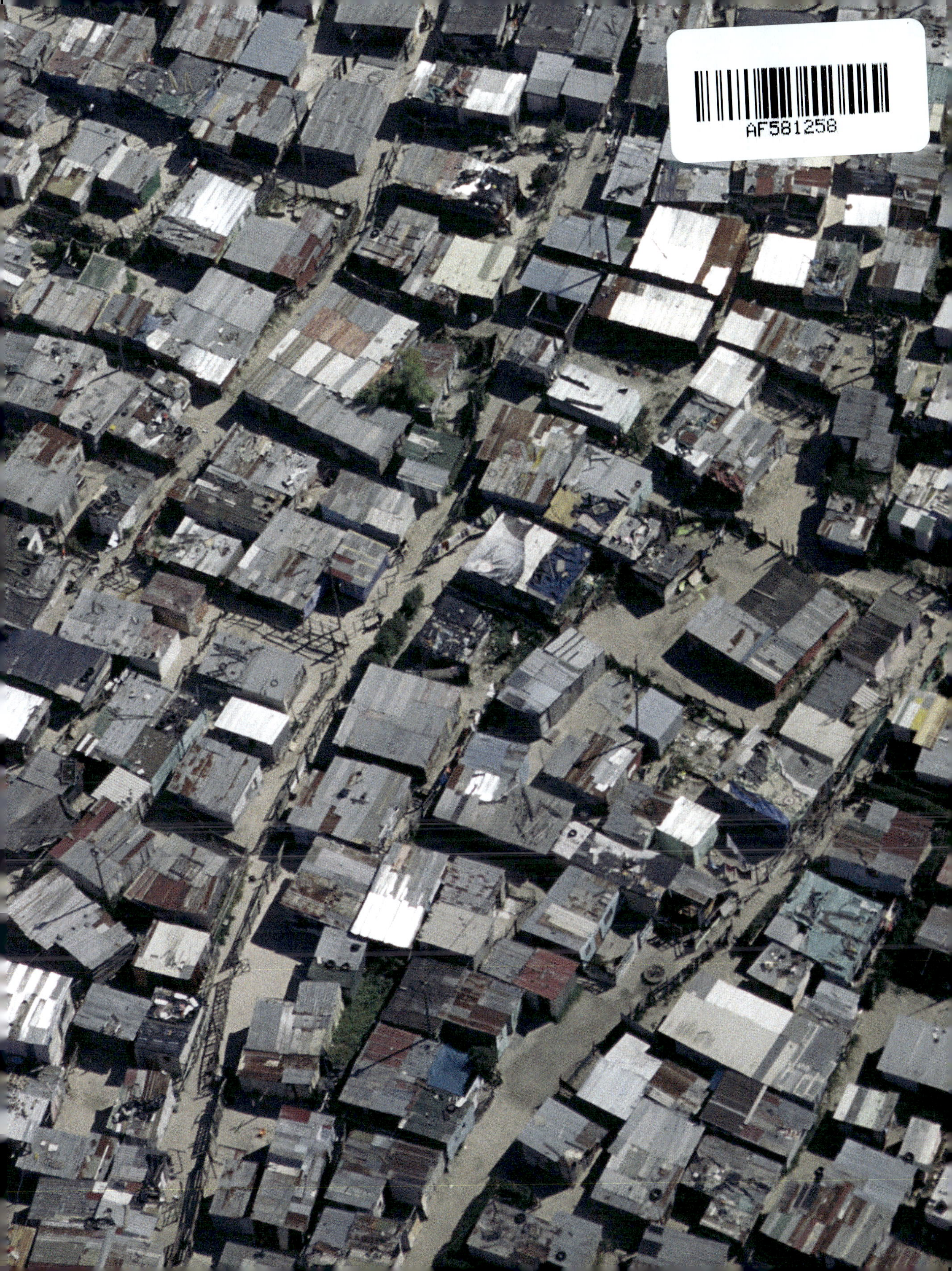

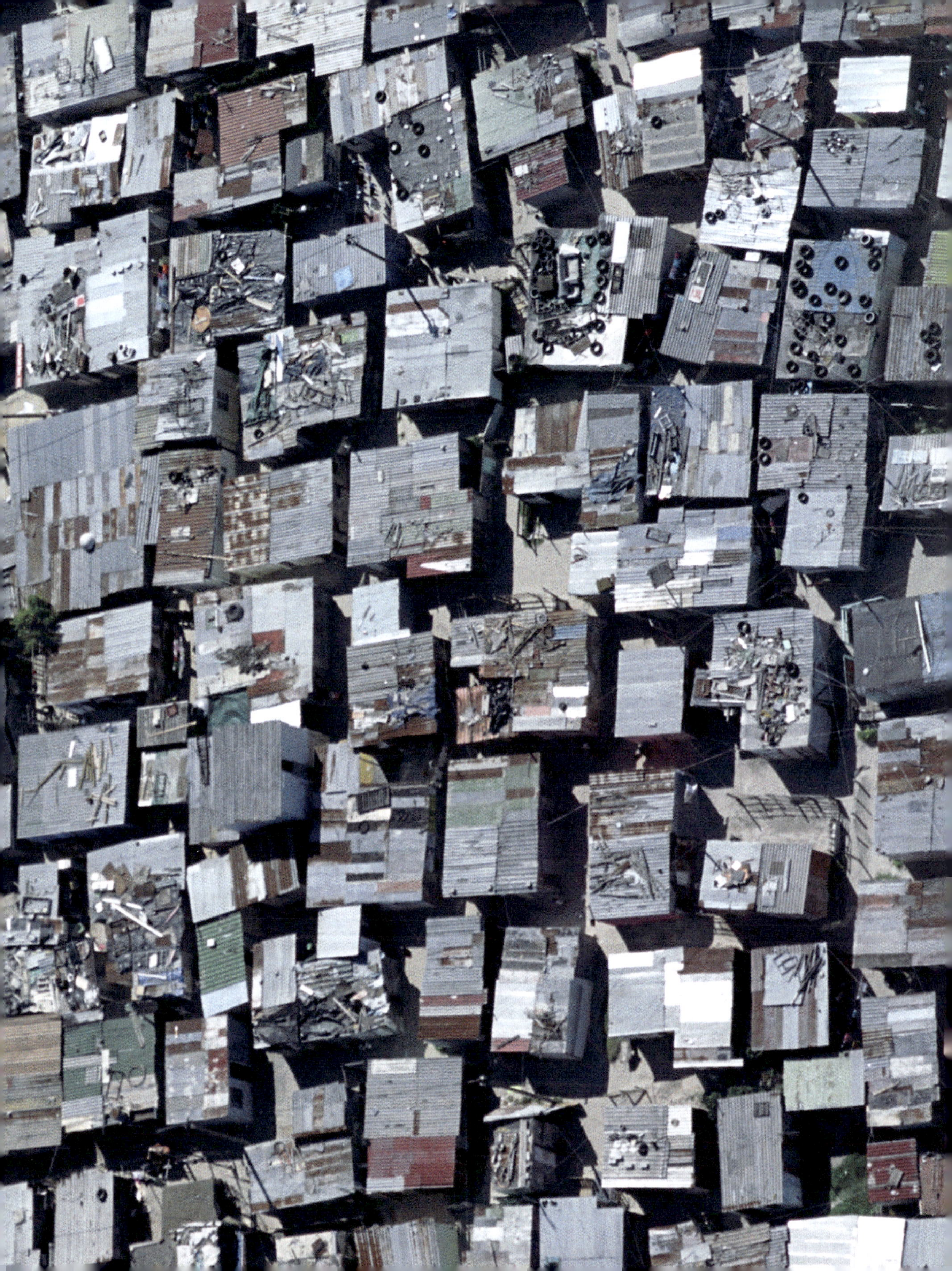

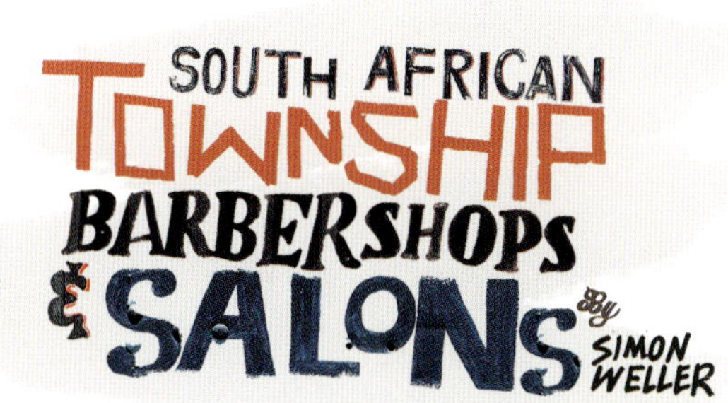
SOUTH AFRICAN
TOWNSHIP
BARBERSHOPS
& SALONS
By
SIMON
WELLER

In memory of my brother

ANDREW RICHARD WELLER

1976–2007

CONTENTS –

PRICE LIST
· AMAFRERHO
· CORNROWS
· BRAIDING
· PIECE/BONDING
· PERM
· RESTORE
· REVLON
· So Fn Free
· Sunsilk
· PRECISE
. AMAREL
. LONG N LASTING
. DARK & LOVELY MIX

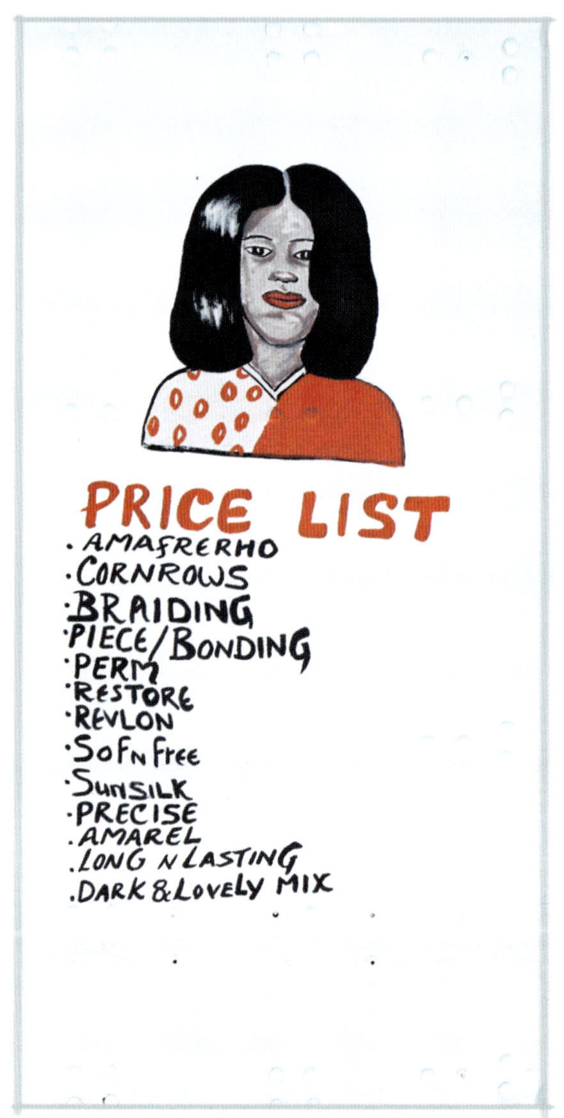

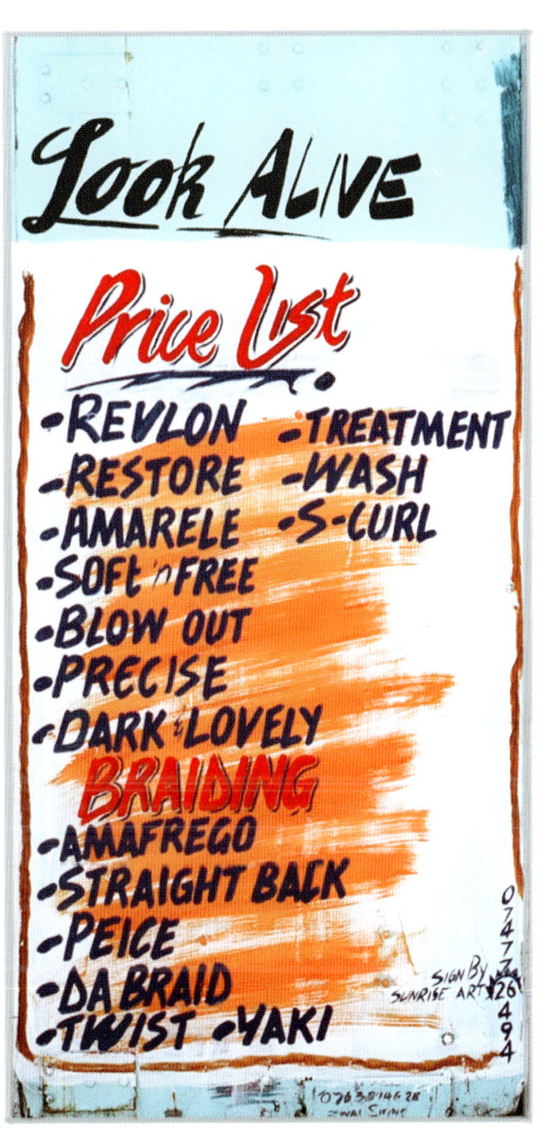
LOOK ALIVE
Price List
•REVLON •TREATMENT
•RESTORE •WASH
•AMARELE •S-CURL
•SOFT 'n FREE
•BLOW OUT
•PRECISE
•DARK & LOVELY
BRAIDING
•AMAFREGO
•STRAIGHT BACK
•PEICE
•DA BRAID
•TWIST •YAKI
SIGN BY
SUNRISE ART
0747726494

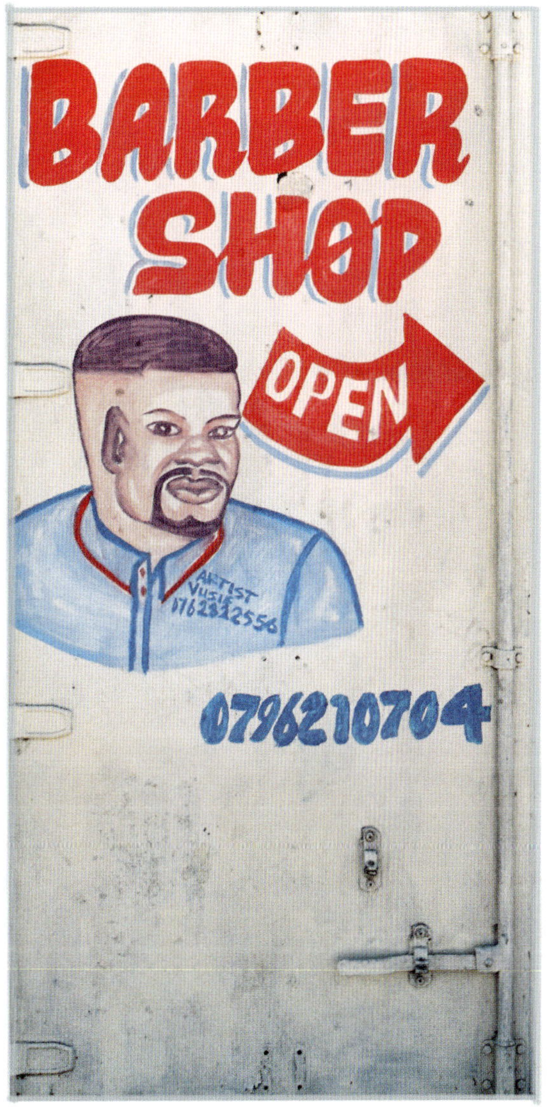
BARBER
SHOP
OPEN
ARTIST
VUSIE
0796210704

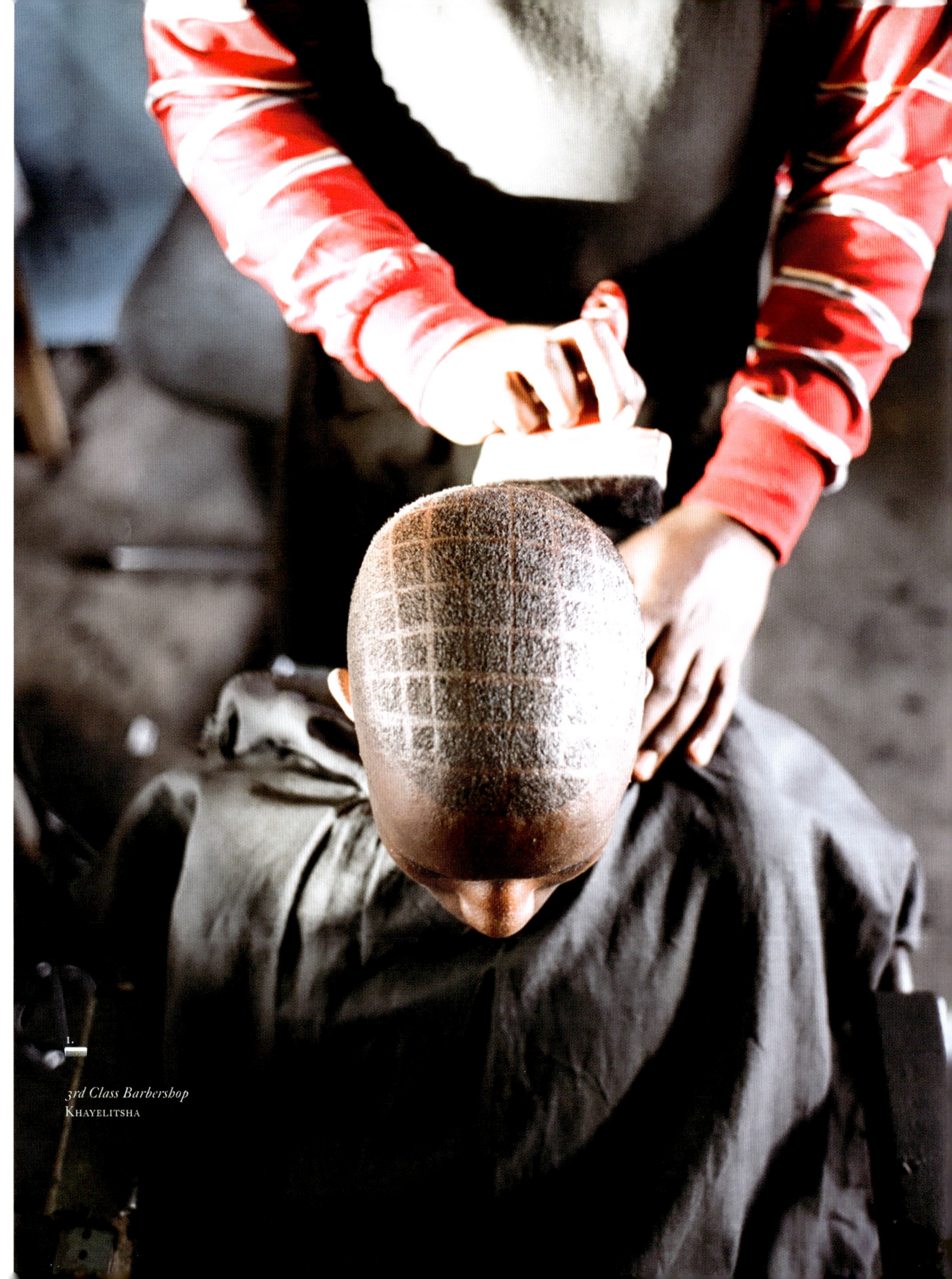

1.

3rd Class Barbershop
KHAYELITSHA

INTRODUCTION

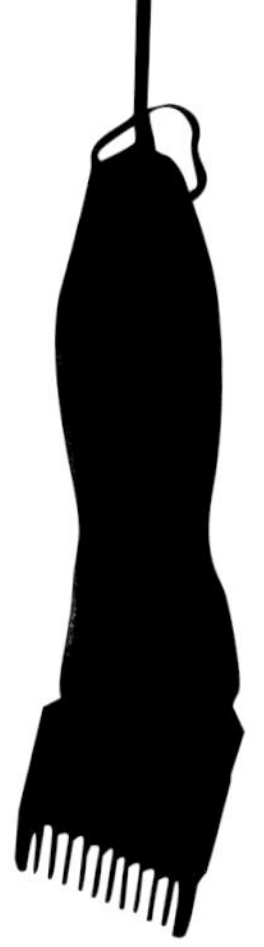

In 2009 I visited my first South African township. Working on a photo shoot in Cape Town I had met David, a local who was eager to take me for a drink in the township of Gugulethu. Having spent a number of weeks in the country I'd had neither the opportunity nor inclination to visit a township. Despite being more than a little nervous, I decided to join him.

Growing up in 1980s England during the height of Apartheid and the State of Emergency imposed in South Africa, I was aware of the dangerous reputations that the black townships had earned. Nightly news showed rioting residents throwing rocks and petrol bombs at the armored police and army vehicles deployed to quell the uprising. In 1990 I sat with my family watching the televised coverage of Nelson Mandela's historic release from prison after twenty-seven years of captivity, the beginning of the end of Apartheid.

Apartheid, an Afrikaans word for "apartness," was the white government's policy of segregation that resulted in worldwide condemnation and led to South Africa becoming a pariah state for many years. The 1950 Group Areas Act No. 41 was a law that forced all non-whites out of the cities and into densely populated slums: townships. To this day the townships are notorious for their crime, disease and poverty and for most white South Africans they are no-go areas that only the brave or foolhardy visit.

But here I was in Mzoli's, a popular township restaurant, with David and hundreds of other people, watching a televised football match, laughing, chatting, drinking and eating. When the home team scored a goal a huge cheer erupted, making for a carnival-like atmosphere. There was no animosity toward me at all, although I was the only white person. Most of my preconceptions had been shattered, but I was still paranoid about my camera bag being snatched. David told me not to worry because the code of honor in the townships works differently. The police have very little presence in these areas so the community relies on its members to enforce the law. The townships have plenty of resident criminals, but committing a crime in their neighborhood is rarely tolerated.

Driving through the township after our meal, I began to notice that one type of business was thriving: barbershops. There were dozens of them housed in an assortment of ramshackle structures and repurposed shipping containers with names like Let's Fix It Barbershop, Try Again Hair Shop and Look Alive Salon. A stunning and enigmatic variety of hand-painted artwork adorned these businesses, illustrating the hairstyles on offer. At the time there was no chance to properly photograph these places, but I promised myself that I would return to South Africa to document this colorful barbershop culture. This book is the fulfillment of that promise.

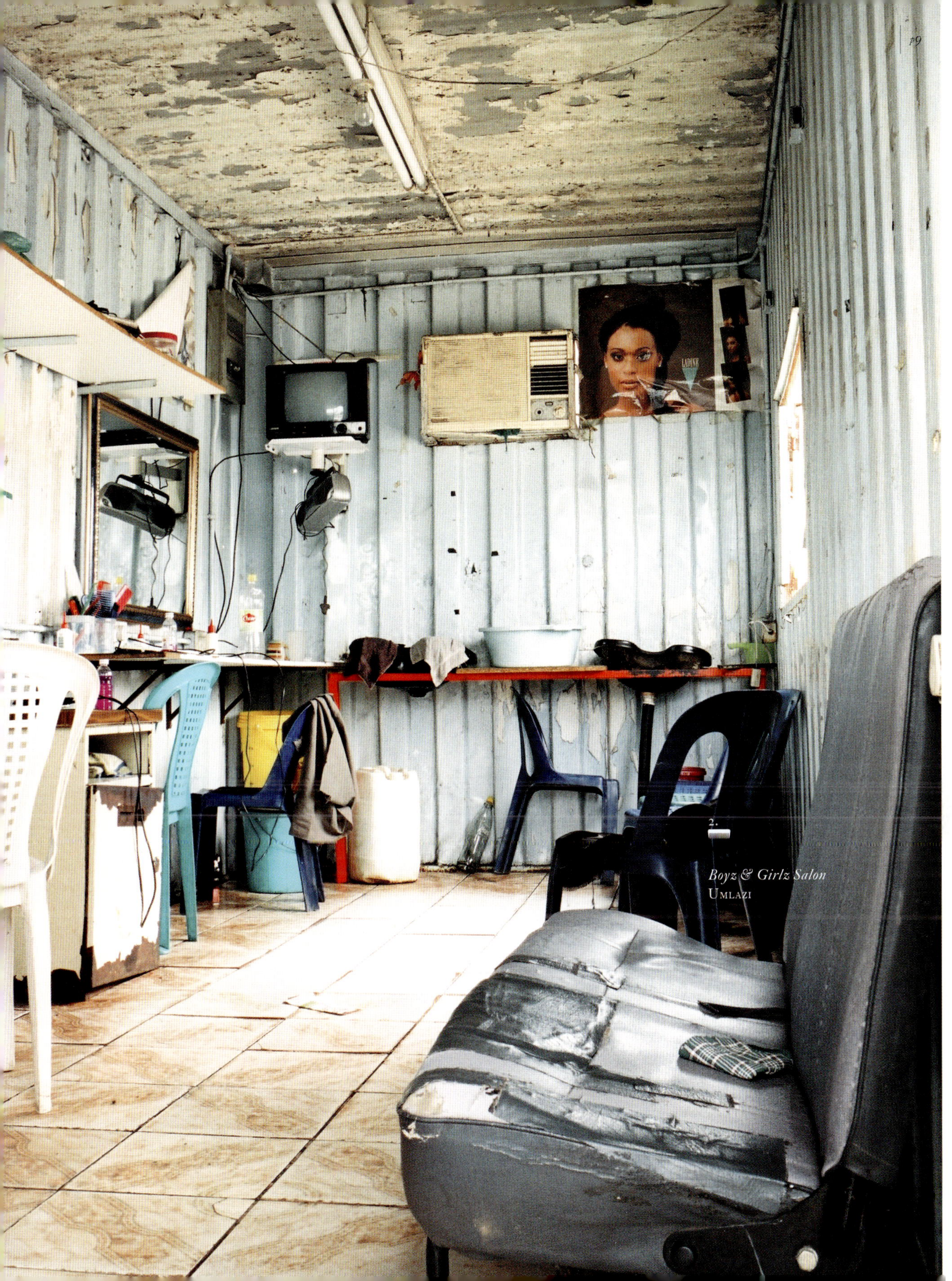

2.

Boyz & Girlz Salon
Umlazi

CHAPTER 1
JOHANNESBURG

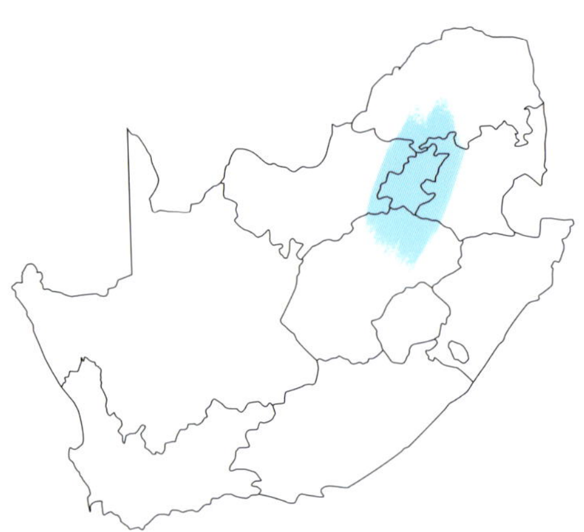

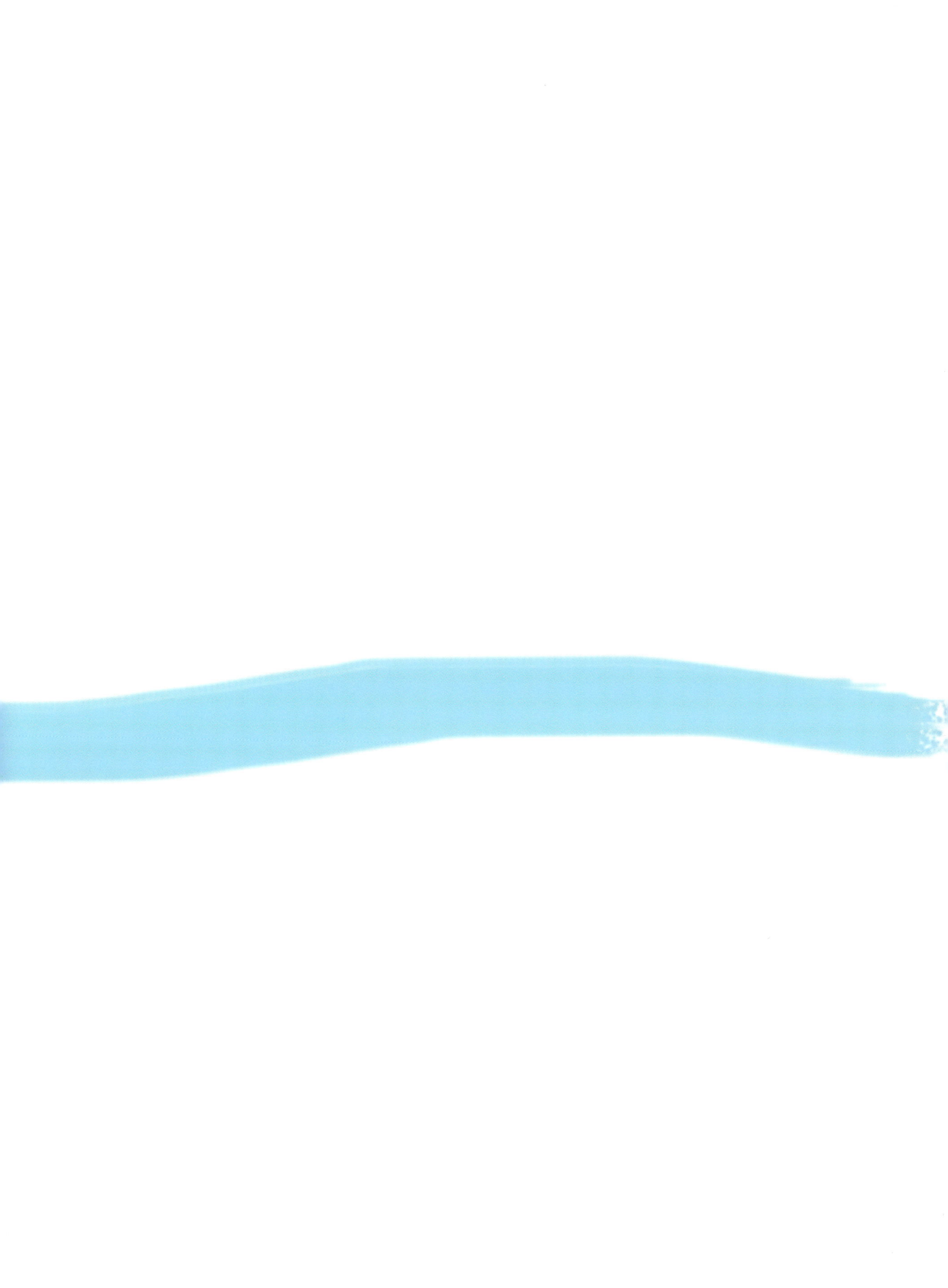

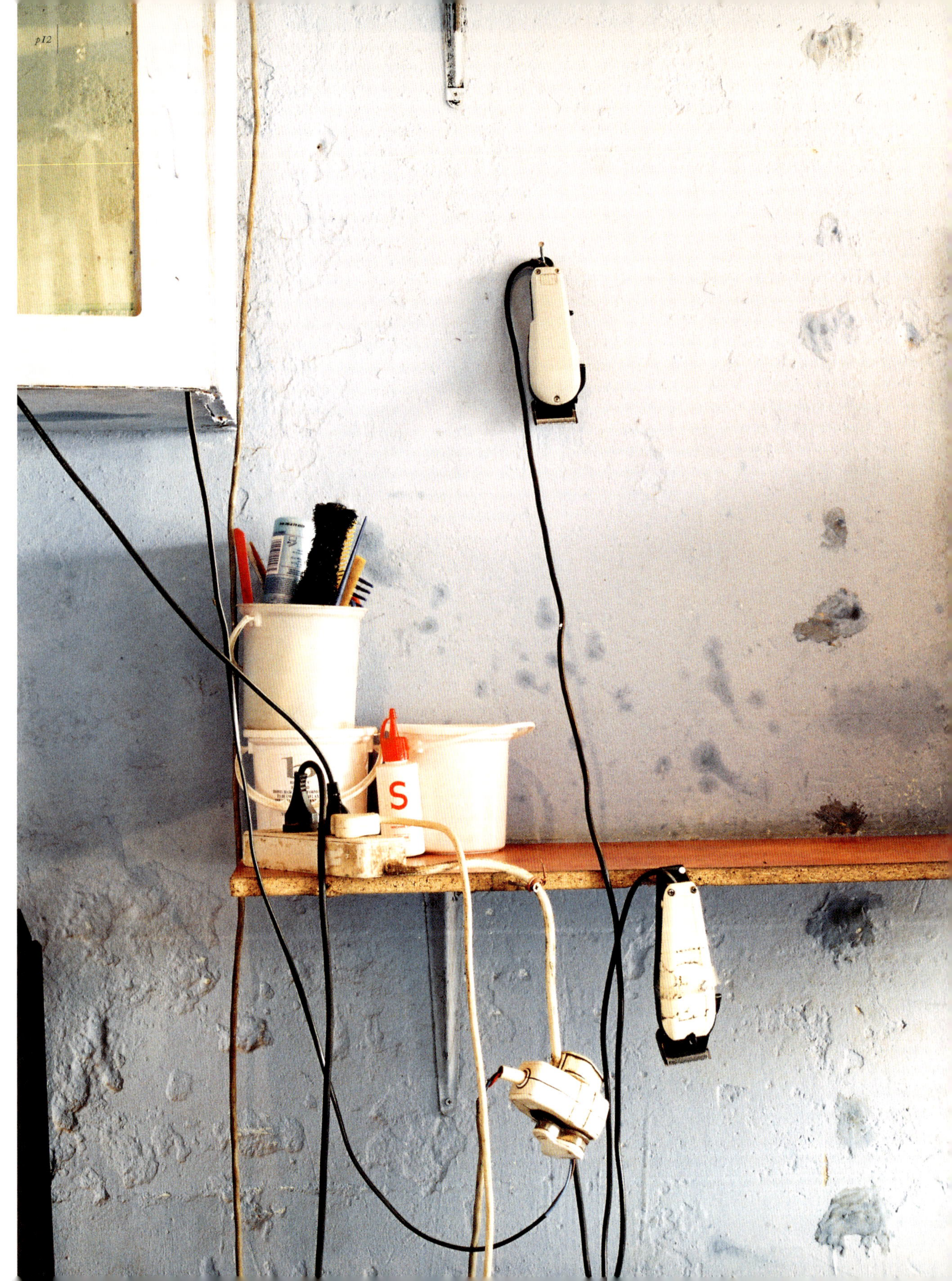
p12
S

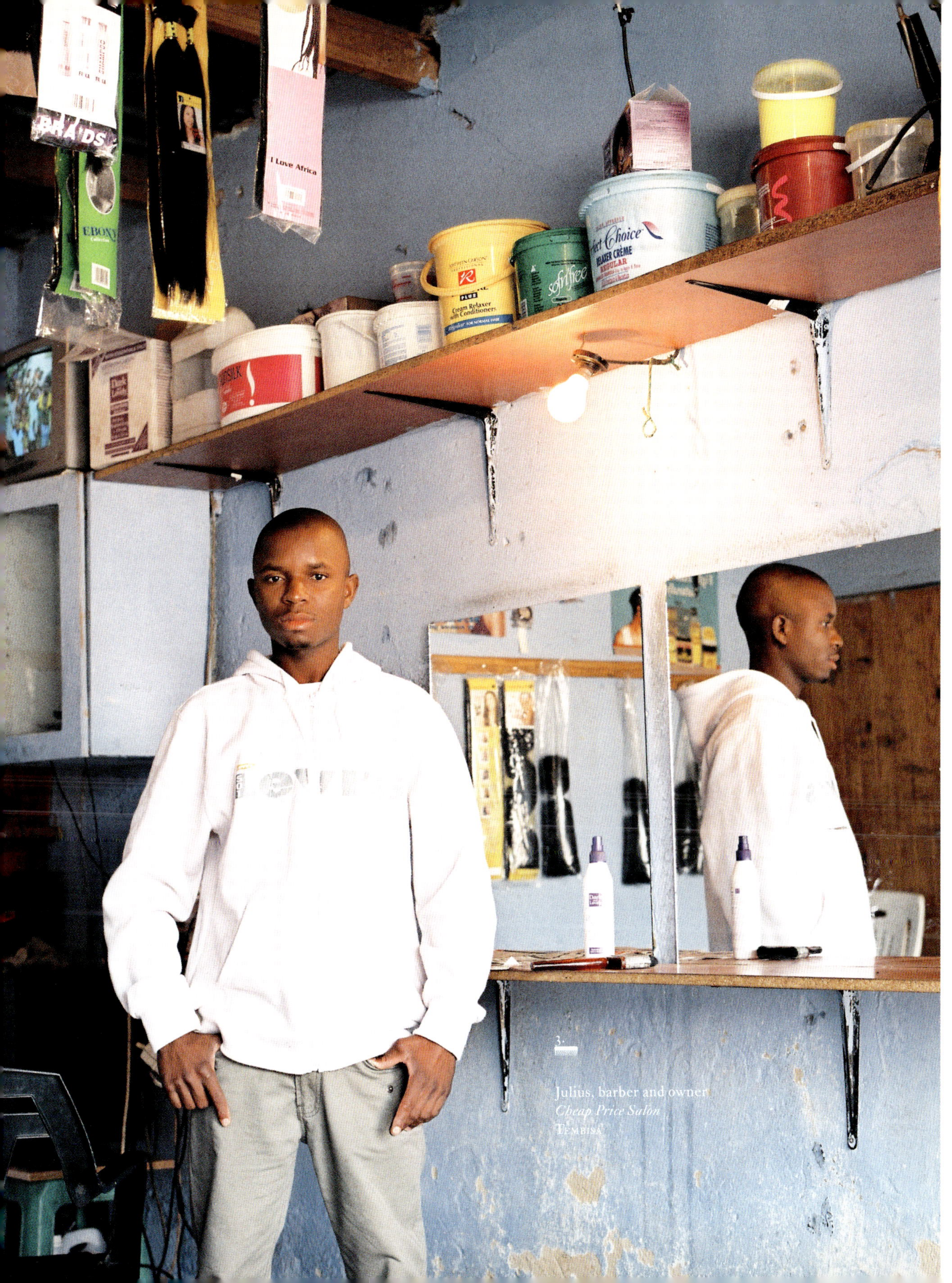

3.

Julius, barber and owner
Cheap Price Salon
Tembisa

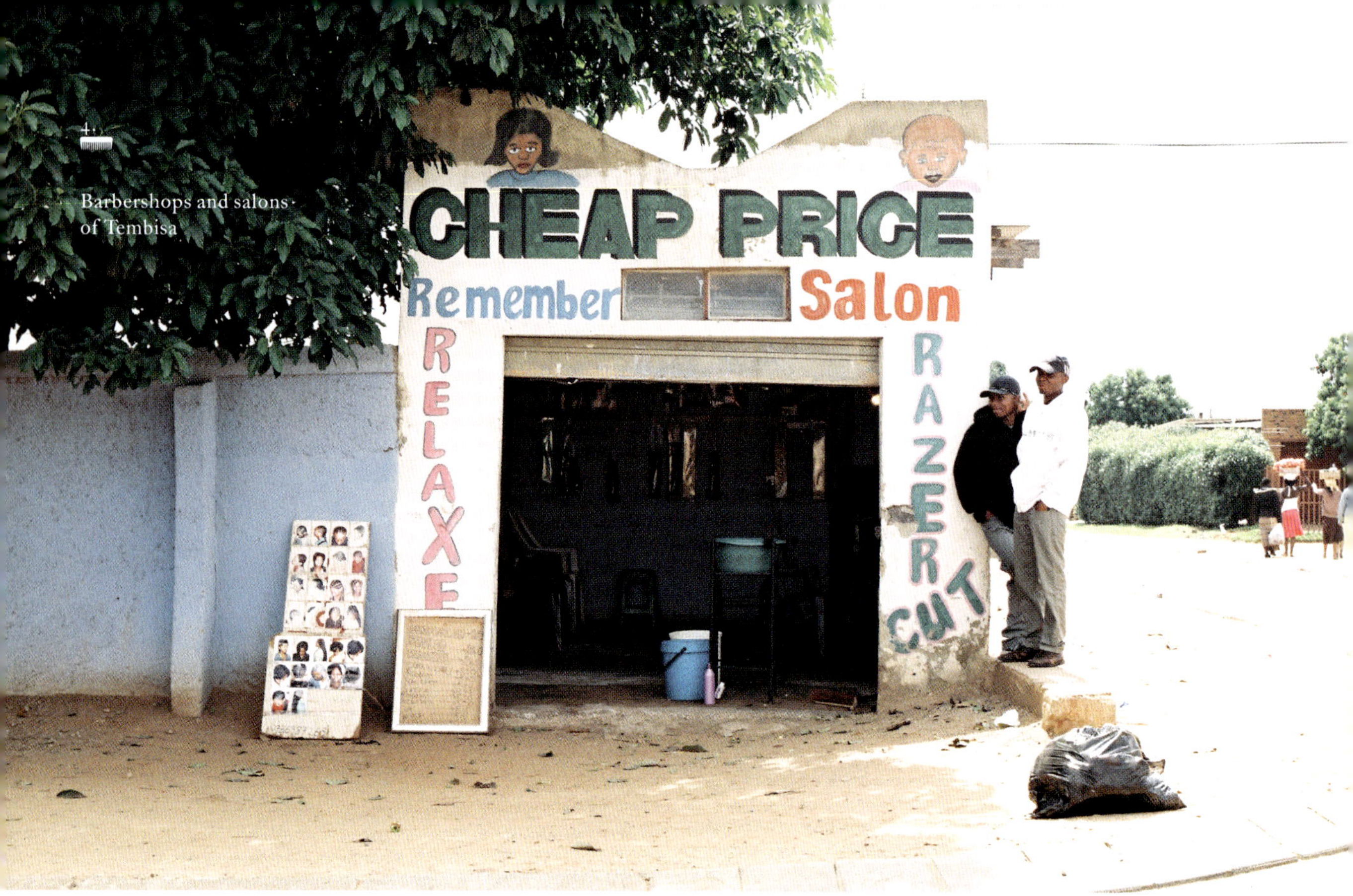

4

Barbershops and salons of Tembisa

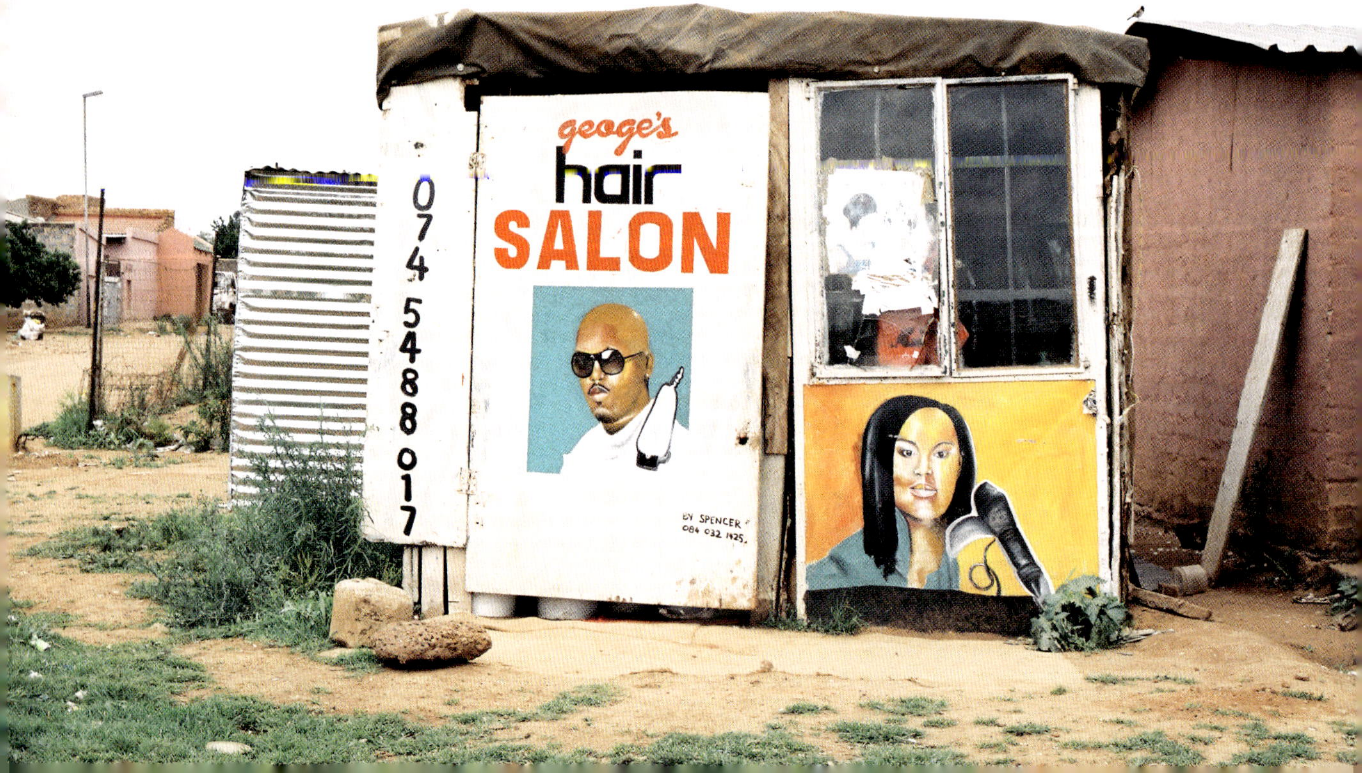

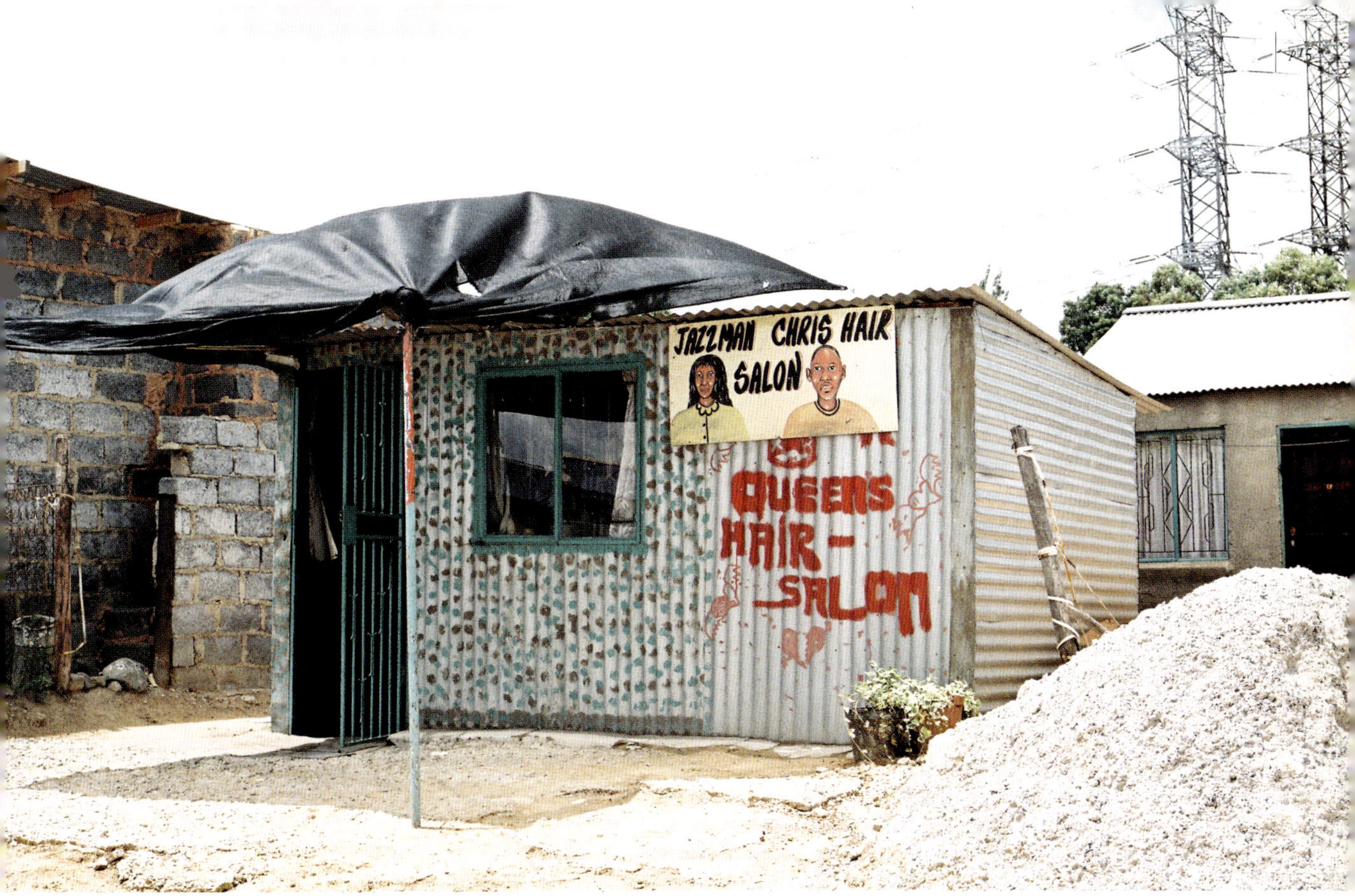

JAZZMAN CHRIS HAIR
SALON
QUEENS
HAIR-
SALOM

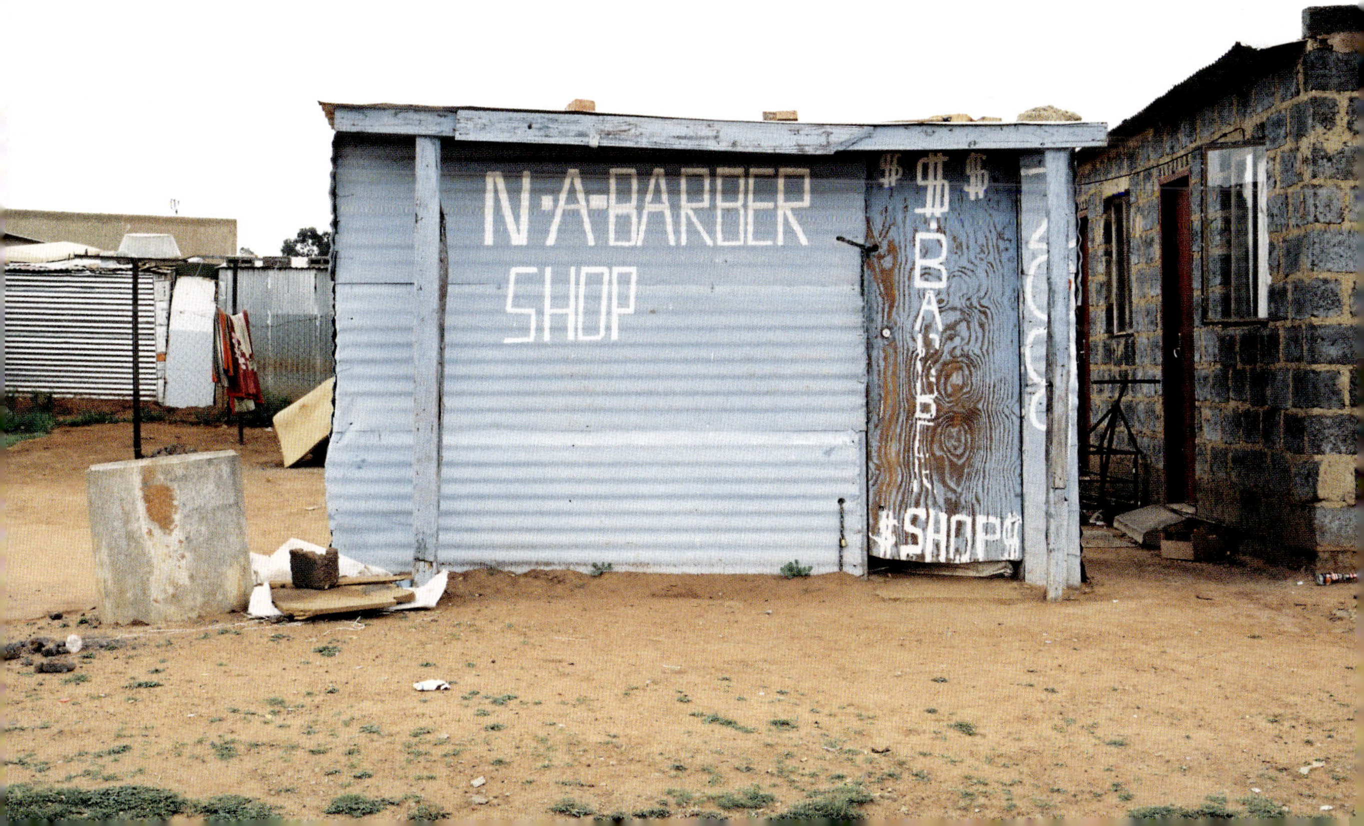

N·A·BARBER
SHOP
$ $ $
$BARBER
$SHOP$

1.1 TEMBISA

Meet Dr Phil. Dr Phil is neither a doctor nor is his name Phil. He is a thirty-eight-year-old black South African businessman and driving instructor actually named Edwin. His favorite American celebrity – the talk show host and TV agony uncle – inspired the nickname. This Dr Phil drives a BMW, is dressed smartly in a black shirt, white chinos and a pair of expensive looking snakeskin shoes. He lives on the border of the large township of Tembisa in northeastern Johannesburg and has offered to act as my escort.

"This one is too professional, we should keep driving," Dr Phil insists, shaking his head. We have just driven past an up-market salon and its very slick Revlon sign and studio photograph of an attractive model. Dr Phil explains that the establishments that have caught my attention are known as "informal barbershops" or "street salons." For the most part, these sorts of barbershops and salons attract customers with vernacular signage and distinctive paintings, typically borne out of visual aspects of African American popular culture, from Hollywood to hip-hop.

Hastily constructed from sheet metal, wood and assorted reclaimed materials, many of these businesses exist rent free, and often lack running water and electricity. The barbers and stylists improvise with buckets of water to wash hair and car batteries to power the clippers. Extremely popular with the community, not only do these places offer cheap haircuts, but they serve as social hubs.

As we begin to visit the shops I notice a trend in behavior: the locals claim to know nothing about who works there, or they just leave. A white officer on patrol with his black partner is not an uncommon sight in South Africa. That we are both wearing sunglasses and driving a flashy BMW gives locals the impression that we are out to make an arrest. Only after Dr Phil explains my project do people open up, very happy to have a stranger take interest in something they take for granted.

By mid afternoon we head to Dr Phil's favorite lunch spot, an old lady's house, with a busy kitchen cooking for a number of people. After eating, Dr Phil drops me off and I reflect on a very successful first day in Johannesburg.

Despite a number of attempts to organize with Dr Phil another day in the Tembisa area he proves impossible to track down. My friend Rudi suggests that I talk to Lydia, the cleaning lady at his office who lives in the township, to see if her son Treasure will show me around. Treasure seems up for the challenge and finds a friend with a car. They pick me up in a battered VW Golf. The driver, Sello, looks about fourteen. It appears that Sello has never driven a car before, stalling constantly, crunching the gears and running through intersections.

Somehow we manage to make it to Tembisa in one piece and begin the search for informal barbershops. Treasure actually seems far more interested in chatting up the young ladies working in the various salons we visit. We drive around for hours and, although I do get some good material, the day is not as fruitful as the previous excursion with Dr Phil. What I do get though is real insight into township life through the eyes of two young men.

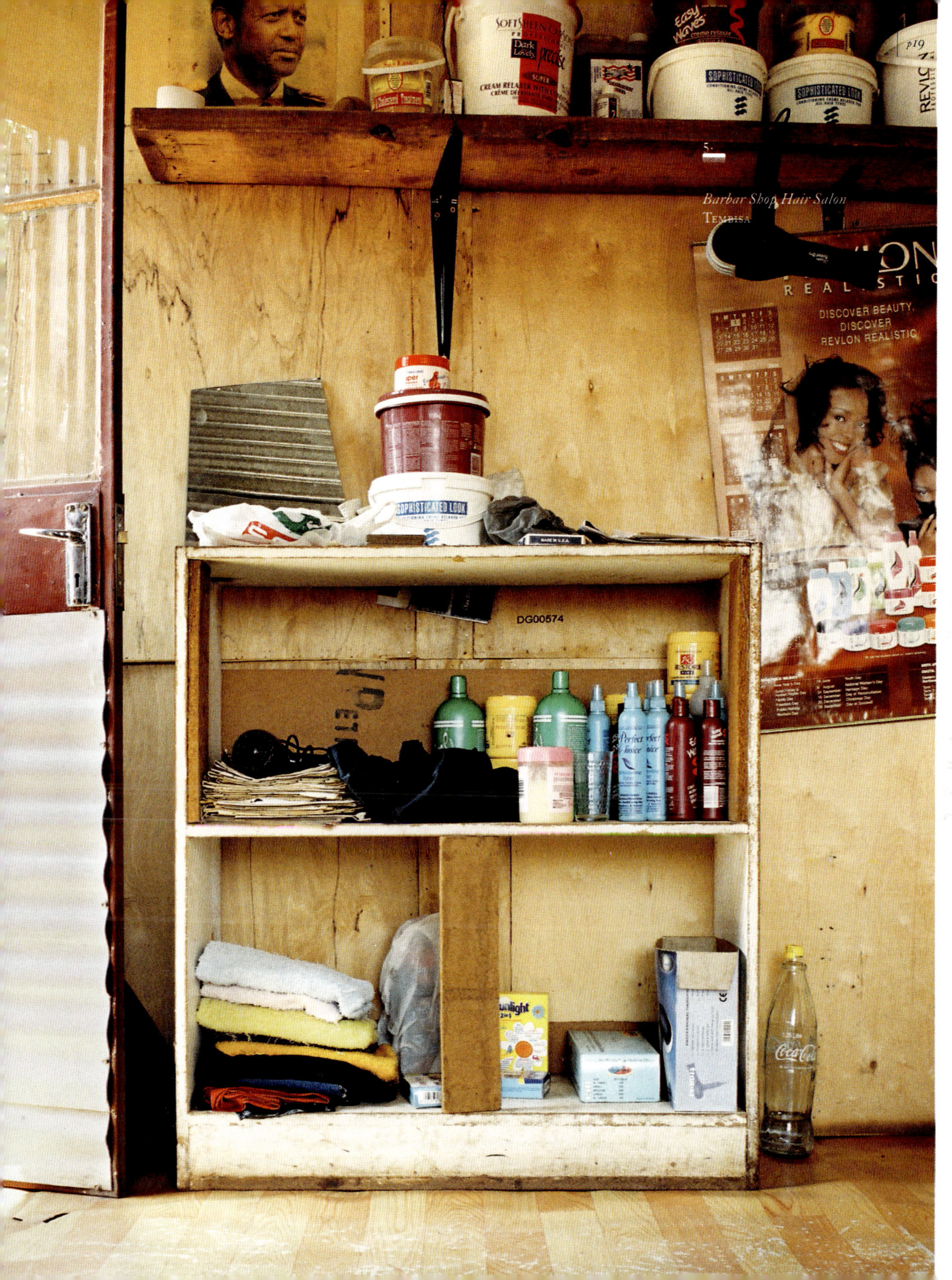

5.

Barbar Shop Hair Salon

Tembisa

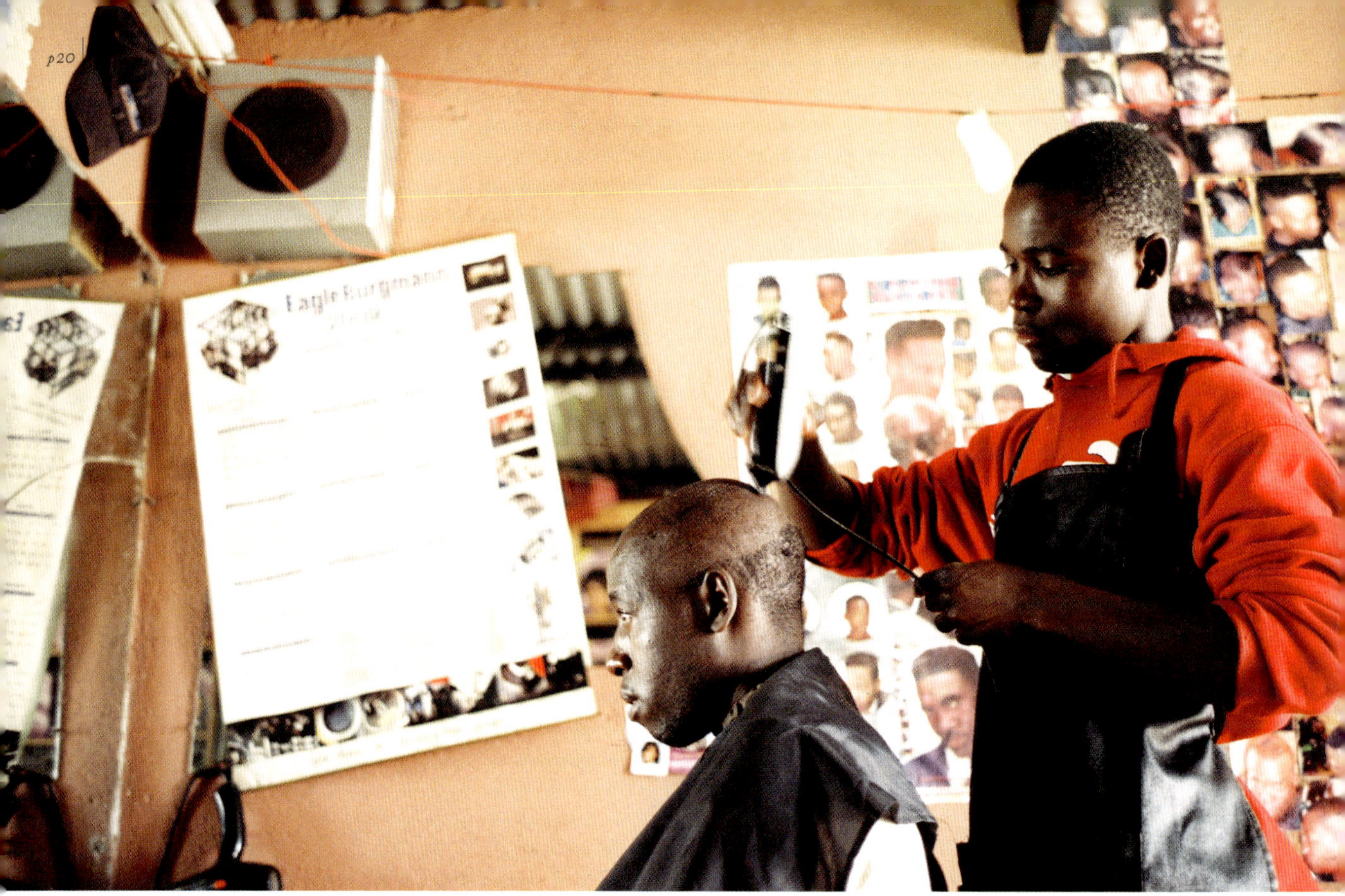

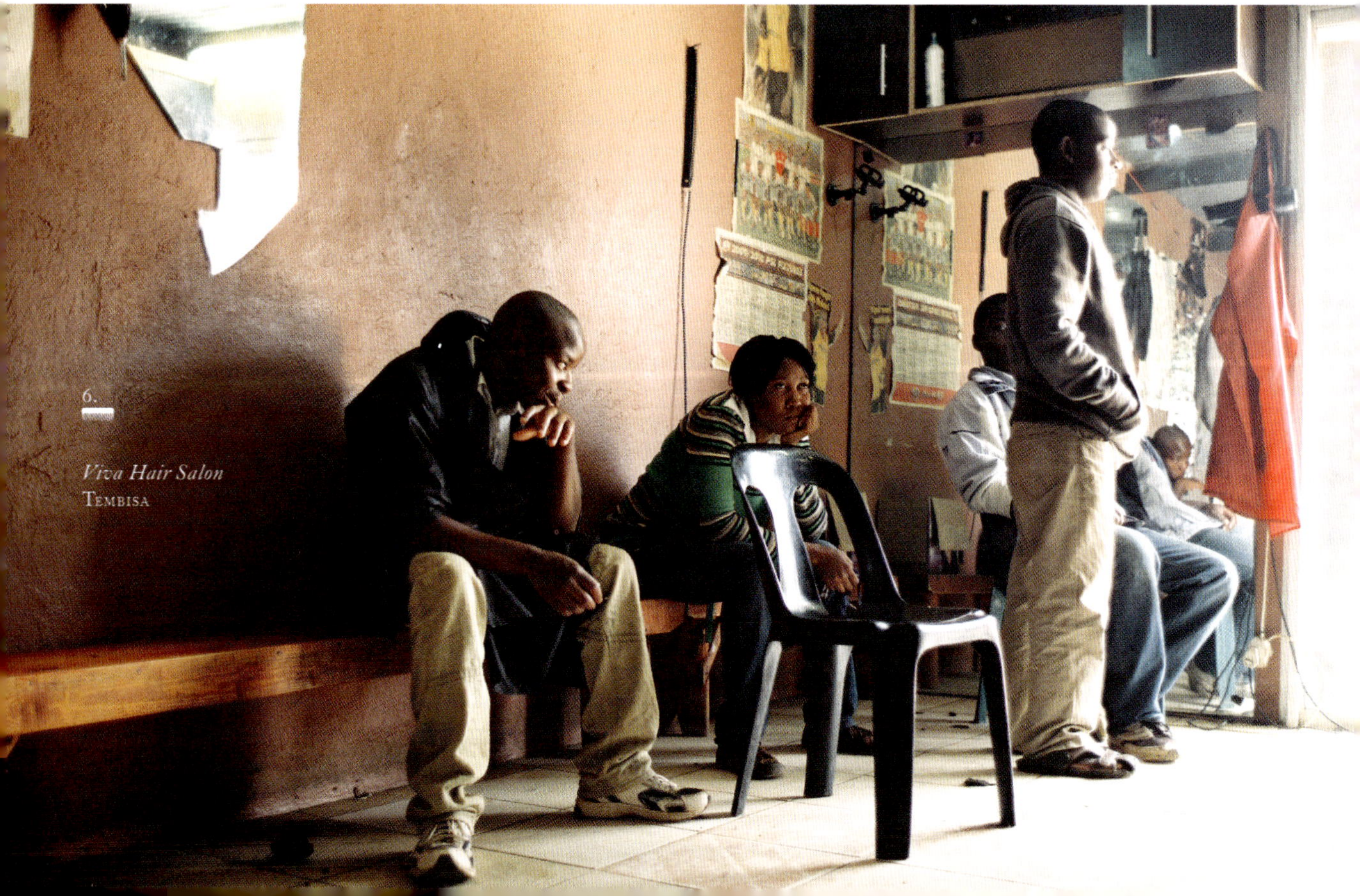

6.

Viva Hair Salon
Tembisa

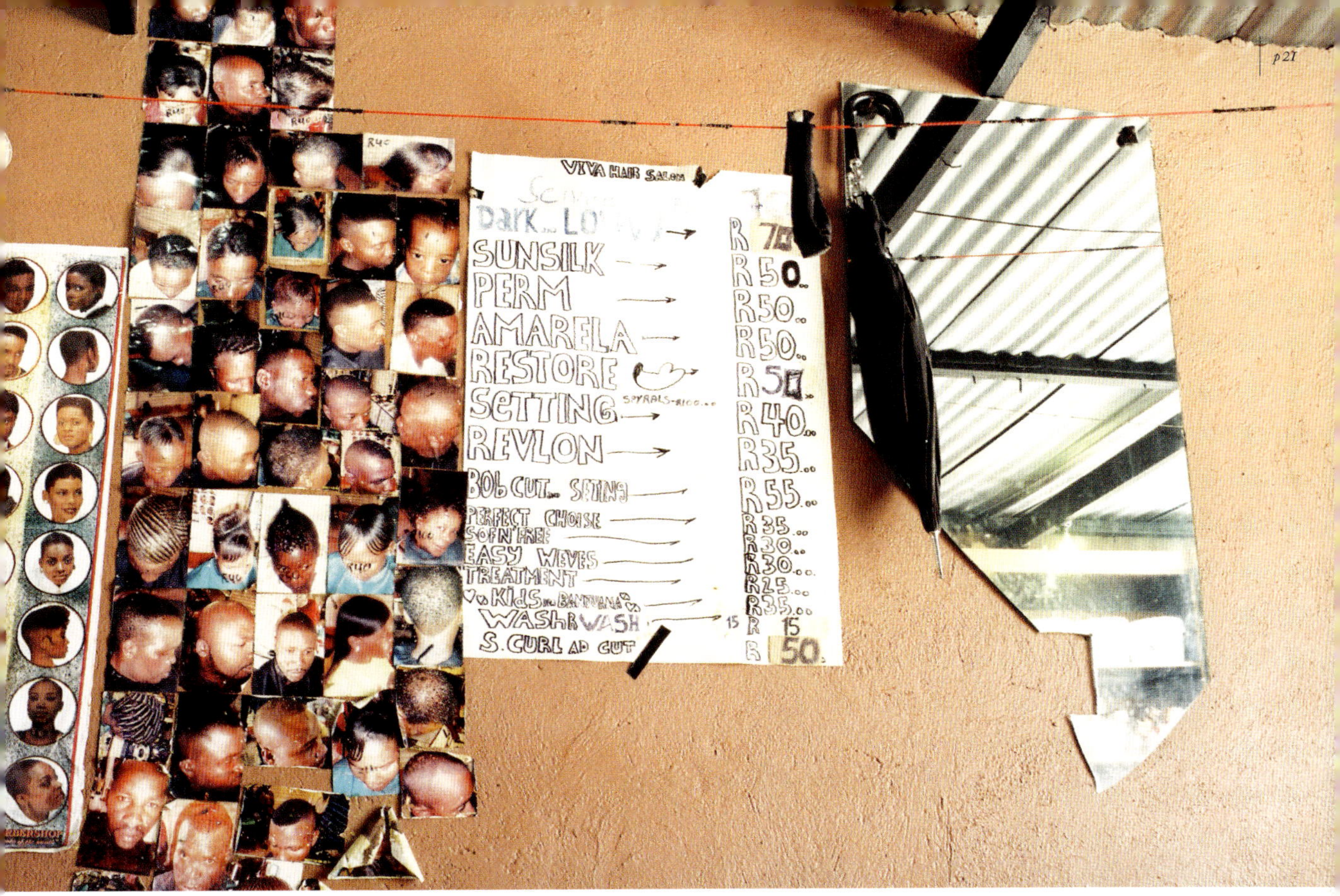

VIVA HAIR SALON
DARK... LOVELY → R 70
SUNSILK → R 50..
PERM → R 50..
AMARELA → R 50..
RESTORE → R 50..
SETTING → R 40..
SPYRALS - R100...
REVLON → R 35..
BOB CUT... SETTING → R 55..
PERFECT CHOISE → R 35..
SOFN'FREE → R 30..
EASY WEVES → R 30..
TREATMENT → R 25..
KIDS ... BANTUANA → R 35..
WASH & WASH → 15 R 15
S. CURL AD CUT R 50
HERITAGE
PAINTS

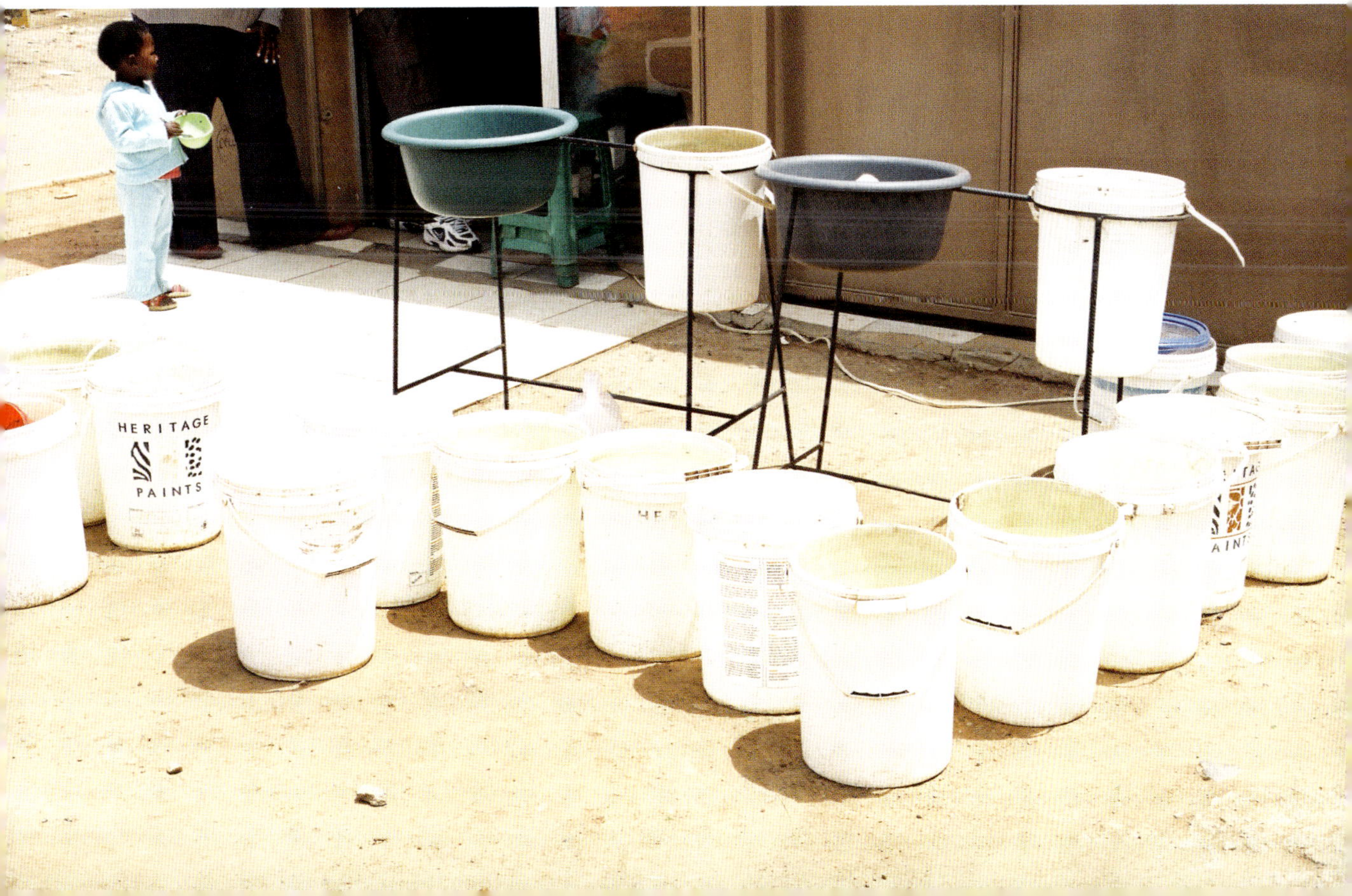

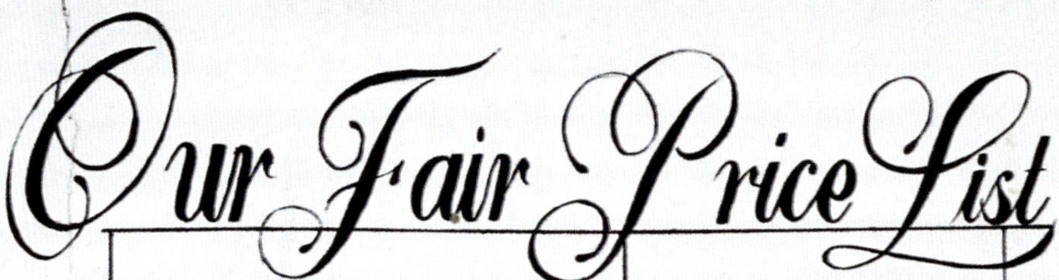
Our Fair Price List
1. Sof n' free R25
2. Revlon R30
3. Dark & Lovely R45
4. Restore R35
5. Easy Waves R30
6. SunSilk R35
7. S. Curl R25
8. Wash (Hair) R10
9. S. Curl N' Cut R30
10. Treatment R20
11. Perfect Choice R35
12. Set. rubbish R15
13. Cut R10
14. Brush R7
15. Chiskop R7
16. Shaving R3
BRADING
1. BONDING R100
2. BOY CUT R150
3. POP CUT R150
4. RAZER-CUT R150
5. STRAIGHT-B R80
6. STRAIGHT-UP R100
Thank You
PAPPAS
(0843548871)
35440736)

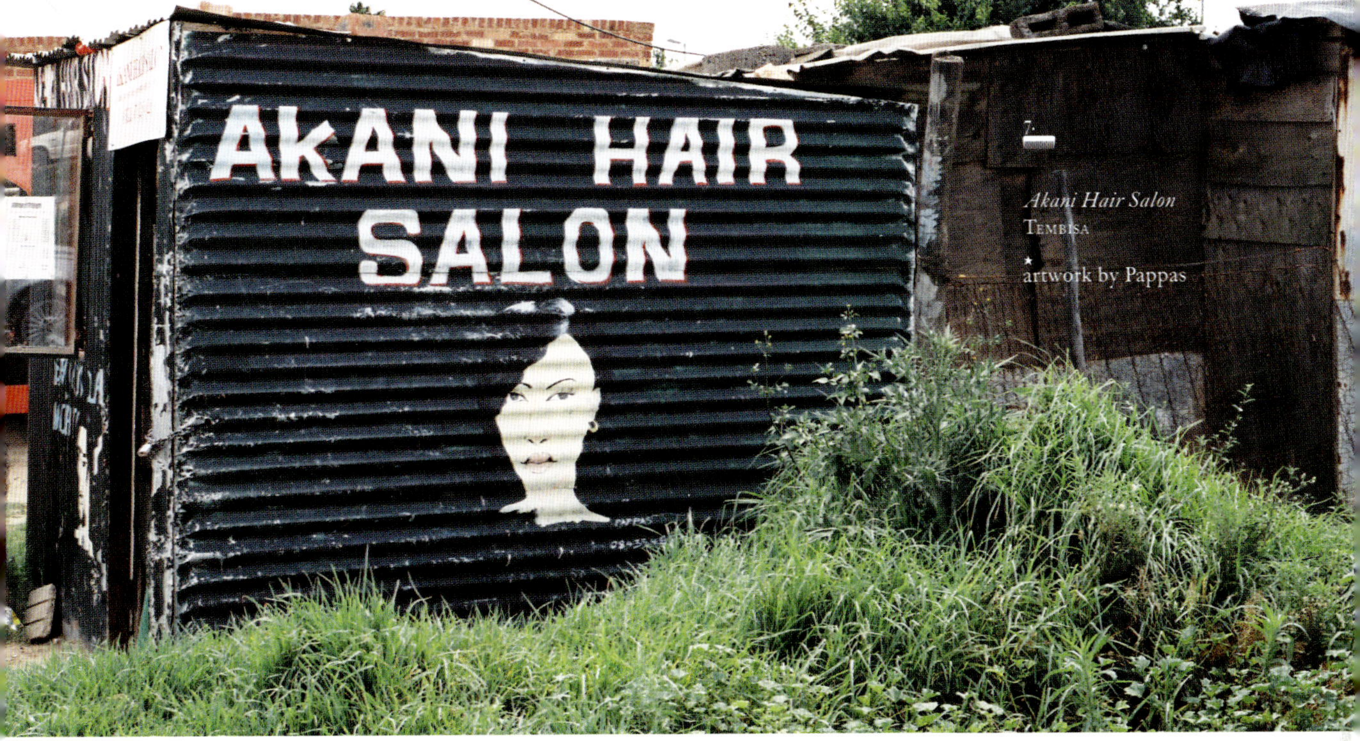

7.

Akani Hair Salon
Tembisa
★
artwork by Pappas

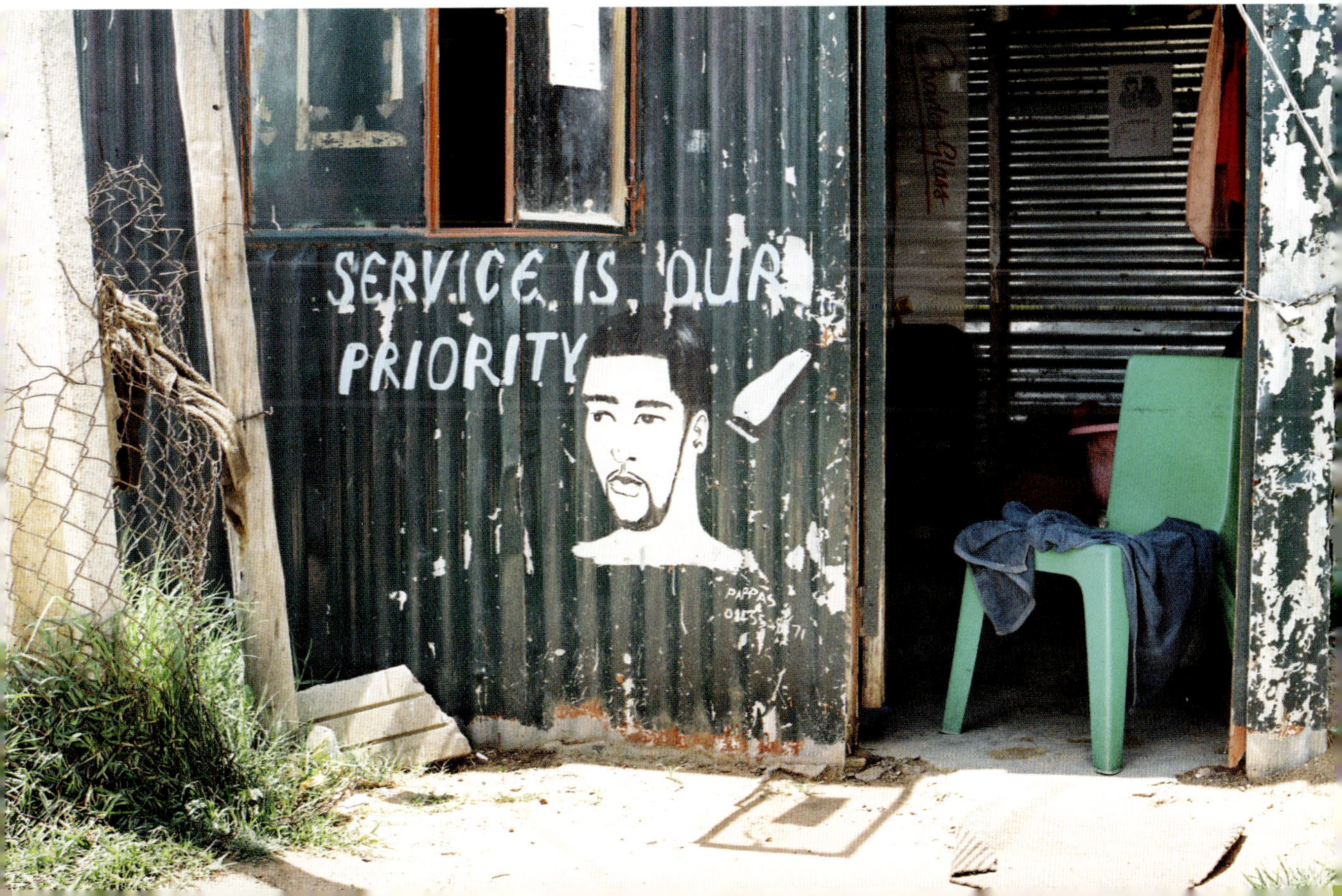

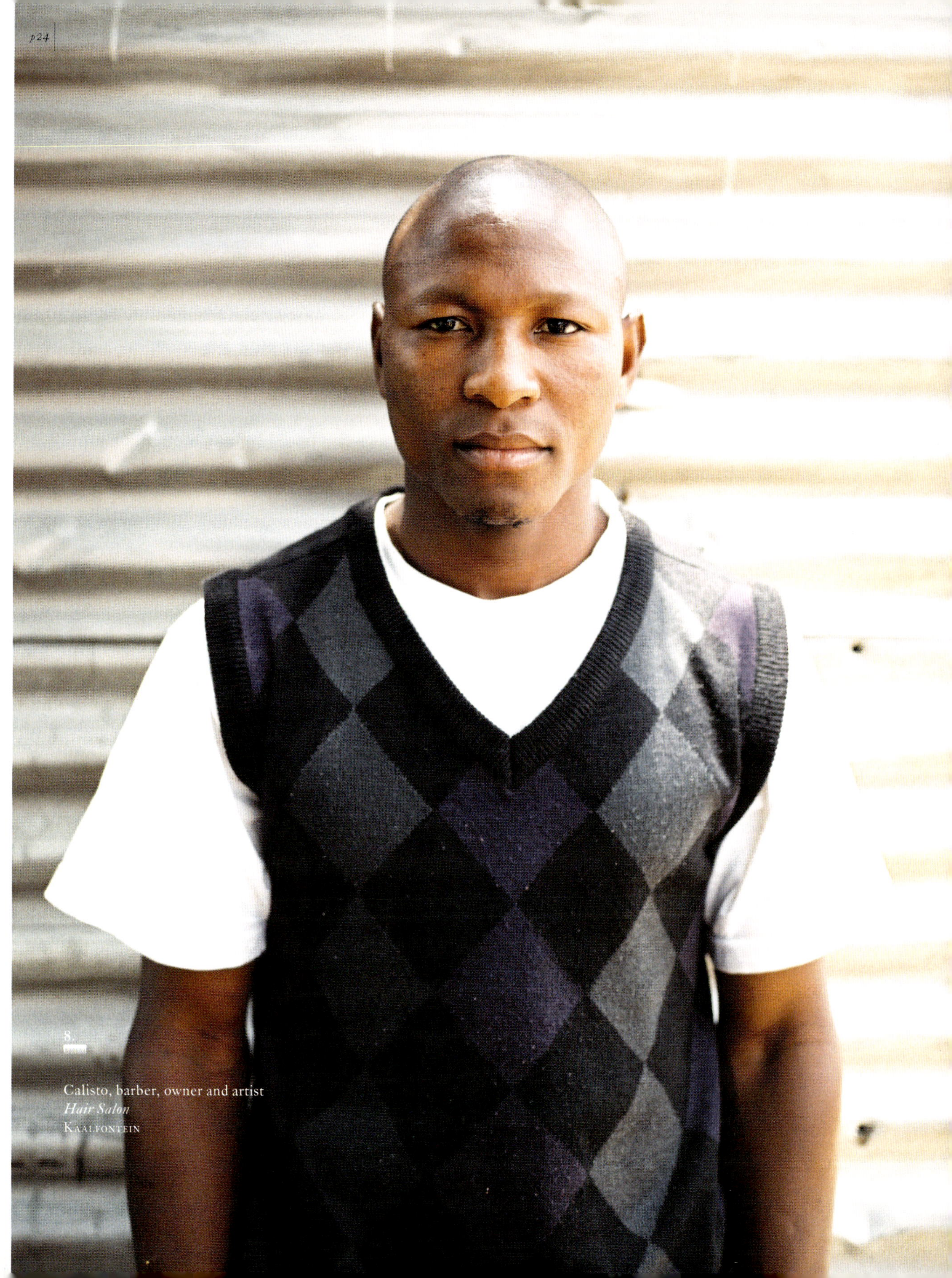

8.

Calisto, barber, owner and artist
Hair Salon
Kaalfontein

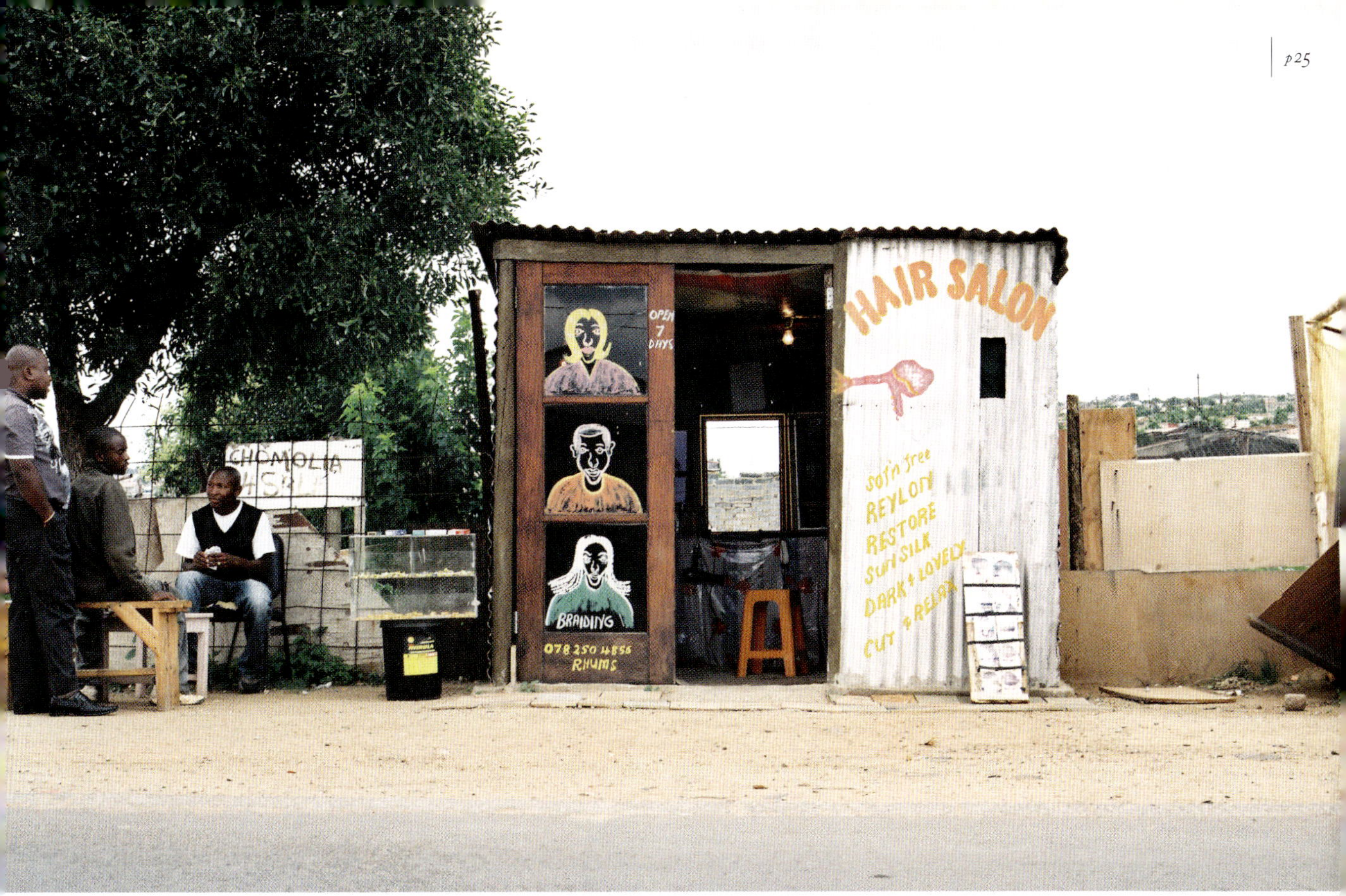
HAIR SALON
OPEN 7 DAYS
BRAIDING
078 250 4856
RHUMS
RESTORE
DARK + LOVELY
CUT + RELAX

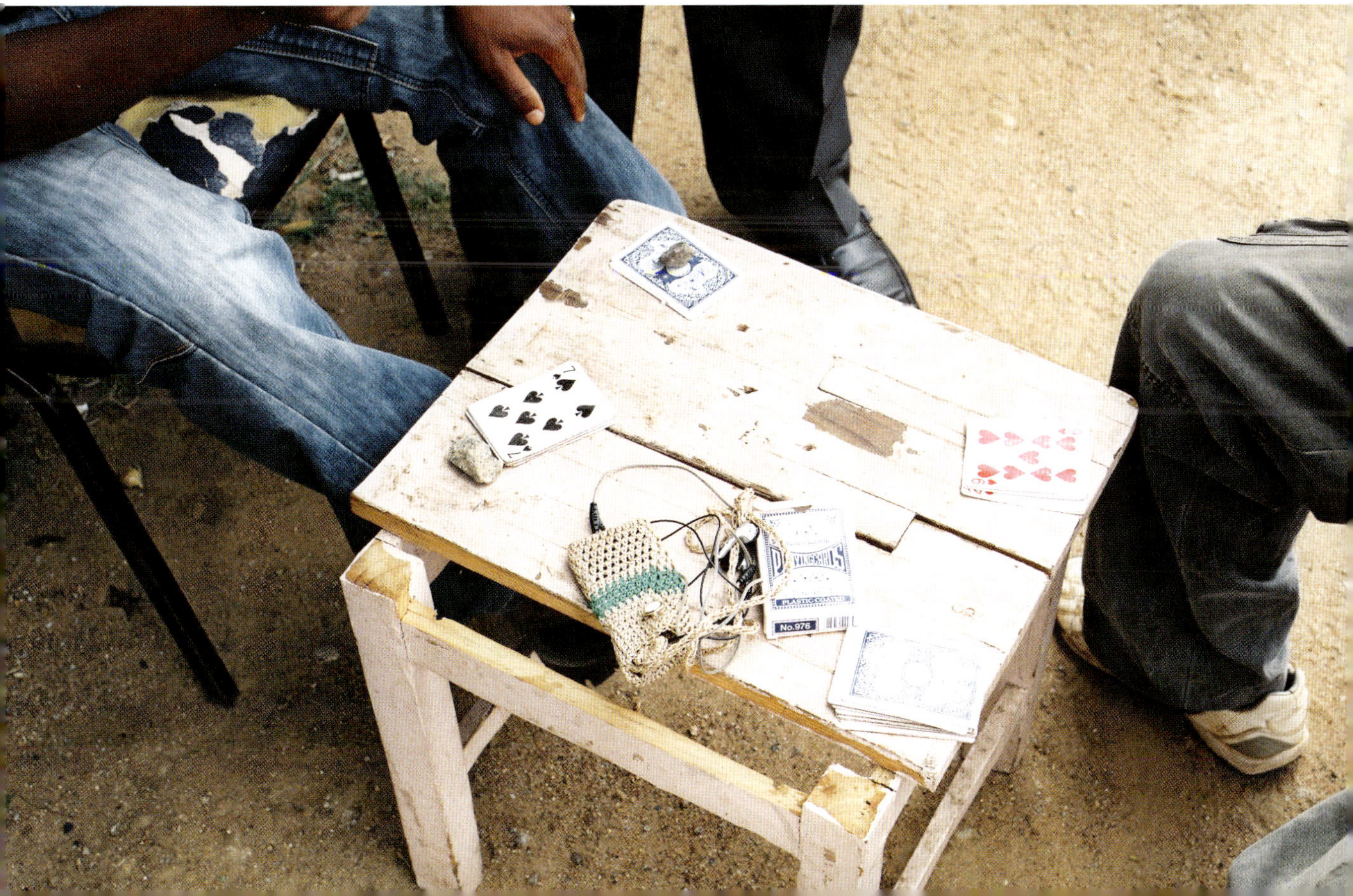

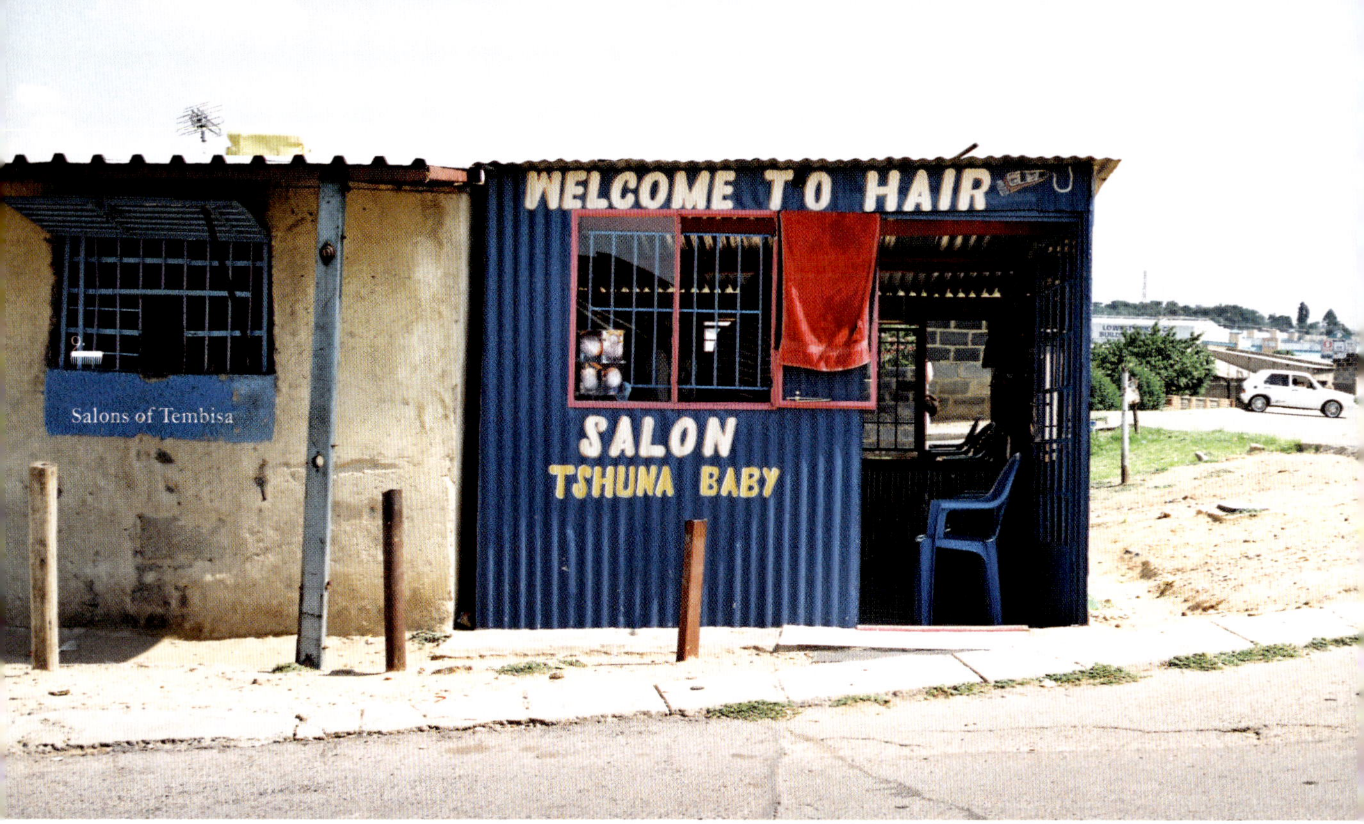

9.

Salons of Tembisa

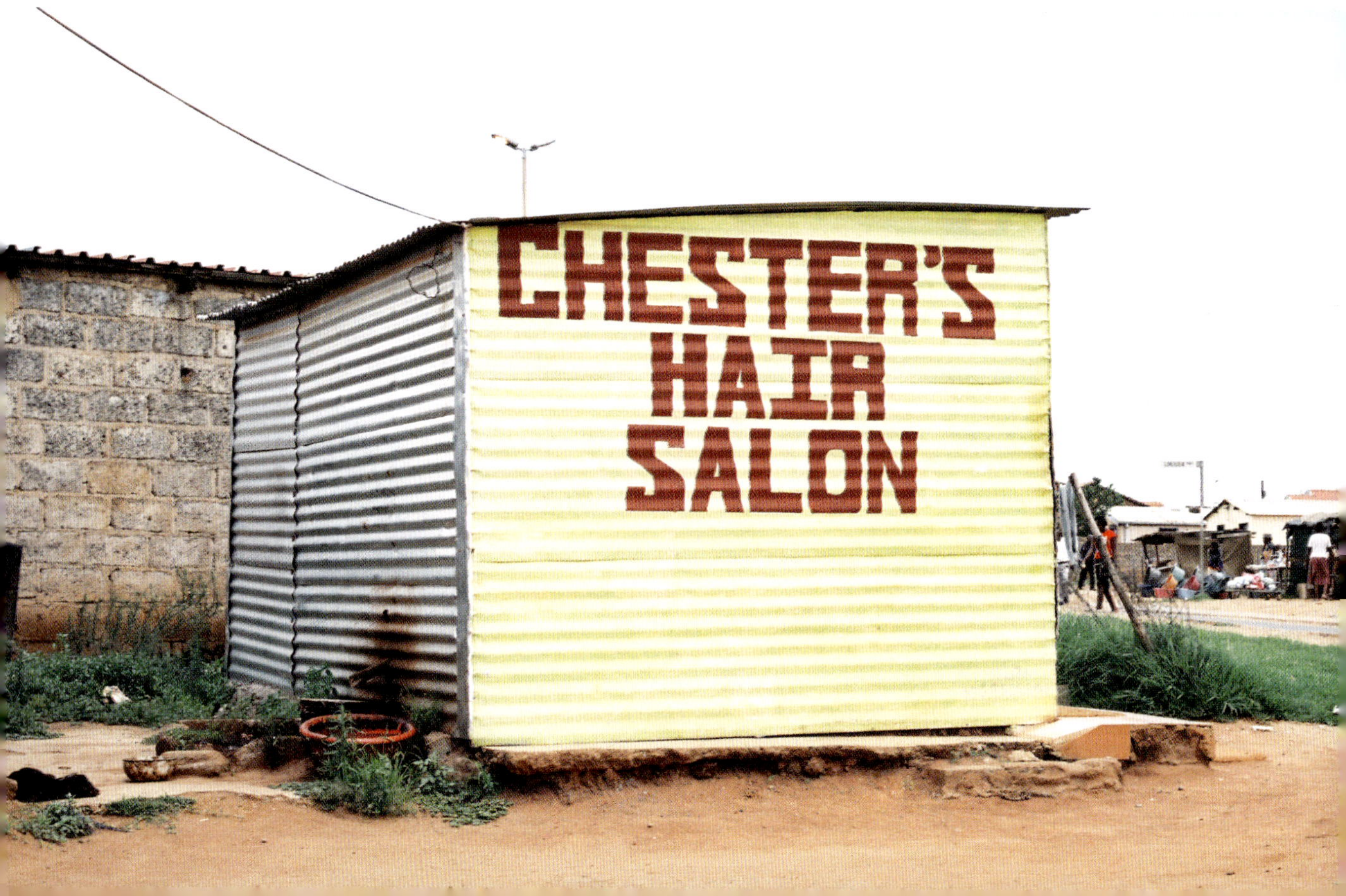

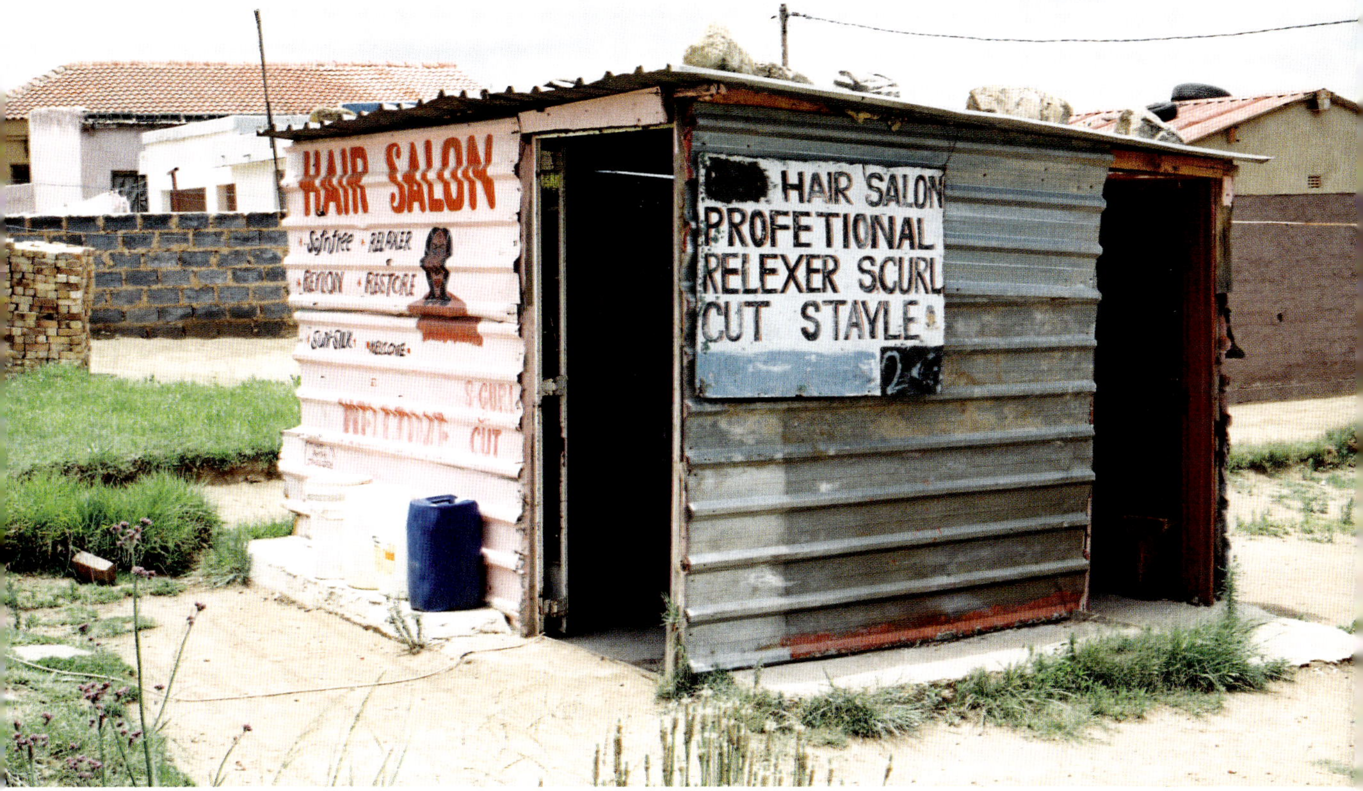

HAIR SALON
HAIR SALON
PROFETIONAL
RELEXER SCURL
CUT STAYLE

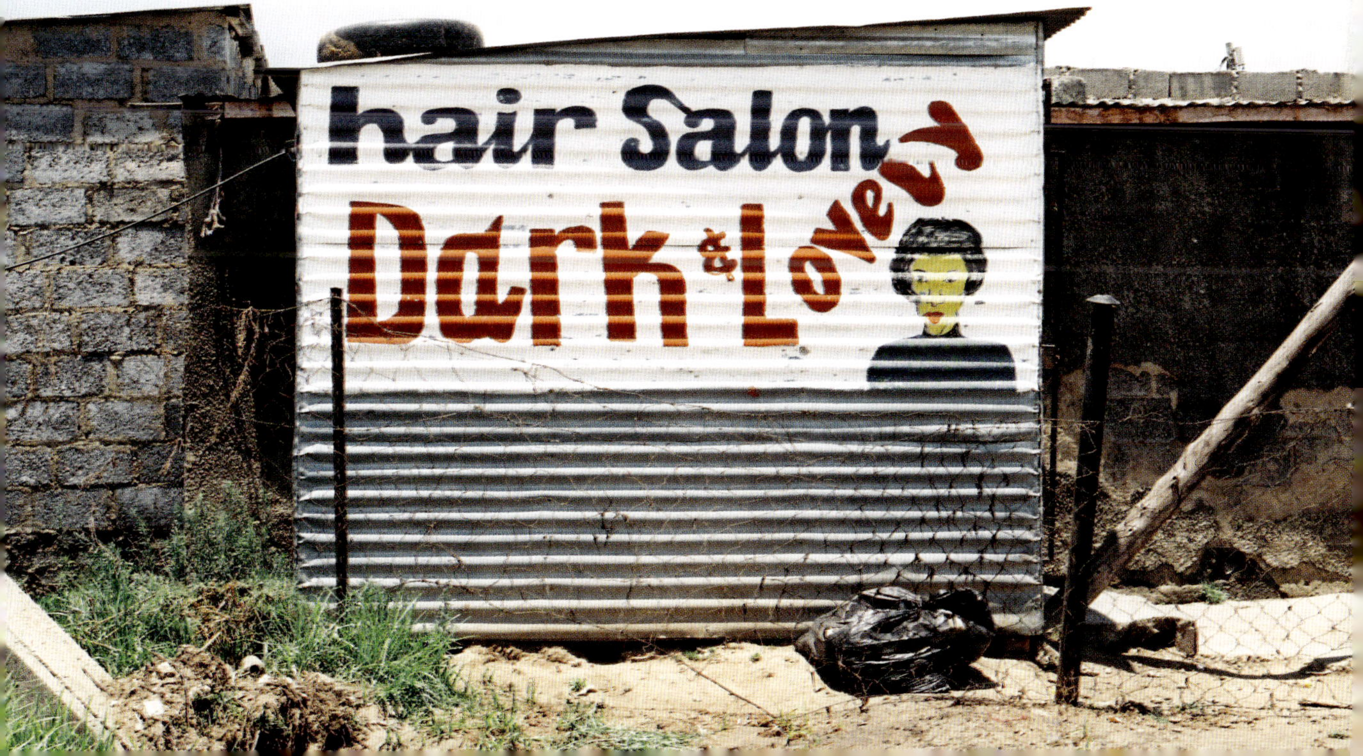

hair Salon
Dark & Lovely

1.2 SOWETO

Soweto, in the southwest of Johannesburg, is without doubt the most famous township in South Africa. The name is abbreviated from "South Western Townships" and the area comprises over twenty neighborhoods. It is known the world over as Nelson Mandela's home for many years, the place where the seeds of uprising against Apartheid first were sown. It also has a rich tradition of sport, art and music, especially jazz. The Mandela effect has understandably made Soweto an increasingly popular destination for visitors on organized bus, bicycle and walking tours. As a result, Soweto is seen as a township success story, despite having its share of crime, disease and poverty.

One example of the area's transition from the center of the black struggle to a tourist destination is Lebo's Soweto Backpackers in Orlando West, situated close to Mandela's former home, and the current residence of Archbishop Desmond Tutu. Lebo Malepa has been welcoming international guests into his home since 1999 and officially launched the hostel in 2003 with the increase of travelers eager to sample a slice of township life.

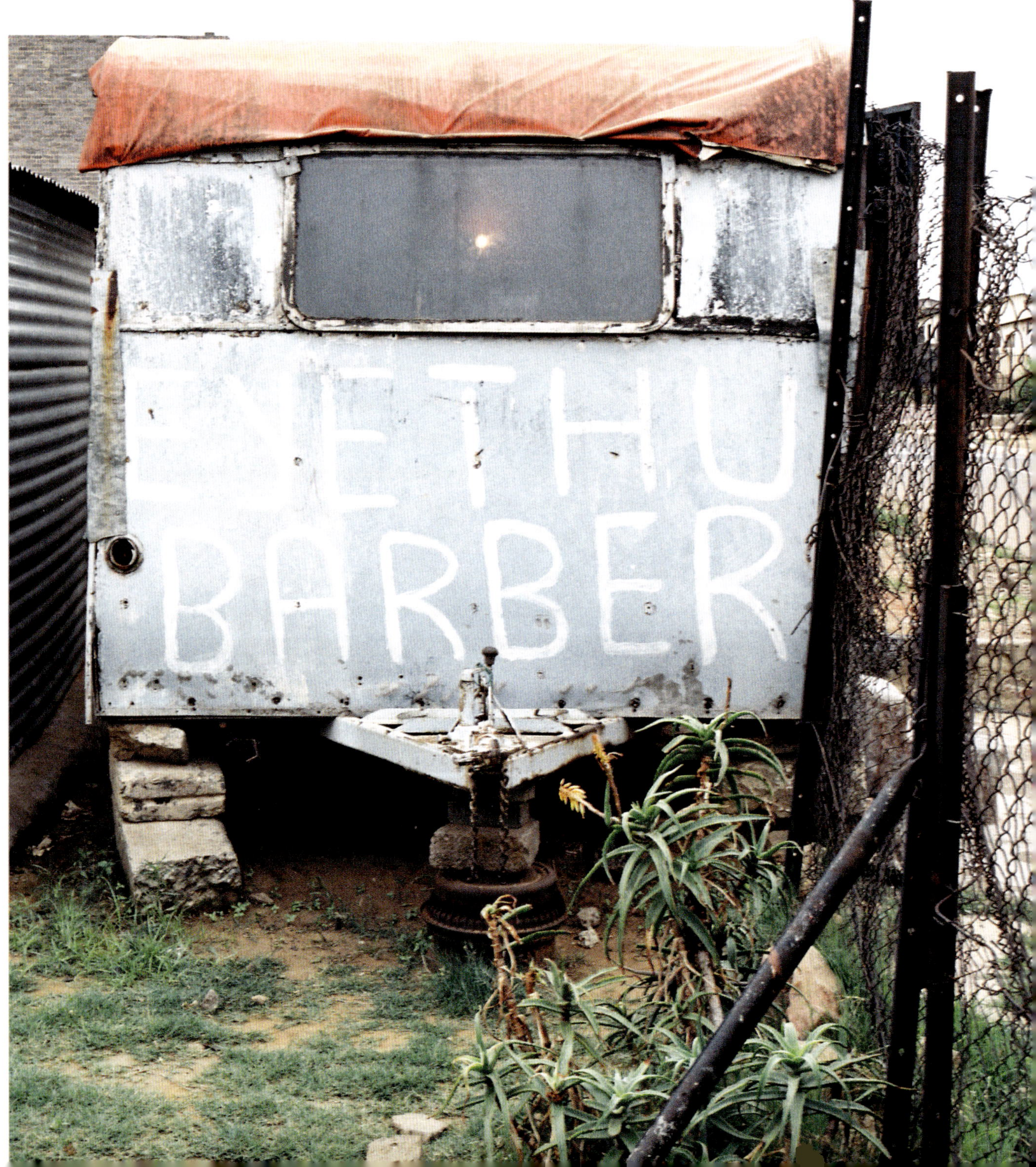
ENETHU
BARBER

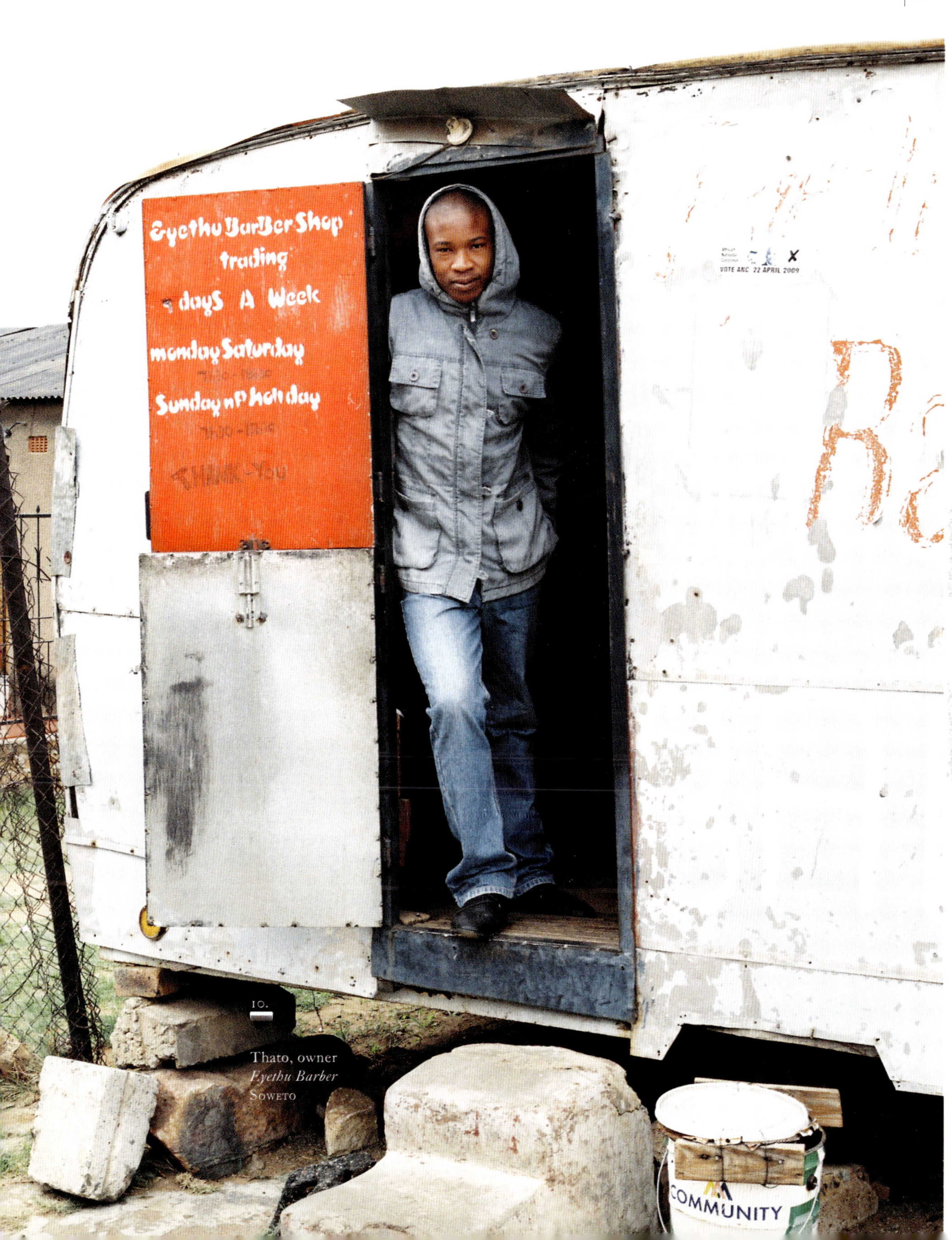

10.

Thato, owner
Eyethu Barber
Soweto

Zama, a young township guide employed by the hostel, agrees to walk me around the neighborhood. Our first destination is the Eyethu barbershop, where Zama gets his hair cut. Eyethu is the first barbershop I have seen housed in a caravan, with most in Soweto usually located in shacks or small buildings. Zama really takes me off the beaten path as we explore the neighboring area of Meadowlands. It is here, far from most township tour routes, where I see the first signs of Soweto's extreme poverty, including squatter shacks and open sewers.

That evening at the hostel I talk to Lebo's younger brother Phillip, who explains the importance of the barbershop: "For us young people it's a place where we get to meet our elders. Over a haircut we get to tell stories, we get to talk about life in general, sports as well. It has that culture of talking, it's not just for hairstyles. I think the best time to go to an informal barber is the day after a very big football match, you know there will always be people and it gets packed and you get everybody talking. It creates a very nice vibe. Unlike a lot of professional salons that have a television, the informal barbershop wouldn't have one. The entertainment comes from talking."

The next day I meet another tour guide, Lungi; he is in his mid forties. If Zama represents the potential of today's South Africa, Lungi's past serves as the foundation for that potential. With a political activist mother and jazz saxophonist father, Lungi was a teenager at school in Orlando West in 1976 when fellow students rioted against the forced teaching of Afrikaans. Known as the Soweto Uprising, security forces killed many students, but the bloodshed revealed the cracks in the government's rule.

For all that has changed, however, driving through Soweto evidences the continuing political and social struggle. Dozens of huge murals shout from the walls: "The Ghetto. Survival Is The Motto"; "United We Stand"; "Say No To Xenophobia Attacks. Africa Unite"; "10 Years Of Freedom! But We Still In The Shacks!"

Lungi explains to me that South Africa has eleven official languages, including isiXhosa, isiZulu and Afrikaans. While the majority of people I meet speak English there are a number for whom Lungi translates. I discover that a number of the barbers and sign writers are not South African but immigrants from neighboring African countries. Lungi tells me why South Africa is so attractive to foreigners, "The reason is for our currency; that's the main advantage in terms of business. We've never had a civil war, so people from most of our neighboring states want to come to South Africa. Here in Soweto we have people from Mozambique who specialize in hair styling, also Zimbabweans who do that. We have guys from Ghana, Lesotho and also Swaziland. It's easy for them to open a business, we don't disturb them."

Although a few black South Africans tell me they resent foreigners living in the townships because they take jobs from locals, it appears that the community accepts the majority of the immigrants. This stands in stark contrast to the xenophobia that exploded in Johannesburg only the year before, resulting in hundreds of perceived "illegals" being driven out of their homes, many badly beaten and a number murdered.

Lungi tells me, "We never had xenophobia in Soweto, even at that time." He goes on to explain that the problems began when big employers began to favor foreign workers over native South Africans. Businesses like barbershops, as Lungi sees it, do not undermine the local workforce: "When they [foreigners] open a business they don't effect employment, they create employment. Actually they give us ideas, we copy from them."

Tracking down the artists responsible for the barbershop signs proves frustrating. Almost without exception the barber or hair stylist has no idea of the artist's name. When I do find a painting that includes contact information, the phone number is usually out of service.

Luckily, Smoky, one of Soweto's most prolific sign writers, is easy to find. He includes his name and phone number on all the walls and businesses he paints, which seem to stand on every corner. Lungi and I travel to the Klipspruit neighborhood to interview Smoky.

We've arranged to meet him at Andris Hair Salon, where I first saw his work. It is hard not to notice him approaching – he is a spitting image of rapper Snoop Dogg, down to the long braided hair, Dickies shirt, baggy jeans and Converse shoes. Laid back, soft spoken and immeasurably cool, Smoky is more than happy to speak with me.

We're in the shade underneath a tree when a brand new BMW pulls up. Three intimidating men get out and one of them opens the car's trunk from

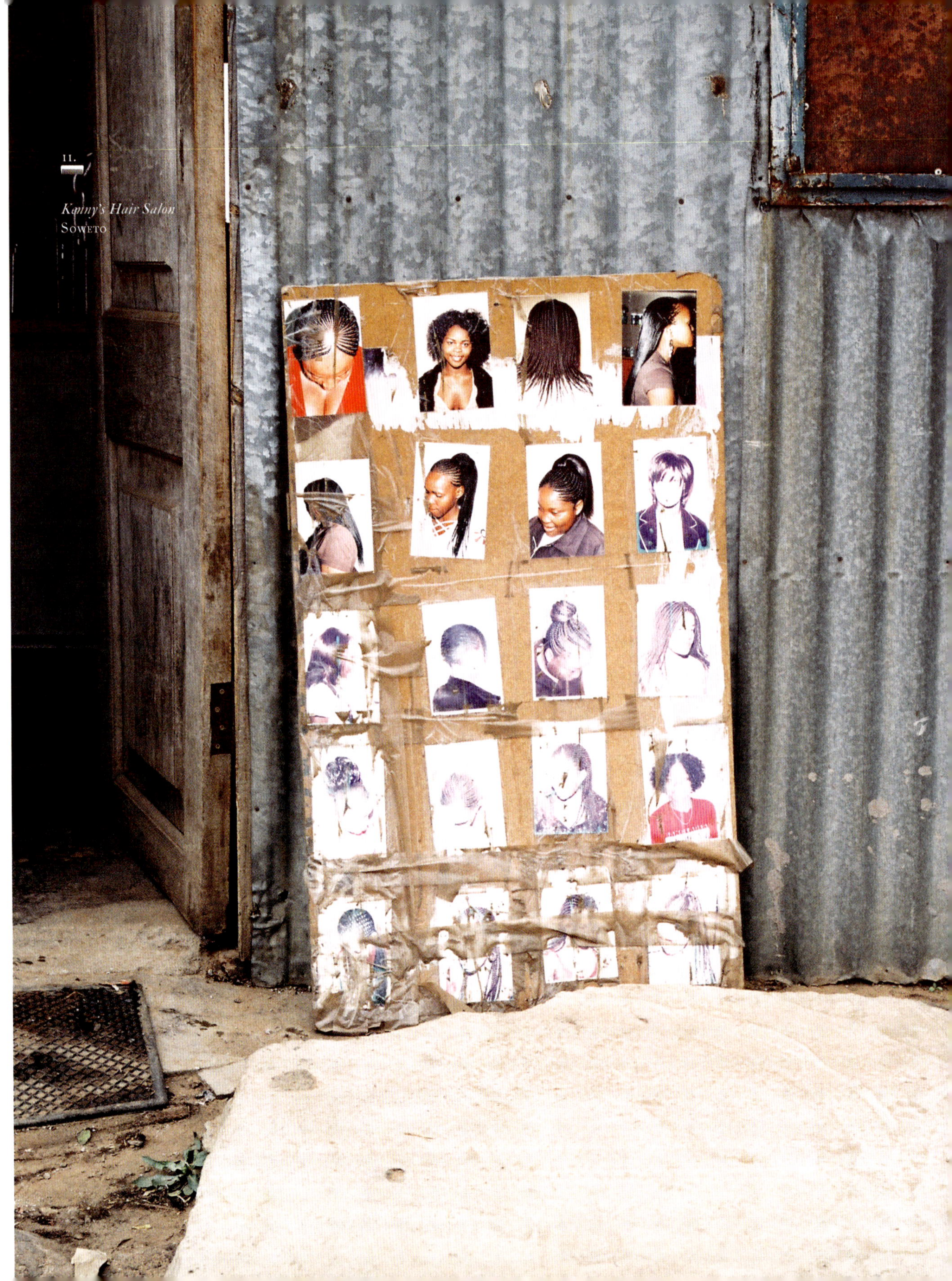

11.

Kenny's Hair Salon
Soweto

which speakers throb house music. The guys lean on the car and rhythmically nod along to the pulsing beat, which is loud enough for me to suggest to Smoky that we move away from the noise. About five minutes later Smoky takes a phone call, so rather than stand around listening to his conversation I approach the men hanging out by the car. "Hey guys, I'm from England," I say, knowing that in townships humor seems to break the ice. "I was wondering if you know what BMW stands for in my country?" All three men look puzzled. I carry on, "If you're a white guy it stands for Break My Windows." They burst out laughing. "If you're a black guy it stands for Black Man's Wheels!" Nerve-wracking silence.

What was I thinking? I wouldn't dream of saying this to anyone in London or New York City and have always found the gag offensive, yet at this moment, for some inexplicable reason, the timing seems strangely appropriate. The three men look at me, smile and nod enthusiastically. One of them asks, "So the black man drives the BMW in England as well? I like that! I like that a lot!"

We all laugh and shake hands. Smoky and Lungi walk up to us and we part ways with the three men. Smoky informs me that the men are carjackers and that their car is probably a recent prize. Carjacking in Johannesburg is a terrible problem and is one of the greatest fears of the city's residents, both white and black. The newspapers regularly report horror stories of merciless criminals; even victims that don't put up fights often find themselves on the wrong end of a bullet.

Smoky tells me his phone call had been about a commission to paint a barbershop. We head to his home so he can pick up his supplies. Smoky lives with his family but one room is crammed with nothing but his canvases, direct but surreal representations of hardships that can plague young men growing up in townships. It is clear that he views his sign writing as a means to an end: "I will tell you the honest truth, I never took barbershop art seriously. For me it was just a job, I would get paid and that was it. It was not my true art. I was just doing it to get paid, but since you came along and talked to me it's shined some light on it for me."

12.

Salons of Soweto

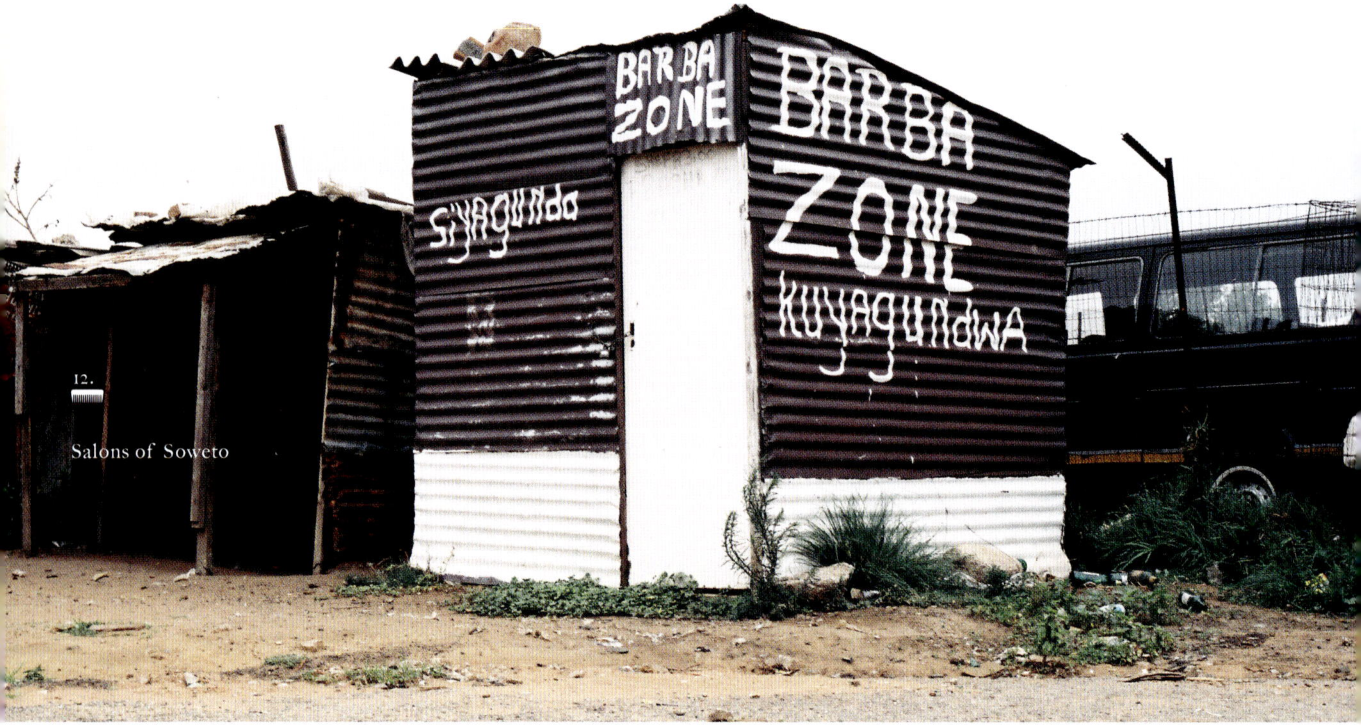

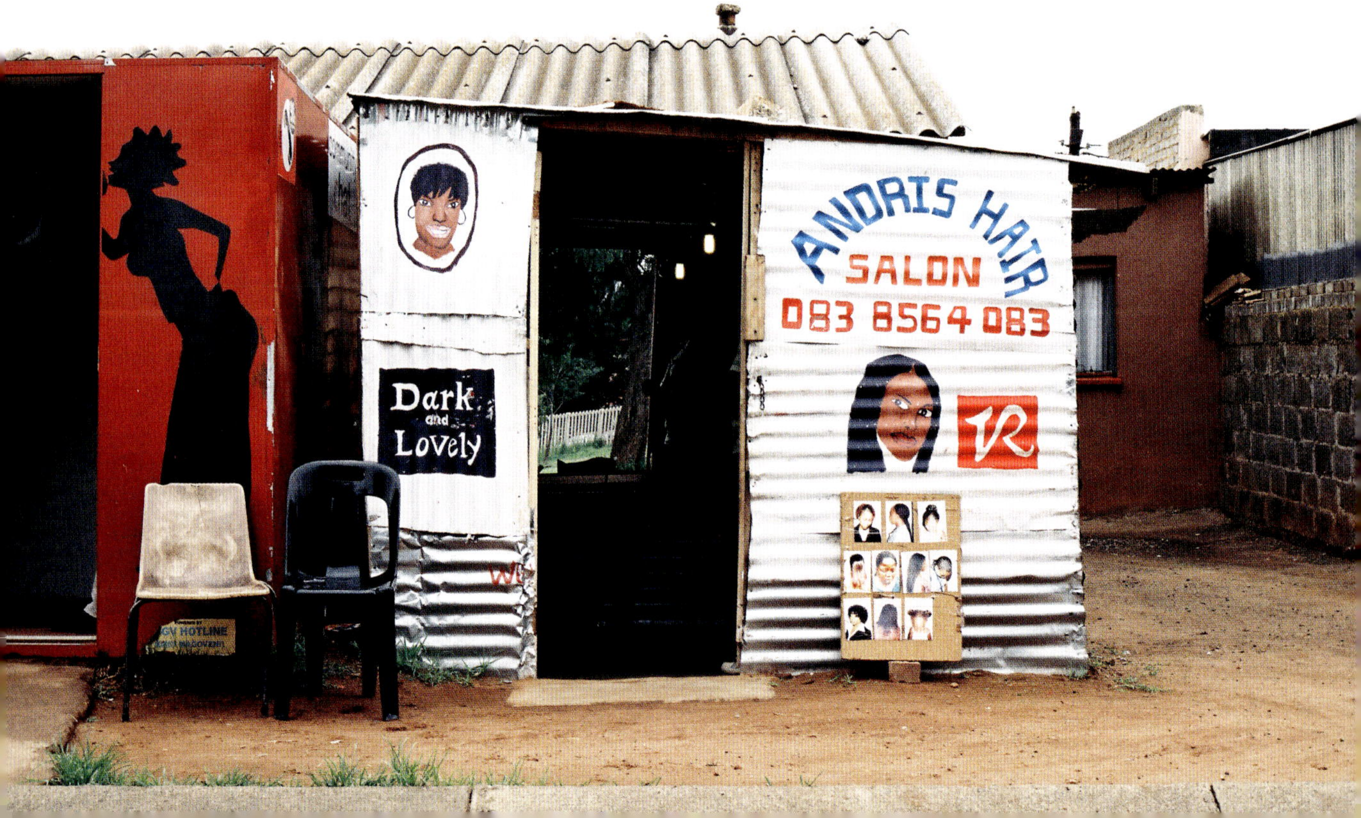

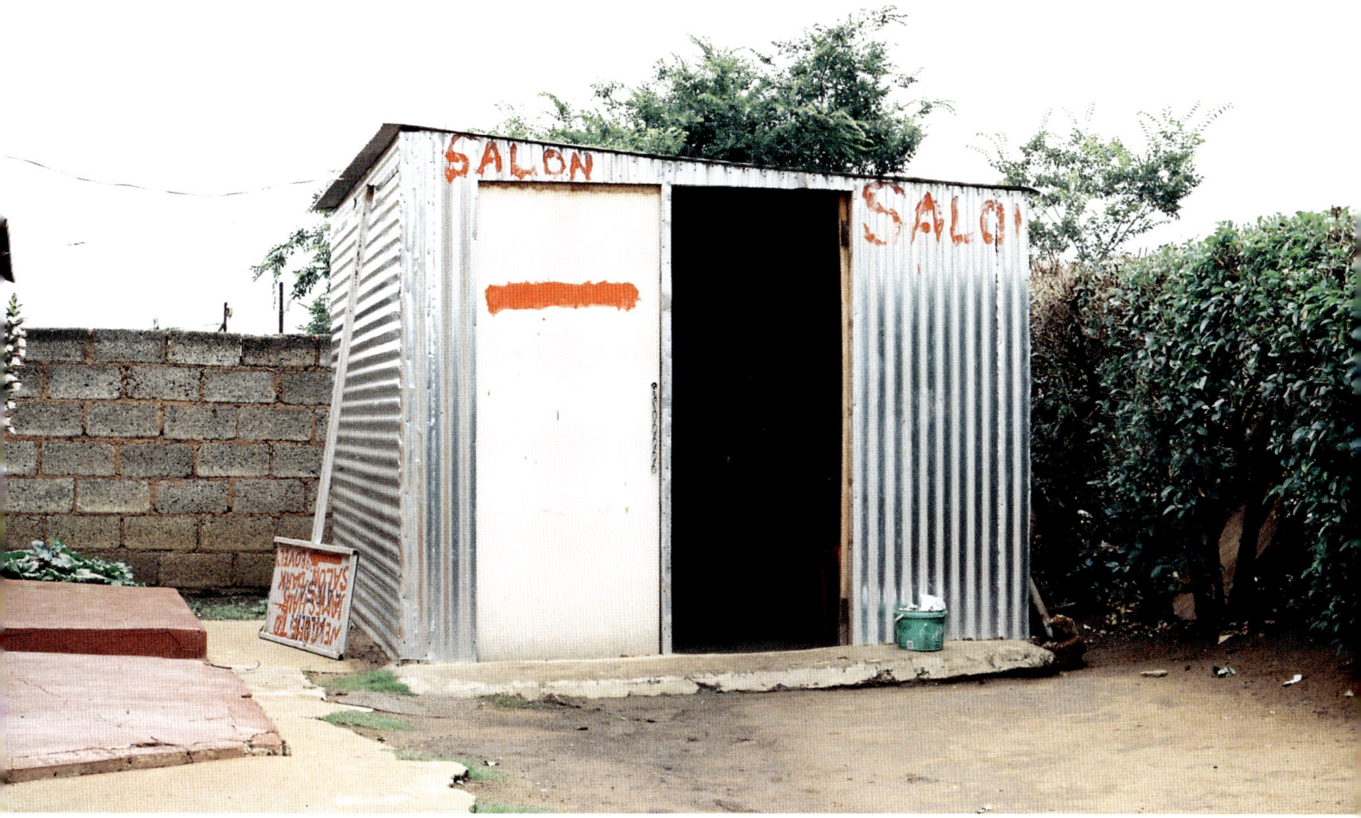

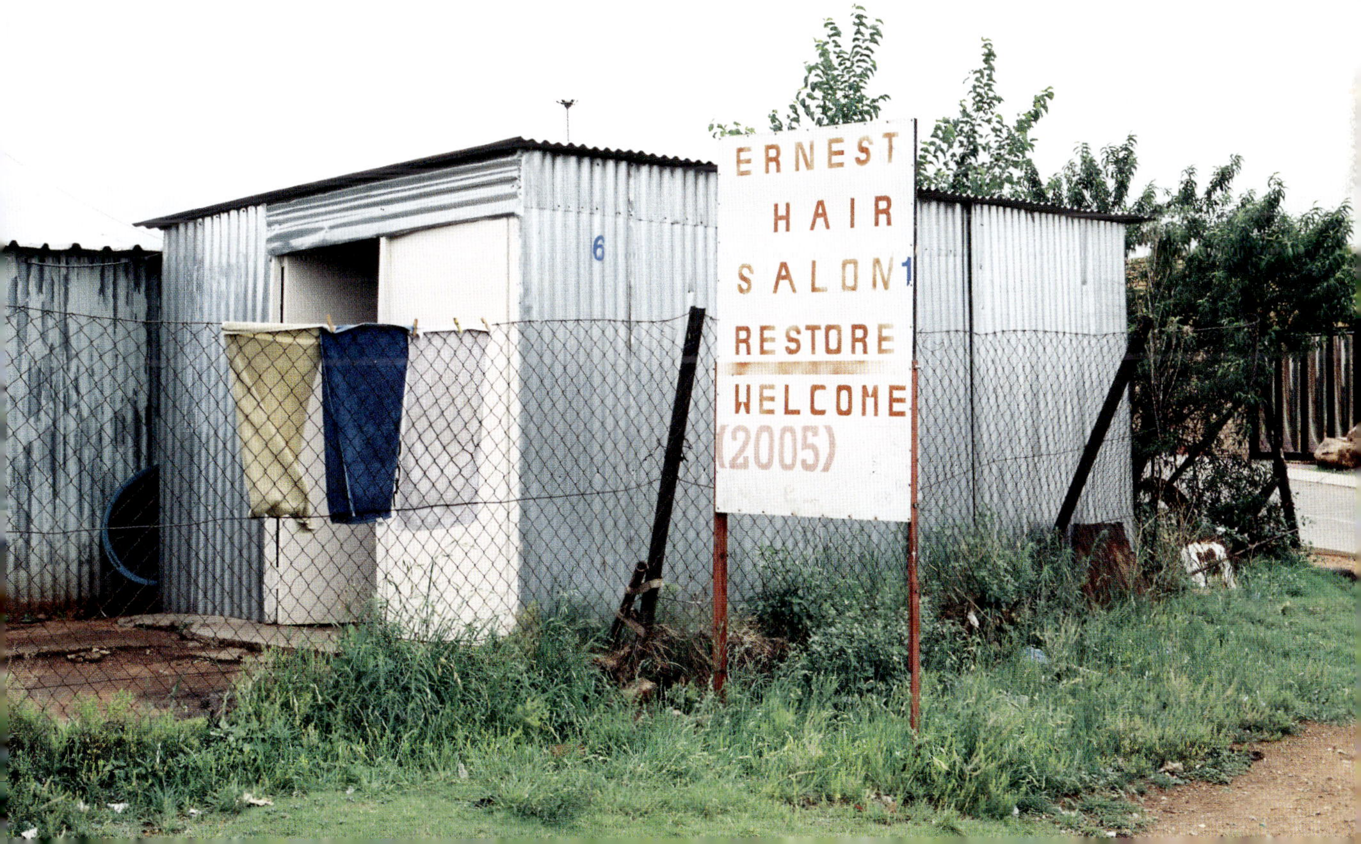

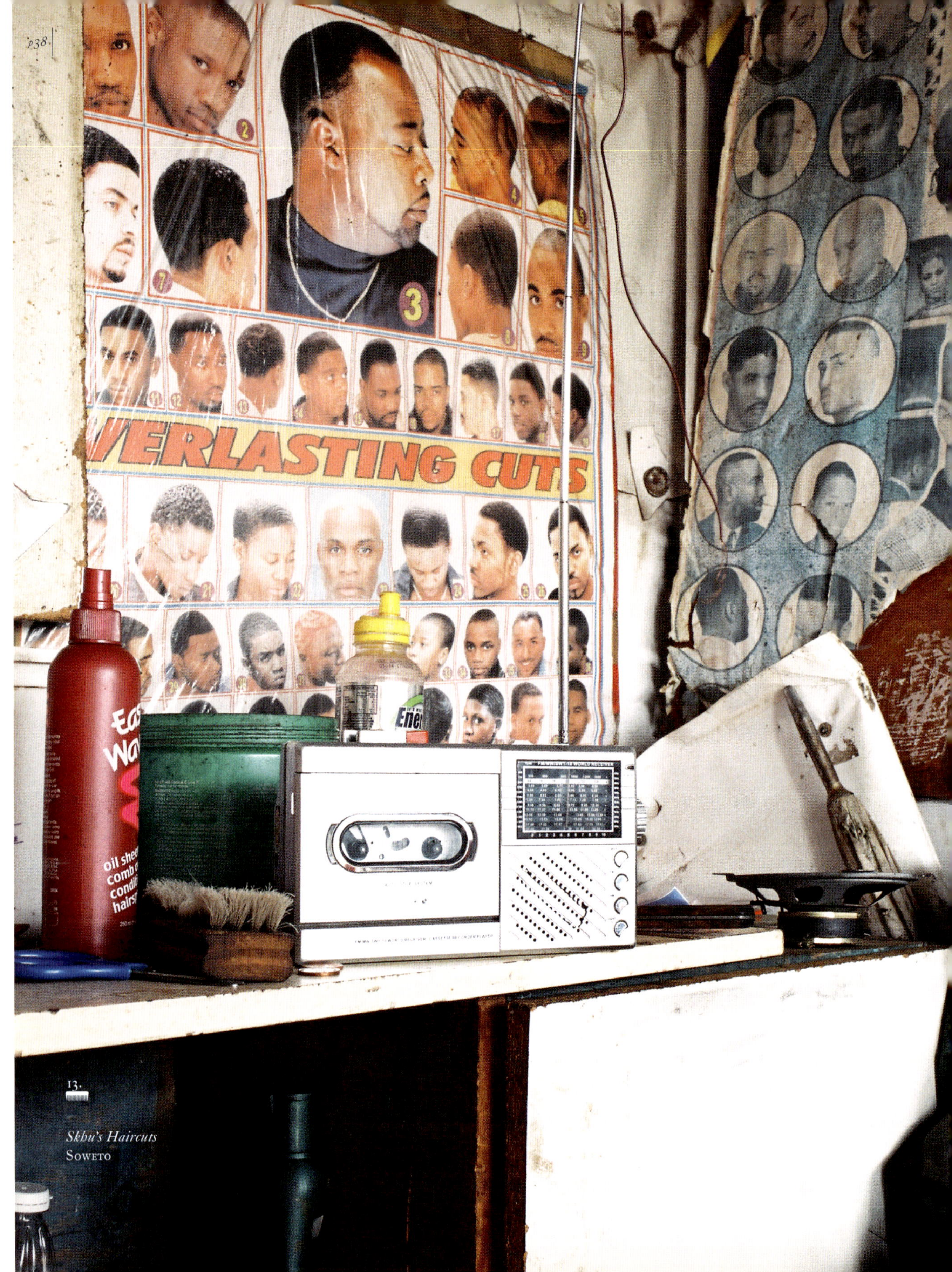

13.

Skhu's Haircuts
Soweto

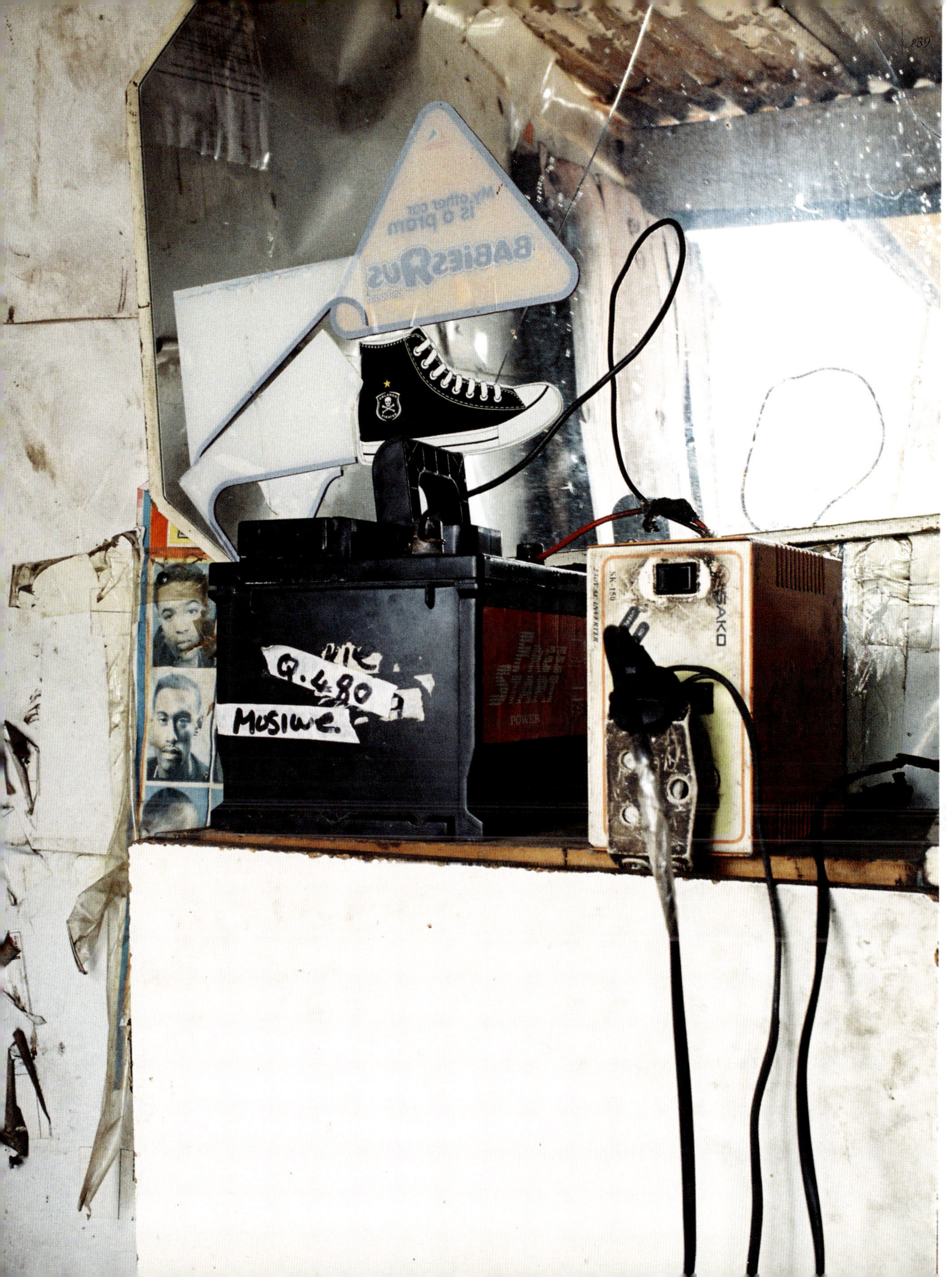
Q.480
Musiwe.
FREE START
POWER
SK-150
SAKO

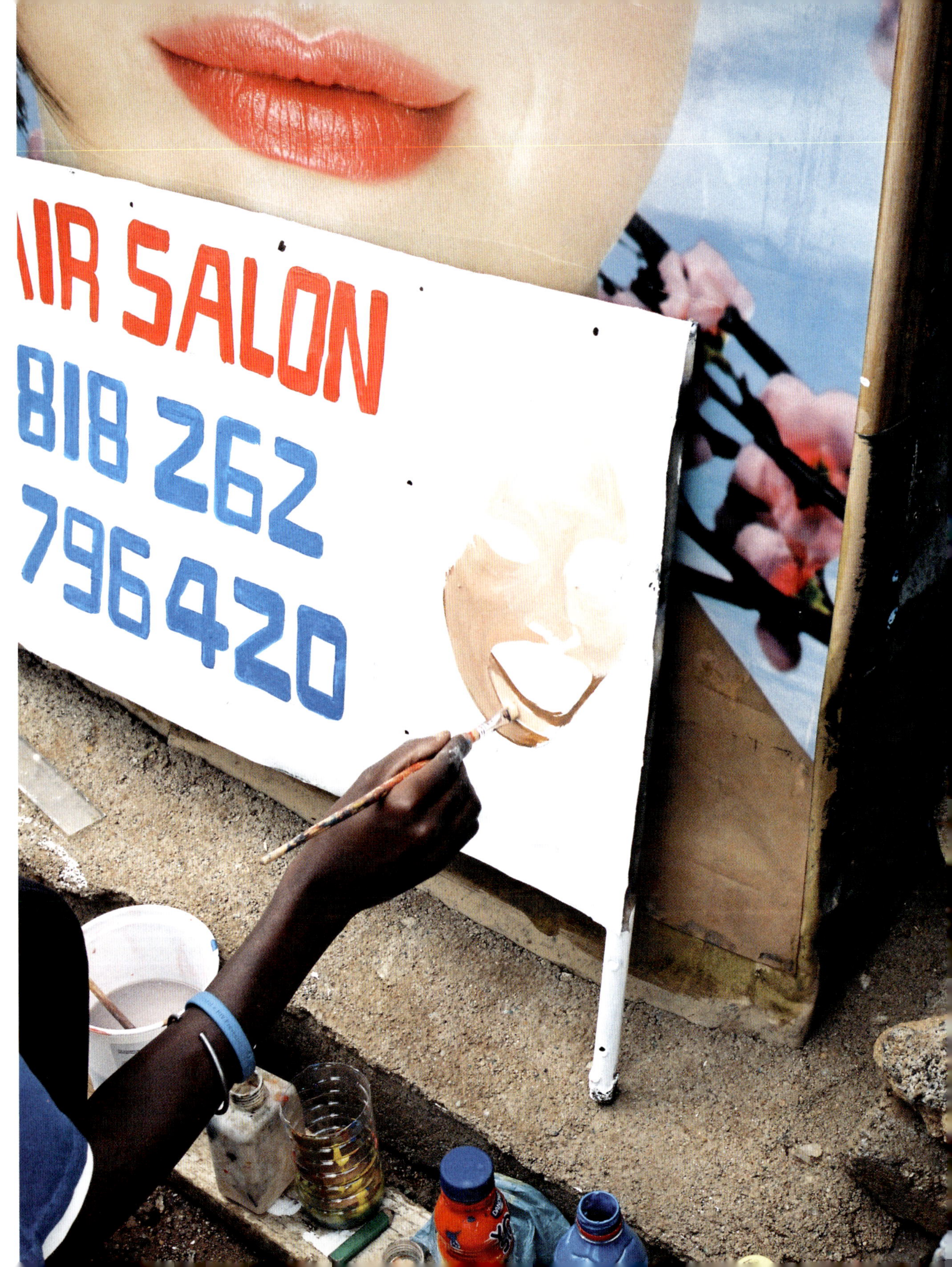
IR SALON
818 262
796420

1.3 Interview with SMOKY

How did you get your name?

I got my name from this hip-hop thing. Sometimes I get on the mic and freestyle and people say that I smoke as I rap.

Did you go to art school?

I studied art from the age of five years old and I've always had a passion for art. If art was a girl I would be married by now! So I've done it since primary school and I've always known what I wanted to do. My mum supported me, she believes in everything I do, especially in art. Then I went to high school, after that I went to the Funda Centre Community College where I studied art for three years. Since then I've engaged myself in various exhibitions. I've exhibited in thirteen galleries as a student, mostly in Johannesburg but there was one in Canada and the other was in London. The Canadian exhibition started off as a workshop, working an educational theme about HIV/AIDS for youth.

Who influenced your art?

I used to go to school with Simphiwe, I will never forget this guy, he was so good at portraits. I had this beef against him – why is there someone better than me? The turning point was when I swallowed my pride and went to him and asked about his technique. He said, "I'll show you." Then I went home and practiced a lot and later became as good as he was. I got so much from him.

I would say that education for me wasn't from a teacher telling me what to do, it was from the people I socialized with. There's more education outside the classroom. If you do something you have to know that there is always someone that does it better than you. Then you don't have to be angry, you just have to find out how he does it, and then just learn from him. You just have to open your heart. You can never know everything.

That's how I learned sign writing. First I saw this guy sign writing and he asked me if I was an artist. I said, "Hell no! I'm just a person who loves art." Then I watched him from scratch, from priming the wall white through to the finished artwork. I didn't miss anything, I absorbed it all like a sponge. At first I wasn't that good, I struggled a lot – some people would only give me half the money and say, "No, no, Smoky, you didn't do okay."

How do you get your sign writing commissions?

Most of the guys, they call me; they get my number from different walls I advertise on. Other people will see me sign writing and stop and ask how much I charge and how to get hold of me. Most of the guys will call me to come and meet them. Some of them will tell me what they want over the phone. I get the details of the barbershop, the name, the phone number and what they specialize in. They give me the measurements of how long the container or the shack is and then I do a rough sketch. I show the sketch and if they like it I do everything else at the shop.

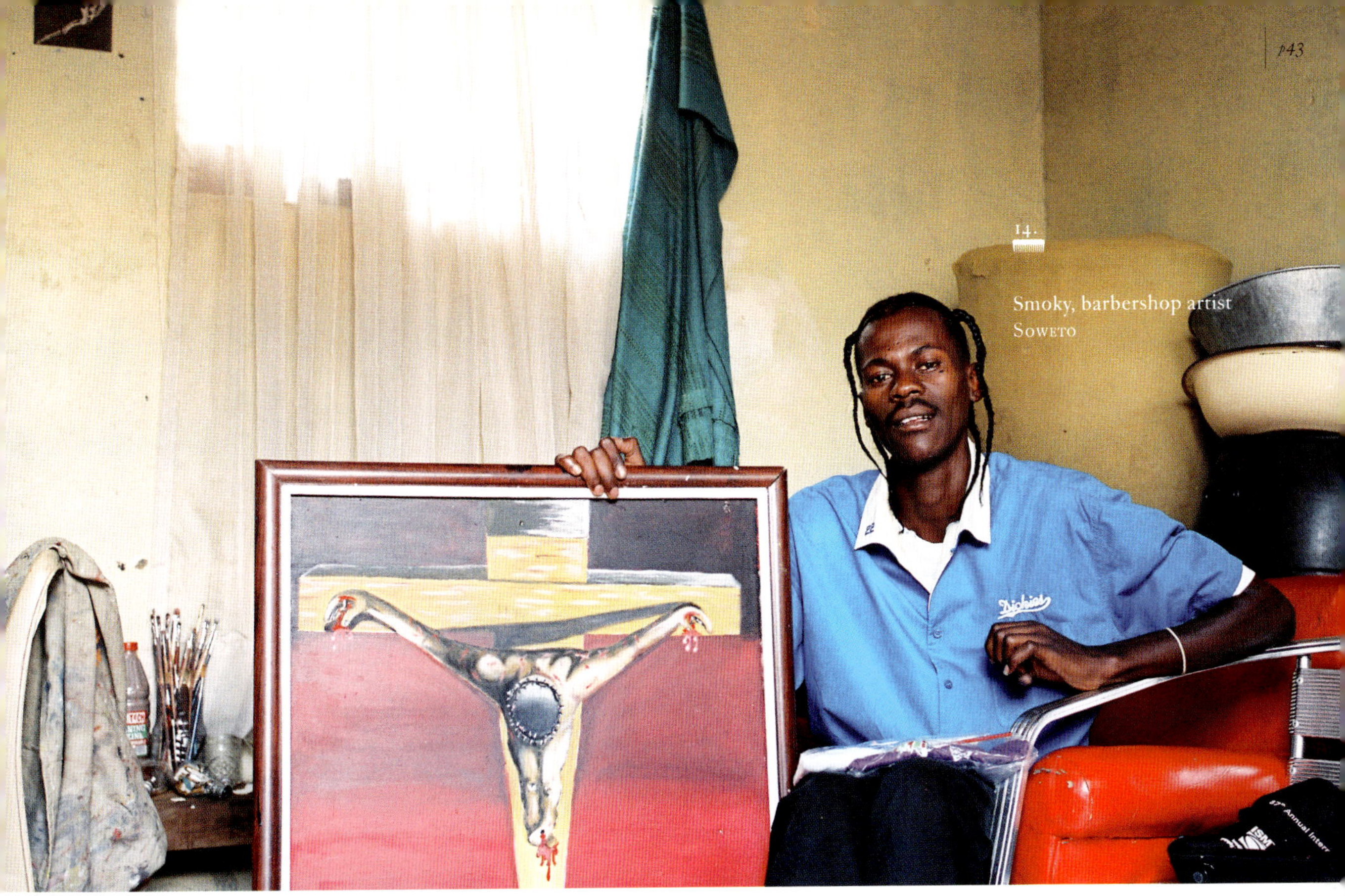

14.

Smoky, barbershop artist
Soweto

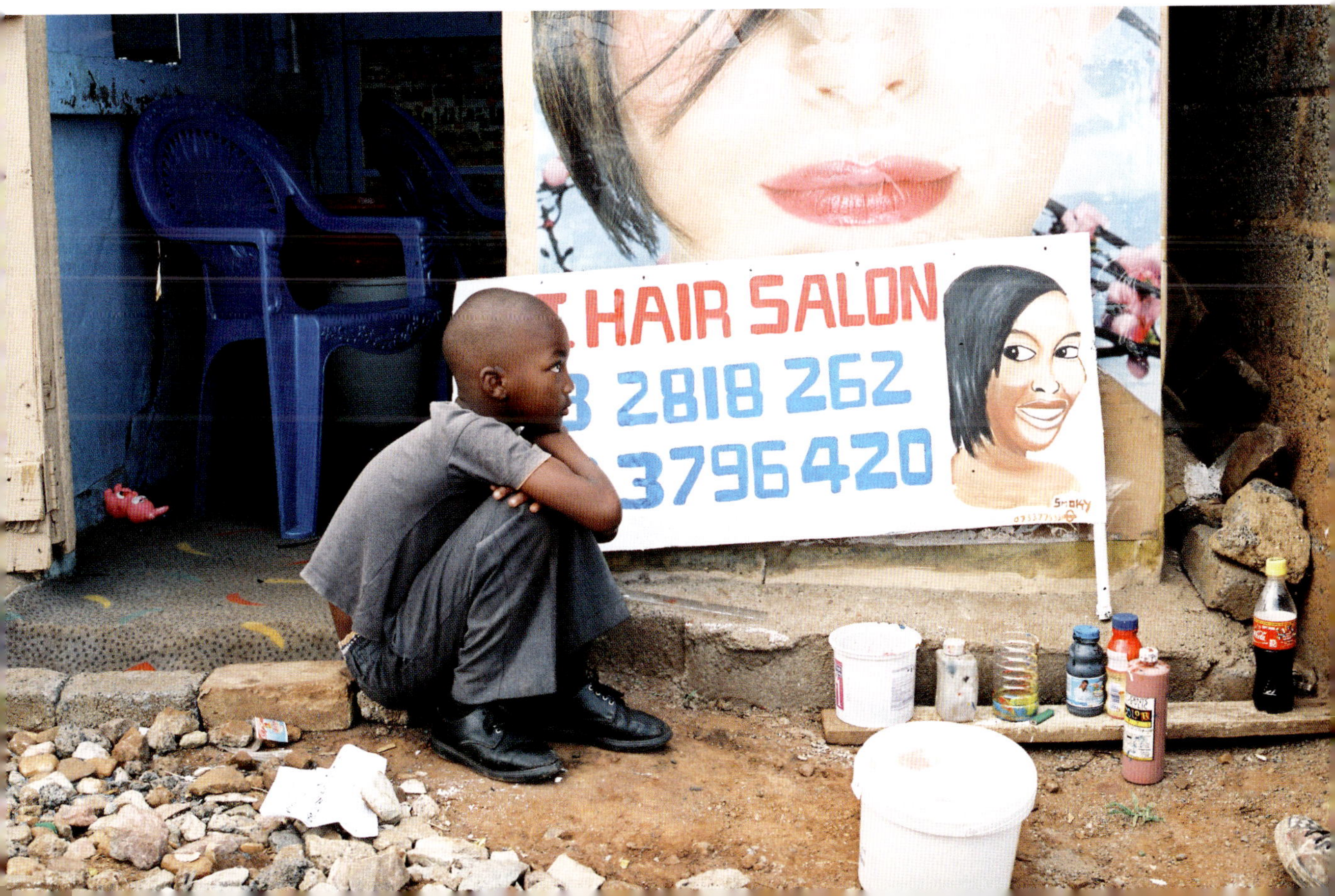

How long does it take to paint a shack?

The Andris shack took me roughly two hours. I wasn't in a hurry, I was relaxed and taking my time because it's my 'hood and I wanted to make sure it looked good. When I'm working outside this area I do them faster, in an hour or even forty-five minutes.

Is there a big American influence here?

There is a whole lot of American influence here. South Africa is in some way converting into America. We dress the same way as American people and if you check most of the hairstyles being done here they are from America, because people saw them on television. Tupac, Biggie, Snoop Dogg, those are favorite characters in the ghetto. I've been asked to paint Alicia Keys, Left Eye from TLC, Jennifer Lopez, a whole lot of them.

What else are you working on?

I'm busy with my comic book, my sign writing and I just recently opened my own company and my own clothing label. I'm planning to do more. For instance the park here has no sculpture and that bothers me, there's no art here and I want to make a sculpture and put it in the park.

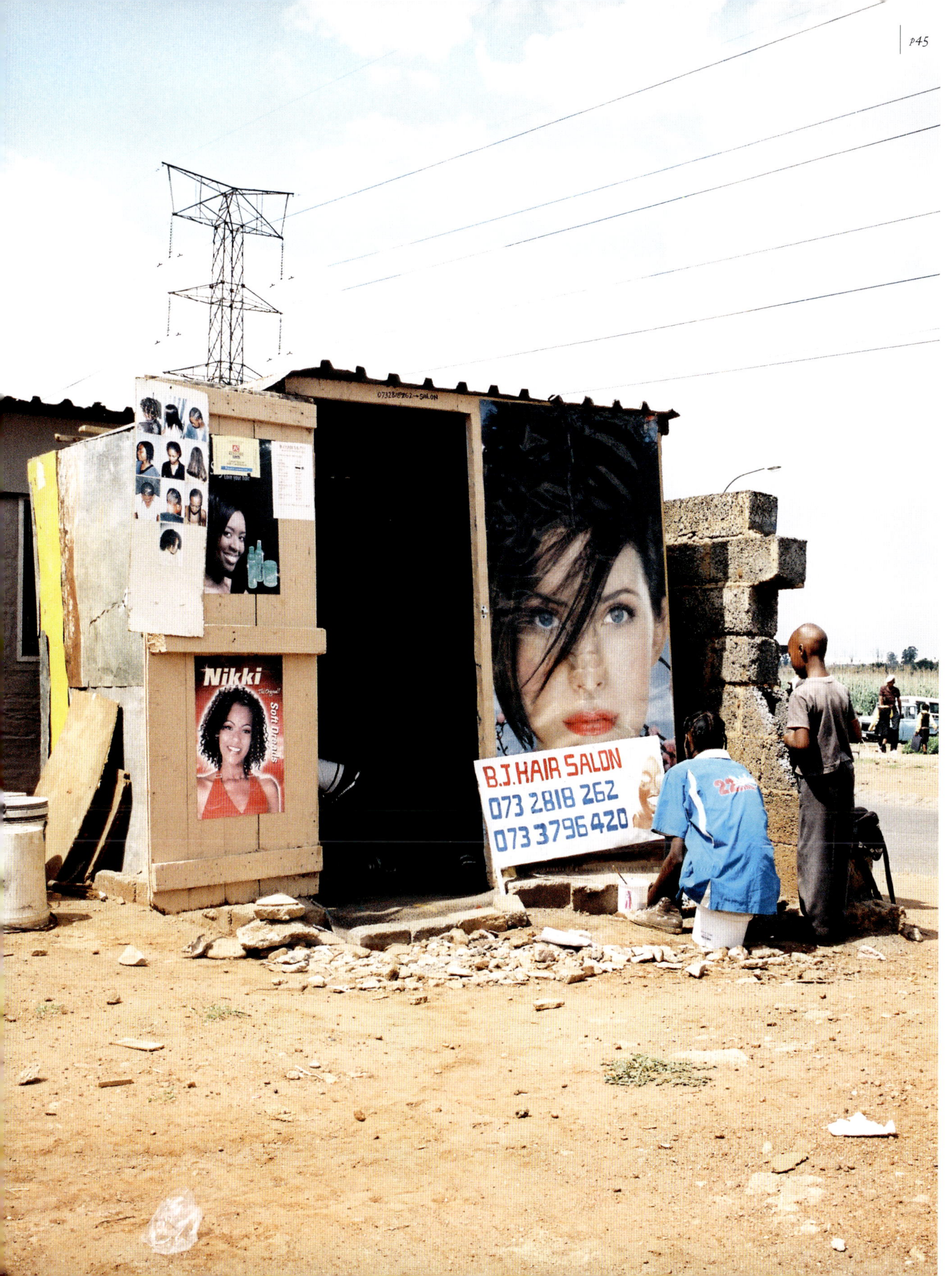
B.J. HAIR SALON
073 2818 262
073 3796420
Nikki
Soft Dreads

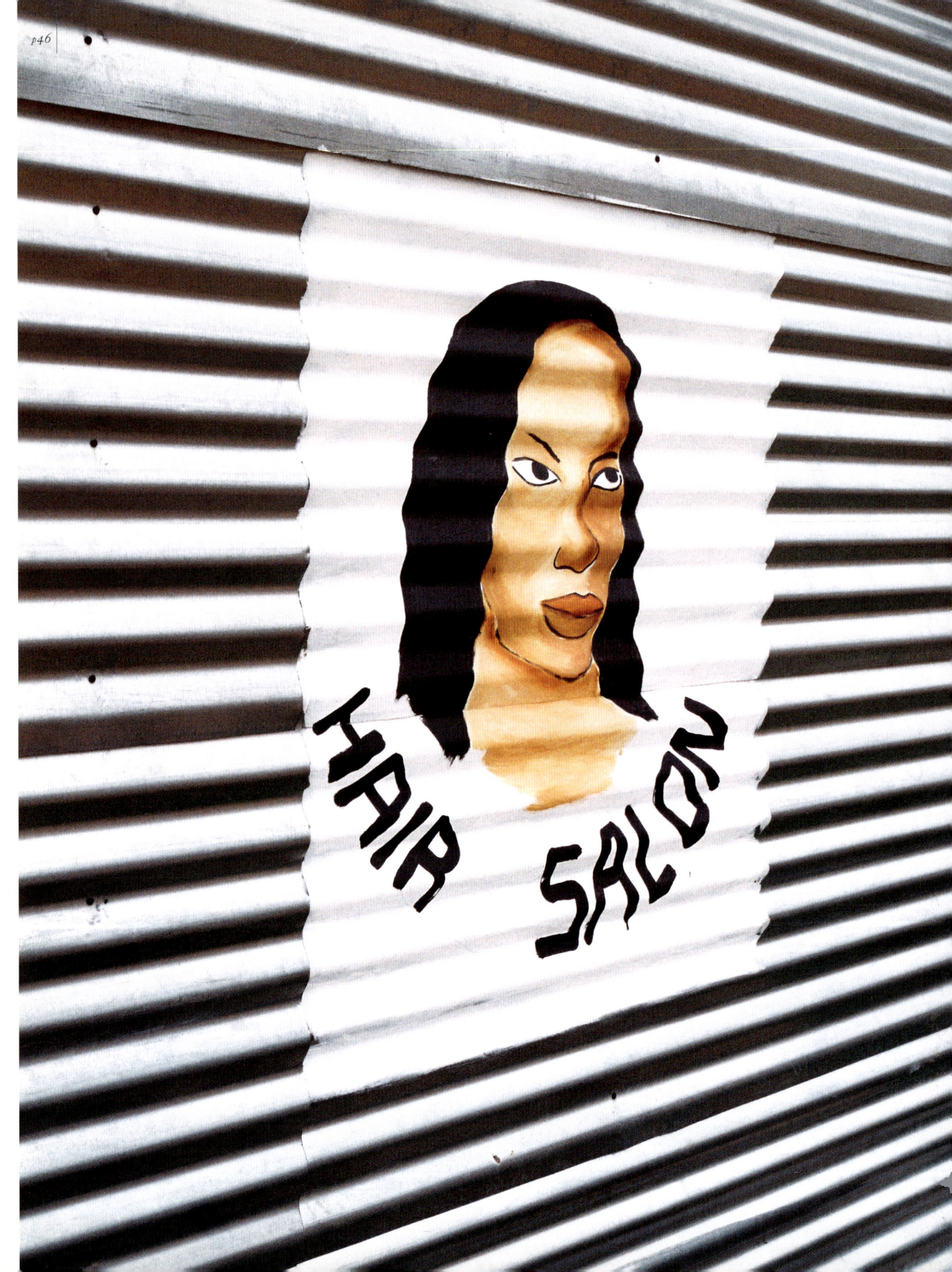
HAIR SALON

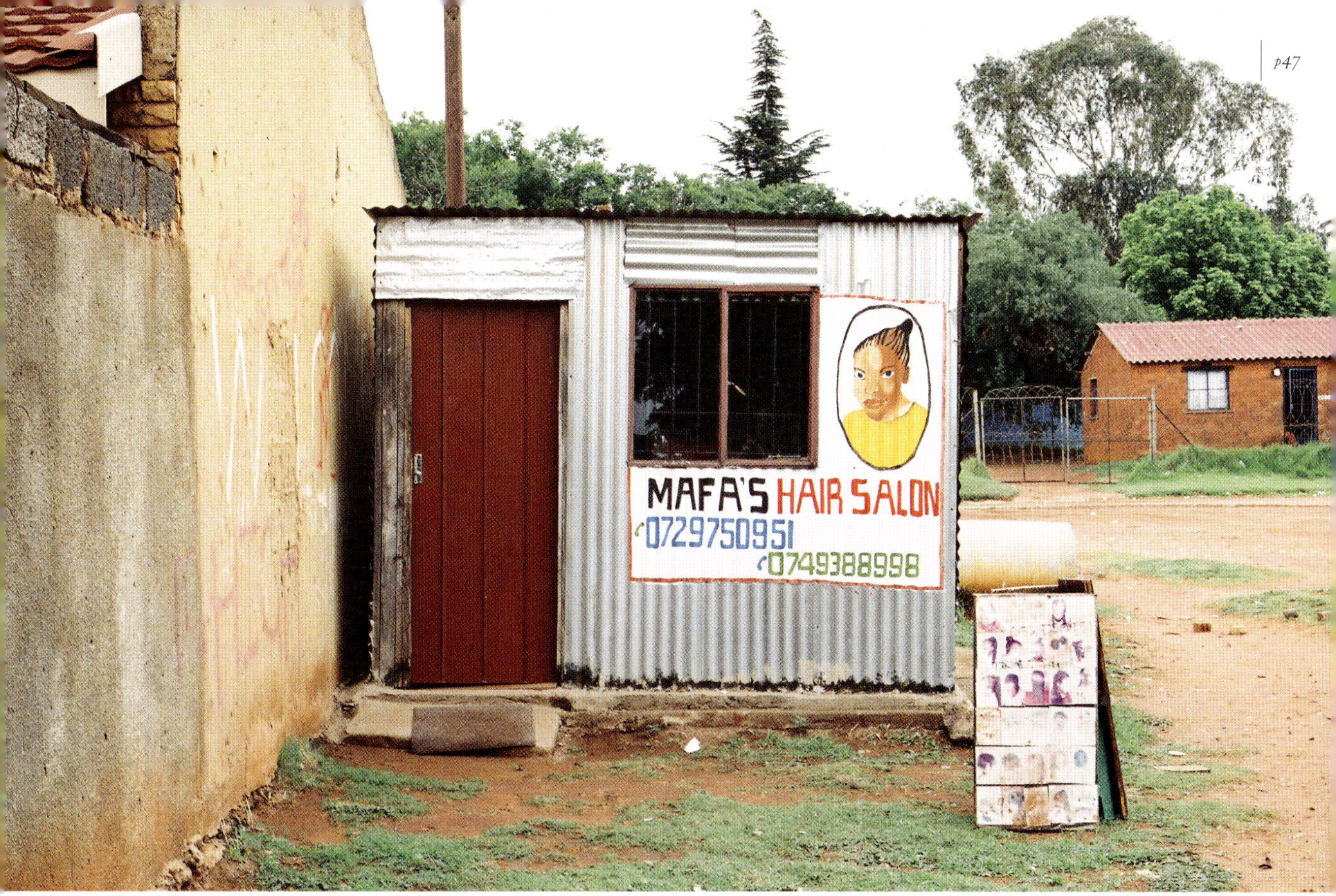

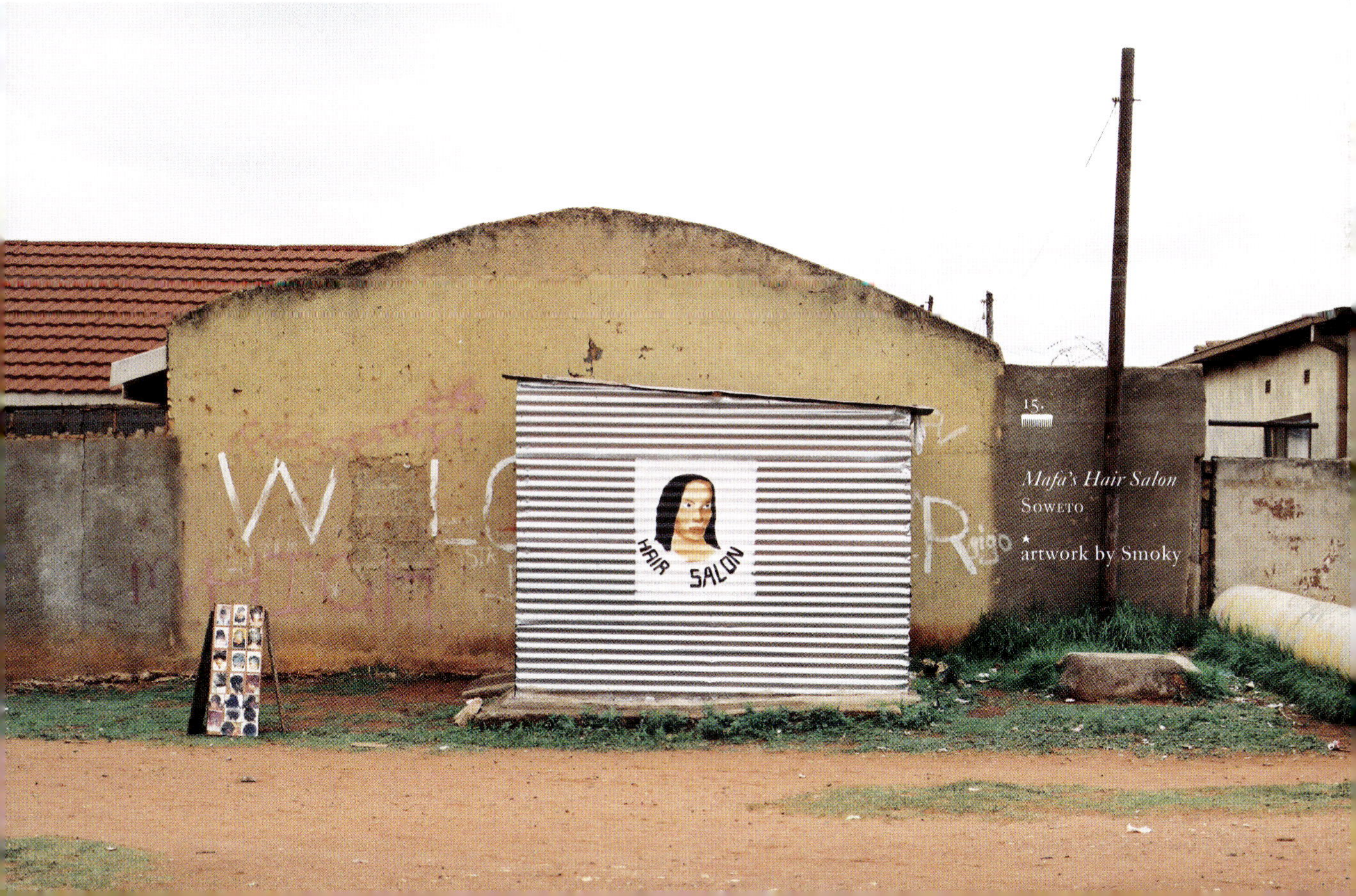

15.

Mafa's Hair Salon
Soweto

* artwork by Smoky

1.4 ALEXANDRA

Alexandra, or Alex as it is commonly called, is situated in the north of the city and lays claim to being one of the most densely populated and deprived urban areas in the country. Ironically it is bordered by affluent residential areas, including Sandton, the wealthiest suburb in South Africa. For many years the township was known as "The Dark City" due to its lack of electricity. Even today, at night the area appears to be a massive black hole in the city's skyline when passing on the nearby freeway. Alex had made the news around the world in 2008 as the flashpoint for the xenophobic violence targeting suspected illegal immigrants, which quickly spread across the country. During my stay in Johannesburg in early 2009, my white South African friends had recounted terrifying media reports of rioting, rape, robbery, racial violence and murder.

On this trip almost everyone I speak to warns me against including it in my itinerary, not least my guides from the previous townships. "Alex is too crazy," Dr Phil had told me, "the streets are narrow, there are too many people and many *tsotsis* (criminals) – you will not be safe there, even with a local guide." Despite the warnings, I still want to visit this important township.

I explain my interest in visiting Alex to Kopano, a young shuttle bus driver from Soweto who thinks his cousin Vusi might take me into Alex. It turns out that Vusi doesn't live in Alex anymore, but he regularly visits his mother there and would be happy to show me around. I arrange to meet Kopano the next Sunday morning at a gas station at the entrance to the township. Kopano is waiting there for me in his trusty VW minibus. I'll happily admit to being scared. All the horror stories have finally started to make me wonder if I'm taking an unnecessary risk.

Surprisingly, my first impression of Alex is a positive one. There are hundreds of smartly dressed families walking the streets, the men in suits, the women in colorful dresses and head scarves. Kopano explains that many of the residents of South Africa's townships are very religious, and here they were in their Sunday best, making their way home from church.

We meet up with Vusi and his friend Dennis. I feel like some kind of minor celebrity with three guys looking after me as we tour the narrow streets of the township. It doesn't take long to see that many of Alex's residents live in terrible poverty. One area of squatter shacks is built on a hill and the structures appear to be stacked perilously on top of each other, creating the effect of a rabbit warren, tiny alleyways snaking between each home. One of the most telling signs of Alex's deprivation is the Nelson Mandela Museum, built on the site of the former leader's old home. Today it stands half finished, after investment and financing dried up.

Despite hardships, the barbershops and salons of Alexandra serve as places where the community can escape. Vusi explains them as places "to chill and catch up on what's going on around you."

Many of the establishments we visit have seen better days: crumbling walls; hand-painted signs worn away by the elements; salon portraits left unfinished, some with eyes, noses, mouths or complete faces missing.

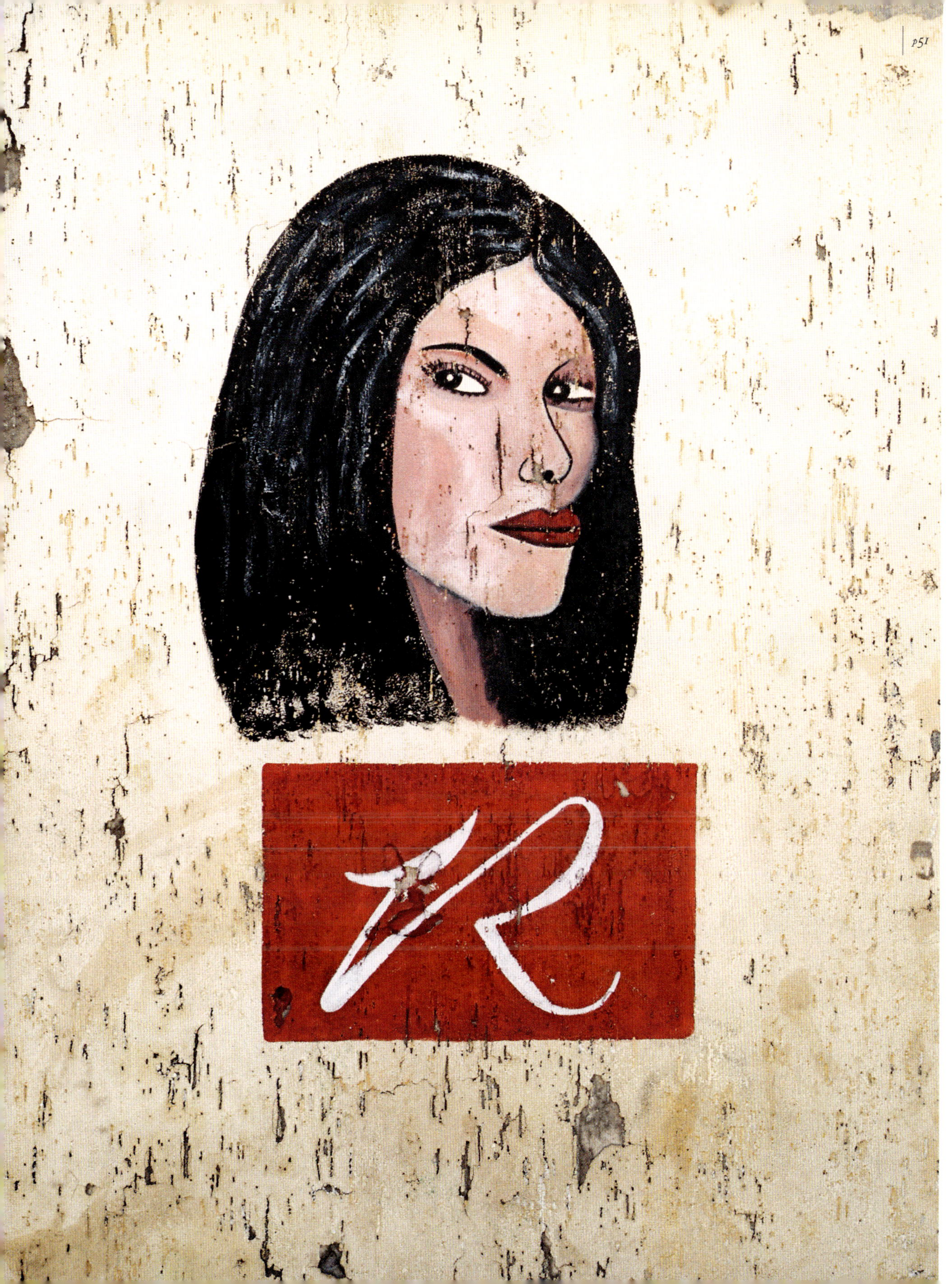
R

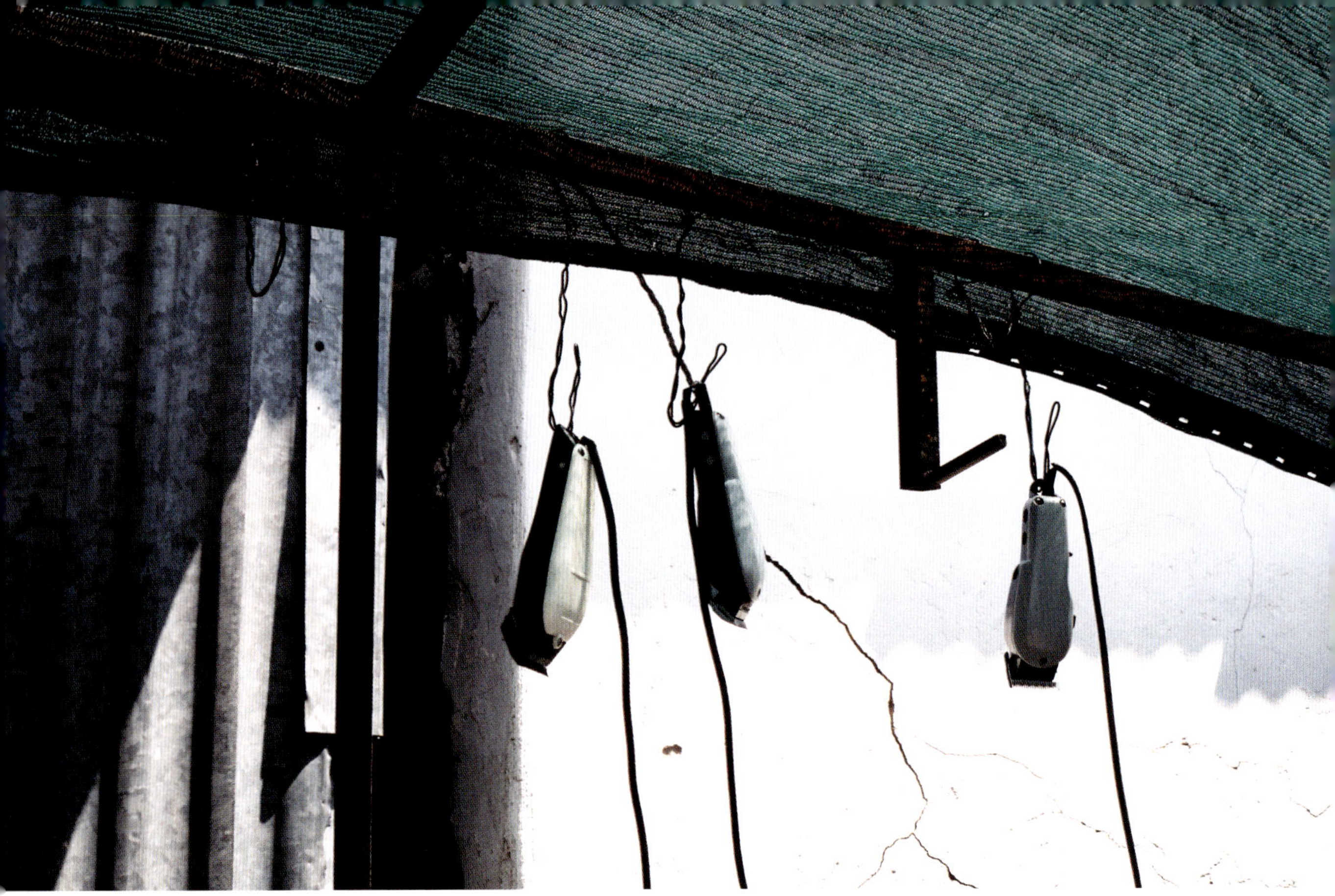

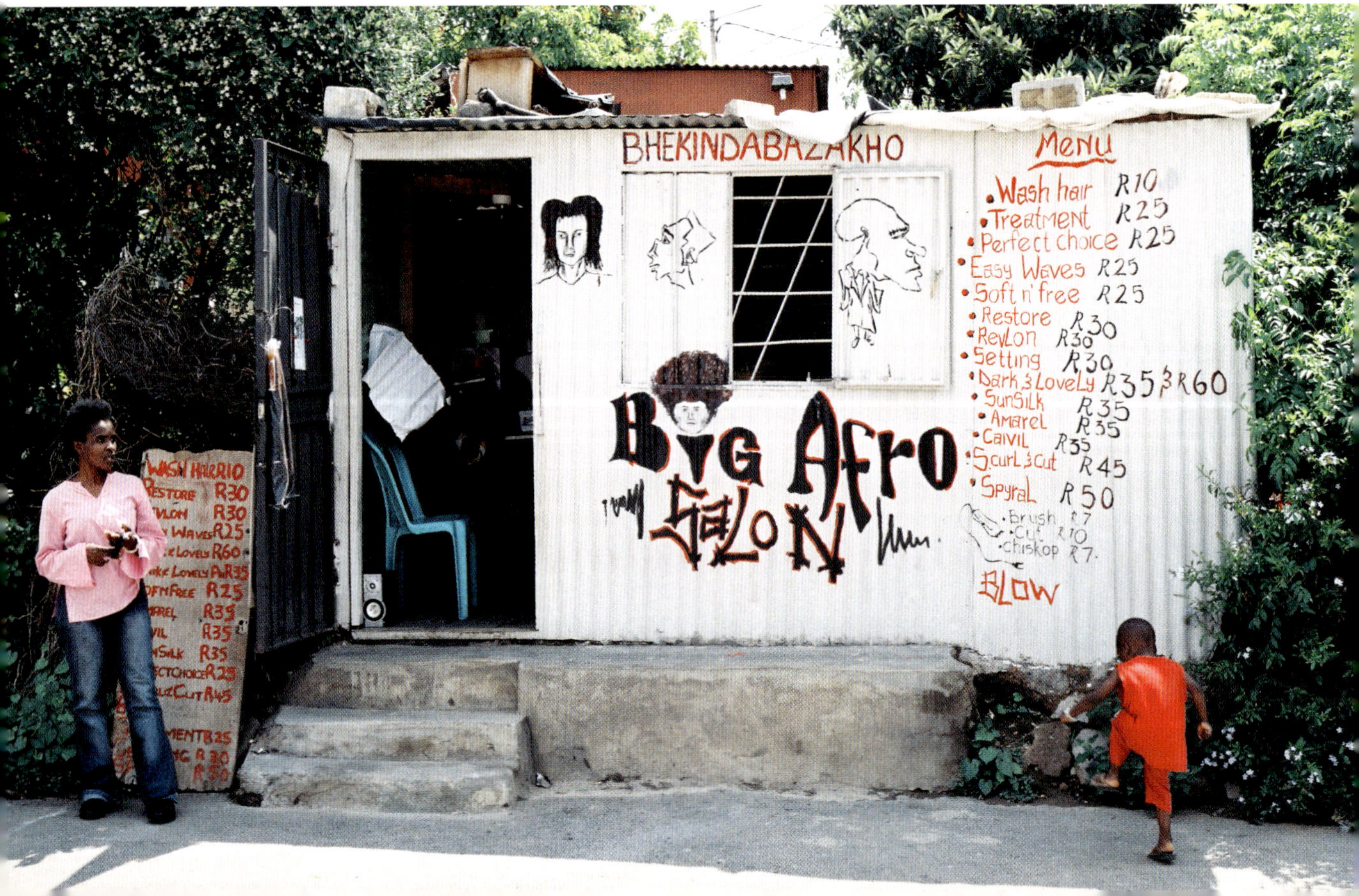

BHEKINDABAZAKHO
Menu
Wash hair R10
Treatment R25
Perfect choice R25
Easy Waves R25
Soft n' free R25
Restore R30
Revlon R30
Setting R30
Dark & Lovely R35 & R60
SunSilk R35
Amarel R35
Caivil R35
S.curl & cut R45
Spyral R50
Brush R7
Cut R10
Chiskop R7
BLOW
Big Afro
SaLON

While photographing one salon I meet Queen. It turns out she was commissioned to paint the portraits I am documenting. Although she is unwilling to be interviewed or photographed it is really good to meet her. During my entire journey across the country she will be the only female artist I encounter.

Despite all the warnings, Alex doesn't live up to its reputation. While some salon owners are unwilling to let me photograph their businesses, most are warm and friendly. Children and teenagers line up to get their photographs taken and one old lady gives me a big hug after I explain my project to her. The key to my positive experience here is thanks to Vusi and Dennis, who seemed to know almost everyone we meet. I will not pretend that everything is okay in Alex, it clearly isn't. But I'm not convinced the community here deserves its bad reputation; most folks here appear to be trying to do their best in an impossible situation. We end our day enjoying a cool drink in the shade beside the banks of the Jukskei River, which divides the township. We all reflect on a successful visit and exchange ideas of how a more organized township tour could really help to bring more hope and pride to the area.

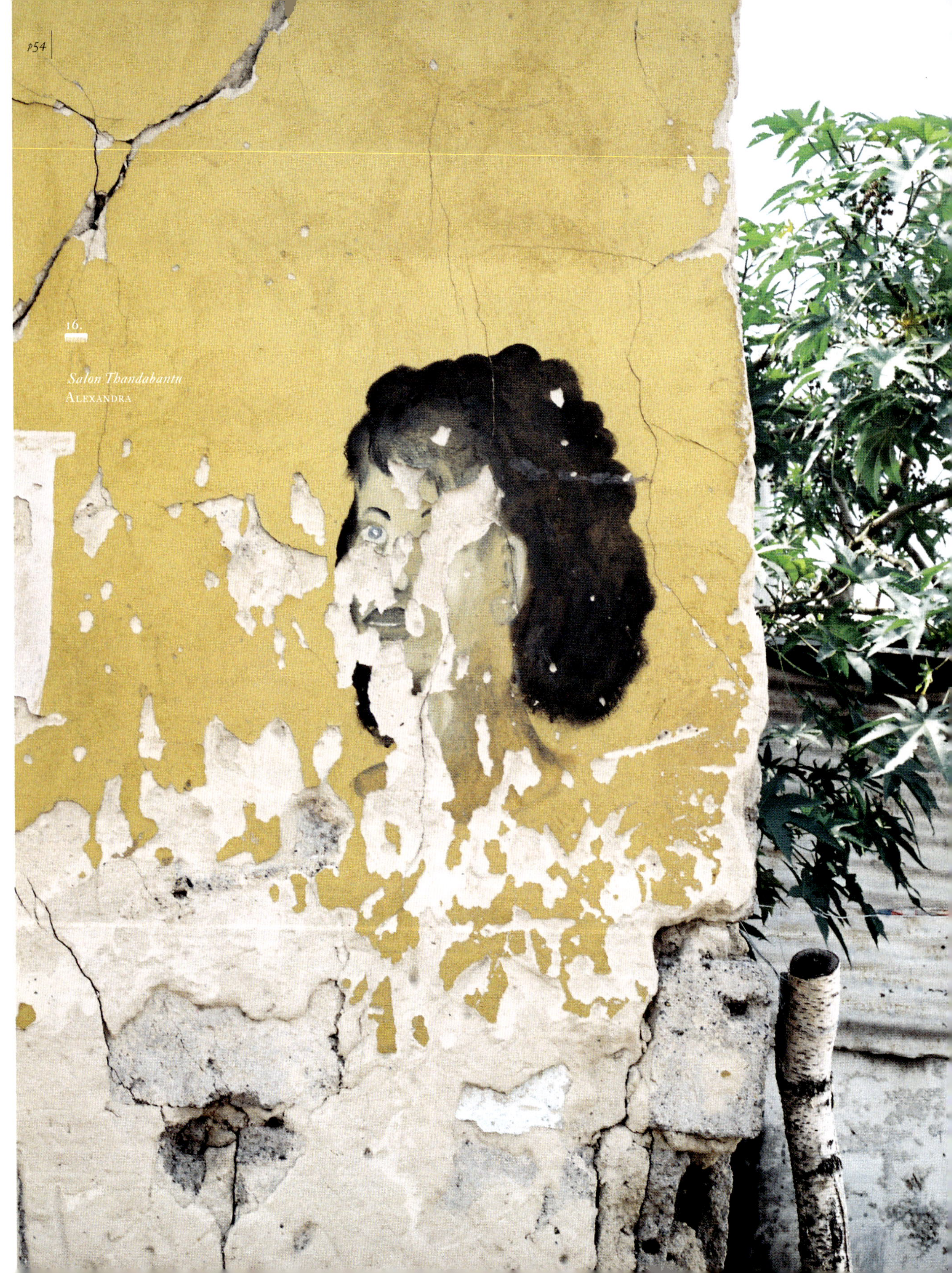

16.

Salon Thandabantu
Alexandra

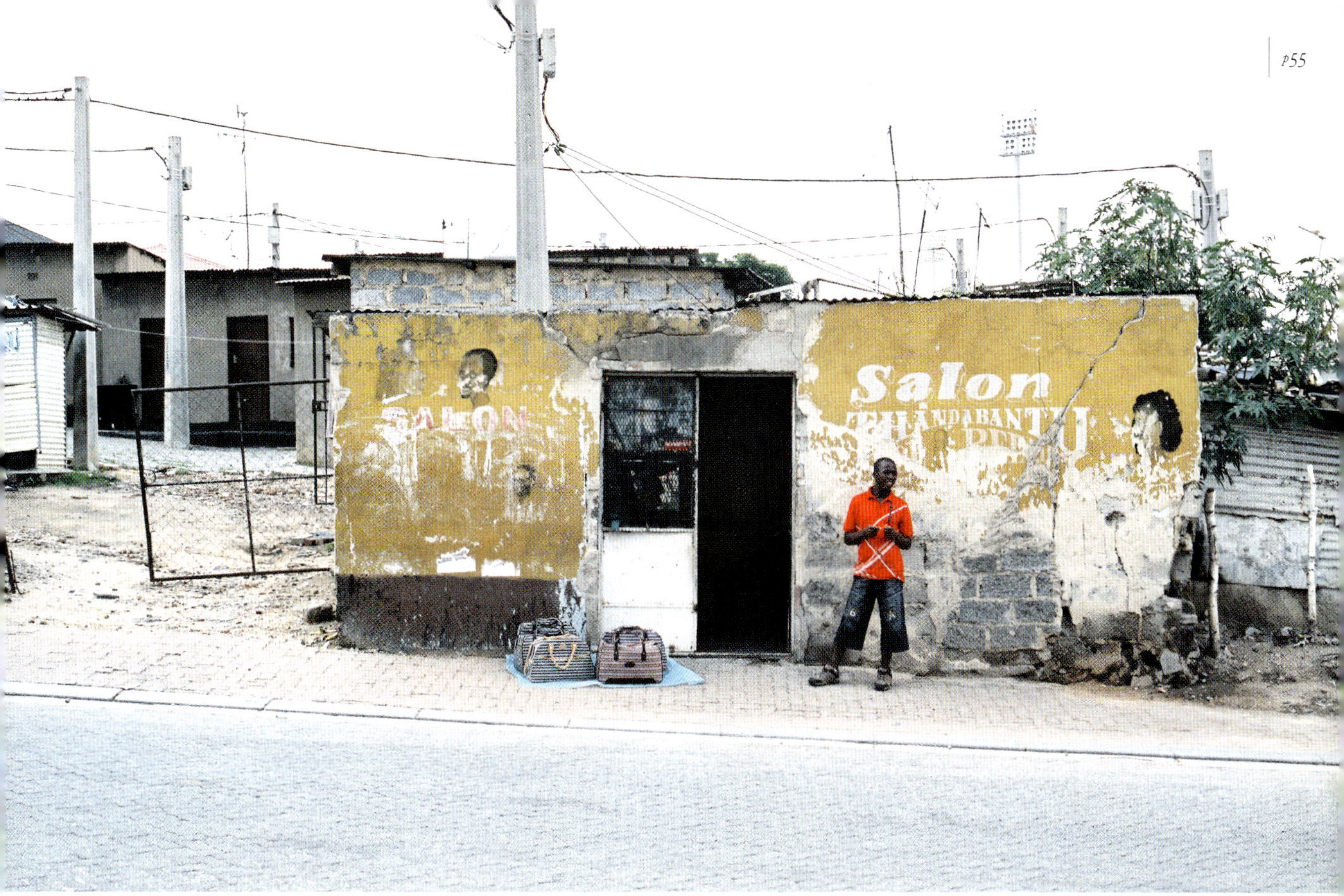

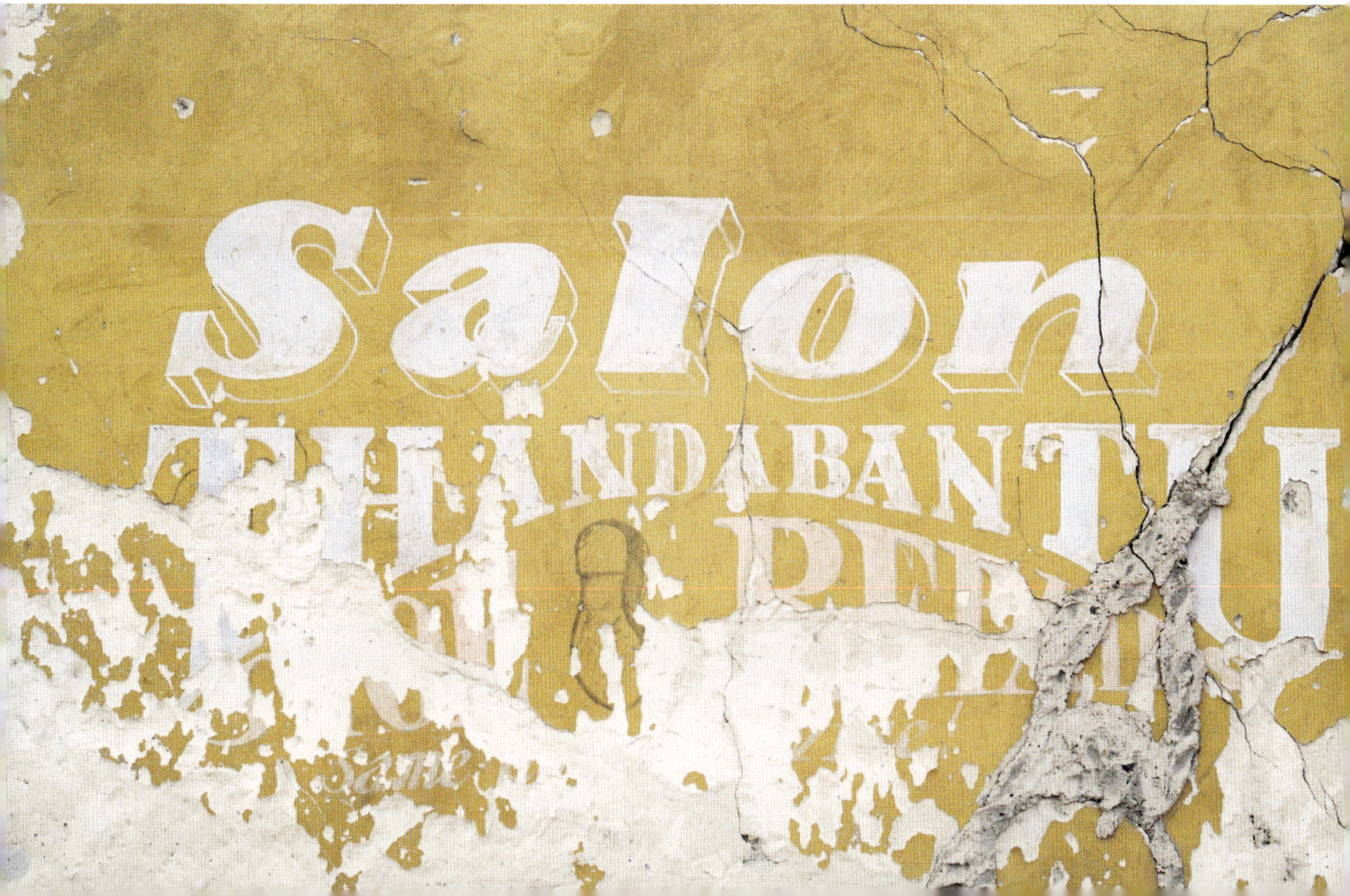

CHAPTER 2
RURAL TOWNSHIPS

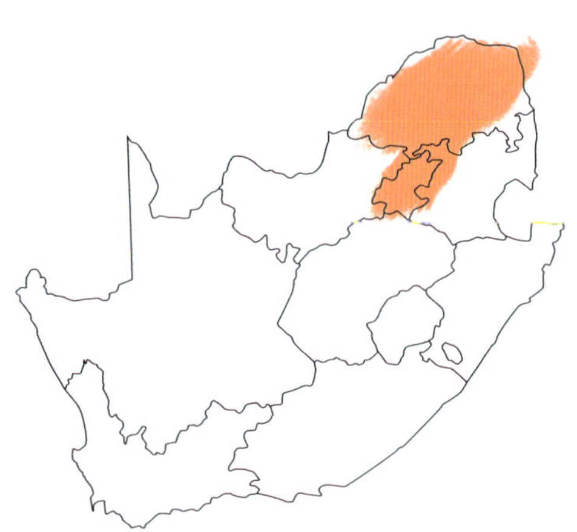

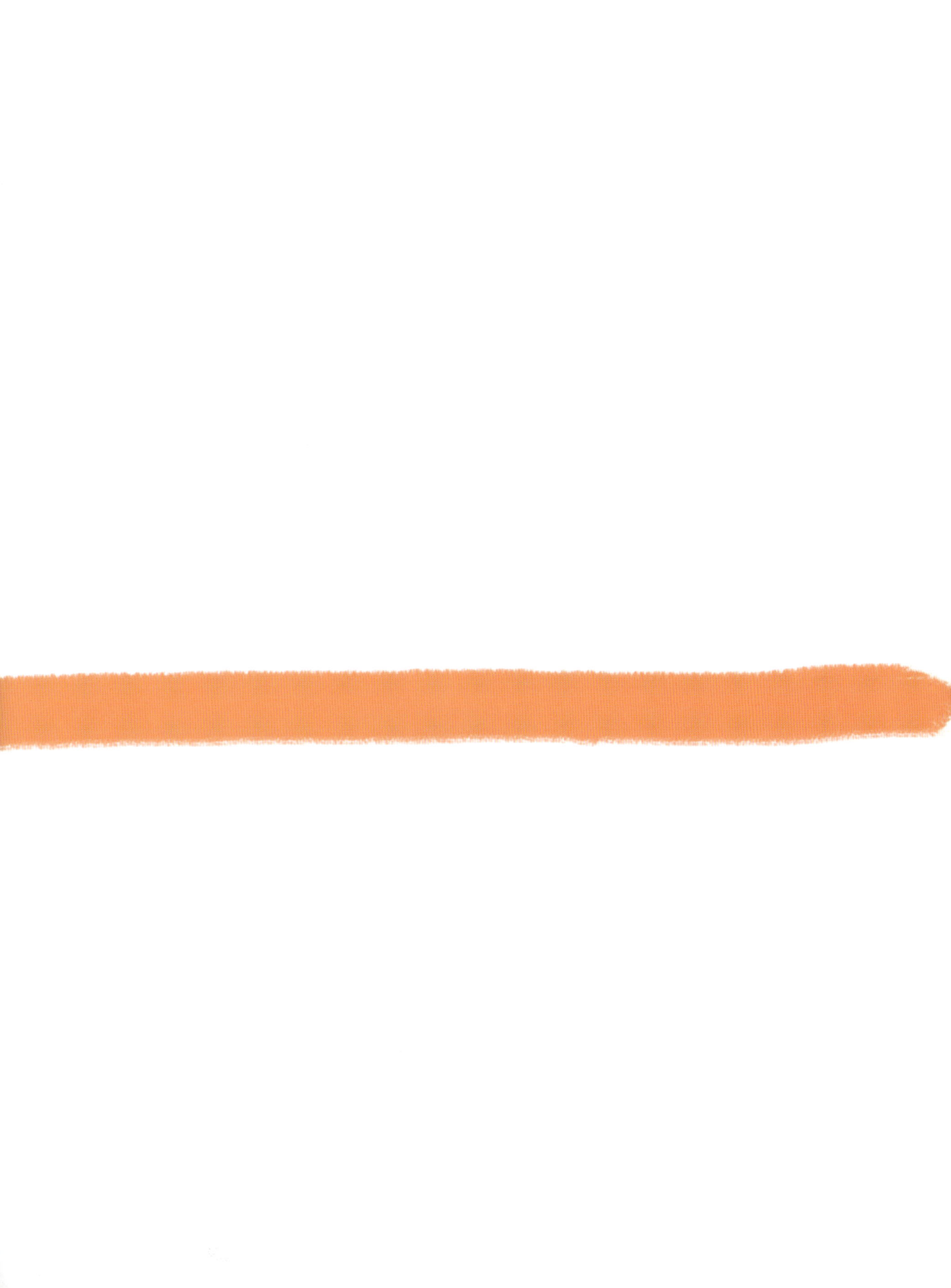

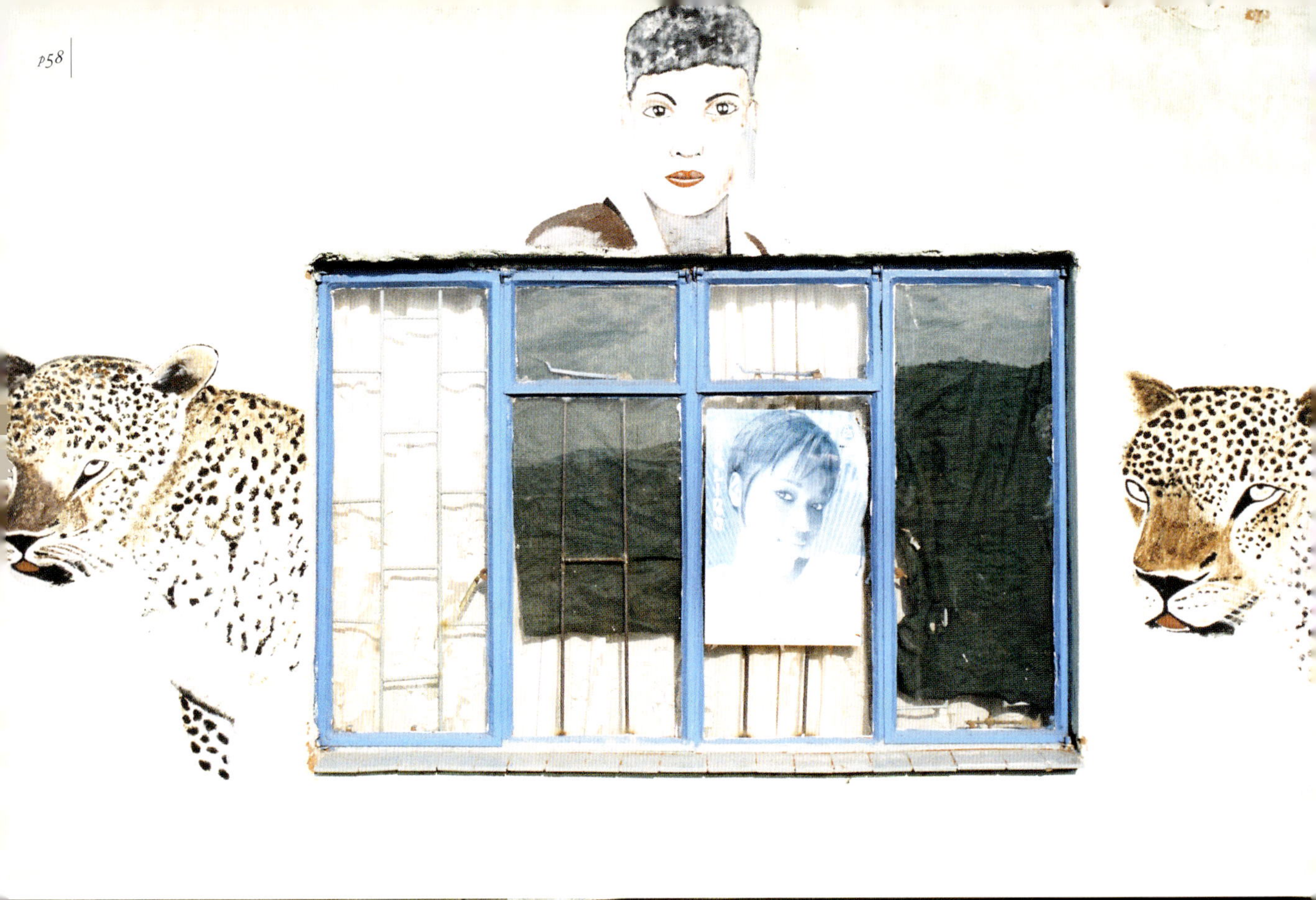

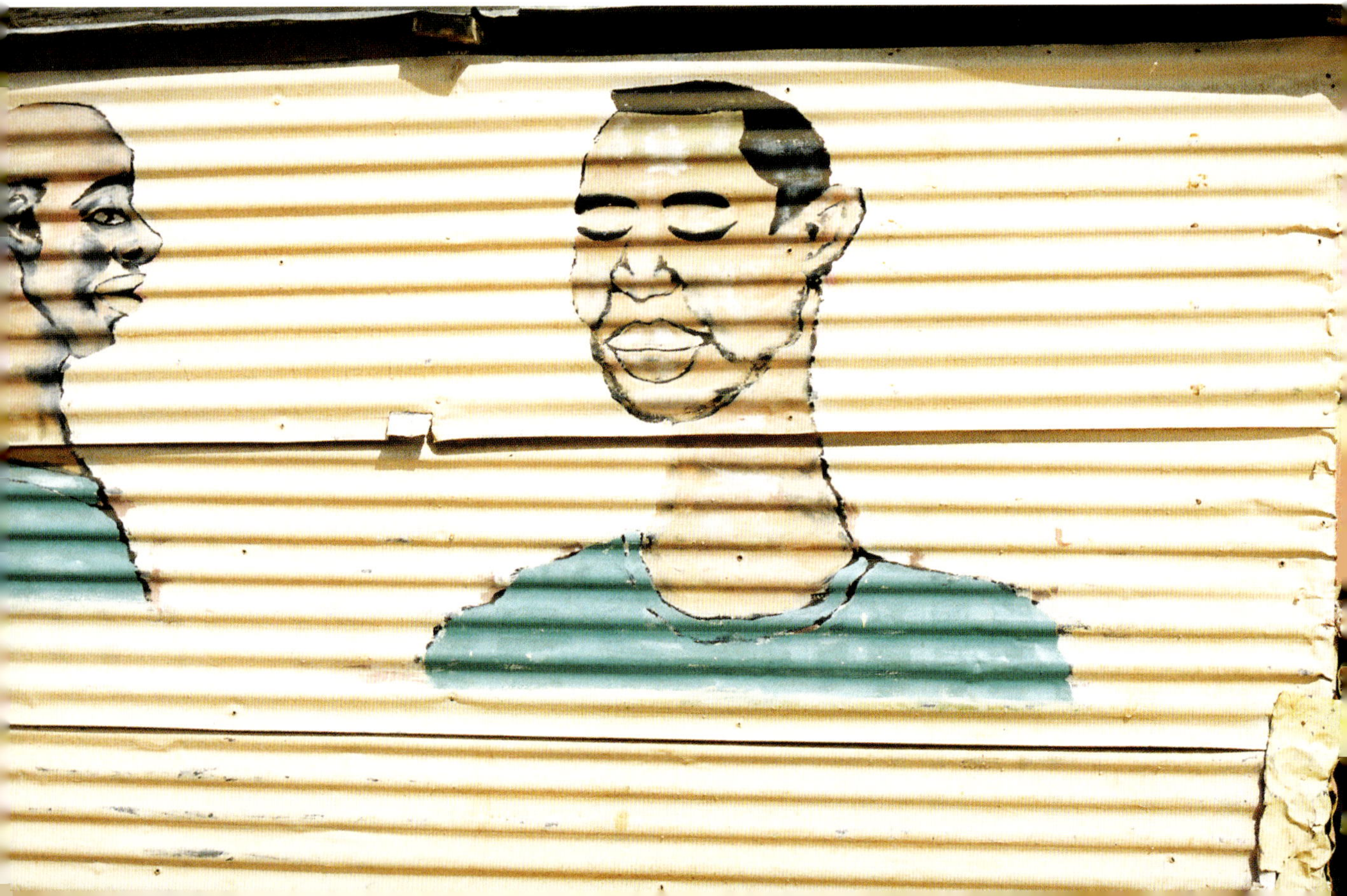

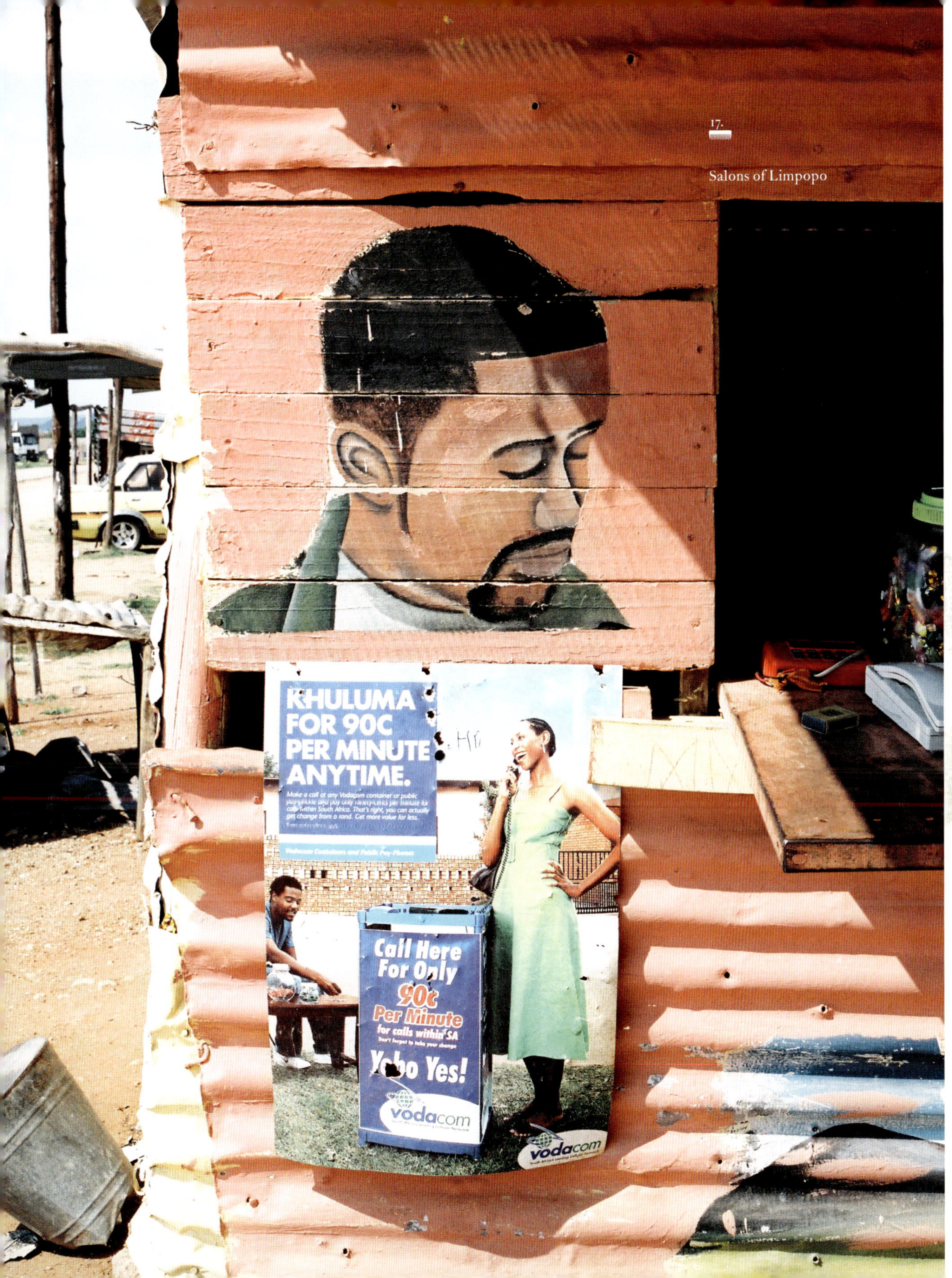

17.

Salons of Limpopo

2.1 SOSHANGUVE

My friend Rudi had told me about a road trip he had taken in Limpopo, South Africa's northernmost province, where there were plenty of rural barbershops. So he and I set out, making our first stop in Soshanguve, outside Pretoria in Northern Gauteng province. I am nervous to be there without a local guide, but Rudi is sure that it will be fine to drive around on our own. We compromise, deciding to befriend a local at the first barbershop we find.

Setswa Se Tsena (which roughly translates as "In and Out") Hair Cut is housed in a ramshackle wooden frame with fabric billowing from the sides. It is a very popular place for locals to meet, and a number of men, both young and old, are standing around chatting, either waiting to get their hair cut or just escaping the blistering midday sun. The barber is preparing to cut the hair of a young boy, probably no more than three years old. The boy sits in a chair with a blue smock around his shoulders, grimacing as the barber shaves his head with electric clippers. We are told that his parents have left him at the barbershop while they go shopping, proving that the community trusts the barber.

I get chatting with Sipho, a local businessman and avid soccer fan who explains the importance of this particular barbershop: "The barbershop is where guys hang out. It's not a matter of where people come to make haircuts, it's about meeting people. It's not like going to the *shebeen* (pub). At the barbershop you meet a different kind of people, where you can make different kinds of friendships."

I am introduced to Donald, a man in his mid twenties who offers to show Rudi and me Soshanguve's other barbershops and salons. We are also on a mission to find Chris Masekela, the artist who produced the sign writing for Setswa Se Tsena as well as a number of other local salons. Despite driving around for almost an hour we can't find Chris. Just as we are driving away we get a call from Sipho – Chris has been spotted walking home, laden down with shopping from a local supermarket. We drive back and meet Chris, who is waiting at the barbershop. My interview with him proves a real insight into the life of an artist in a rural township.

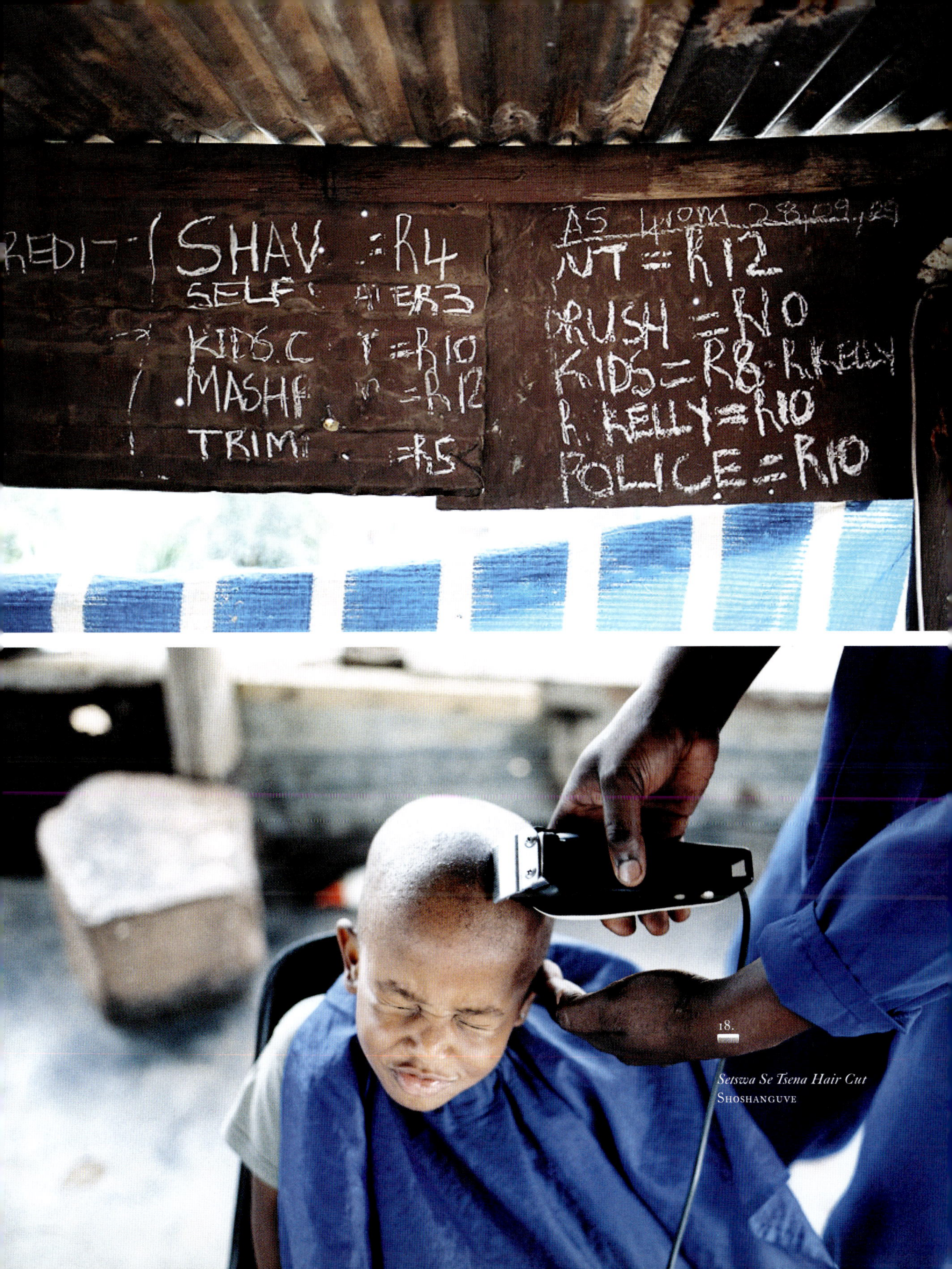

18.

Setswa Se Tsena Hair Cut
Shoshanguve

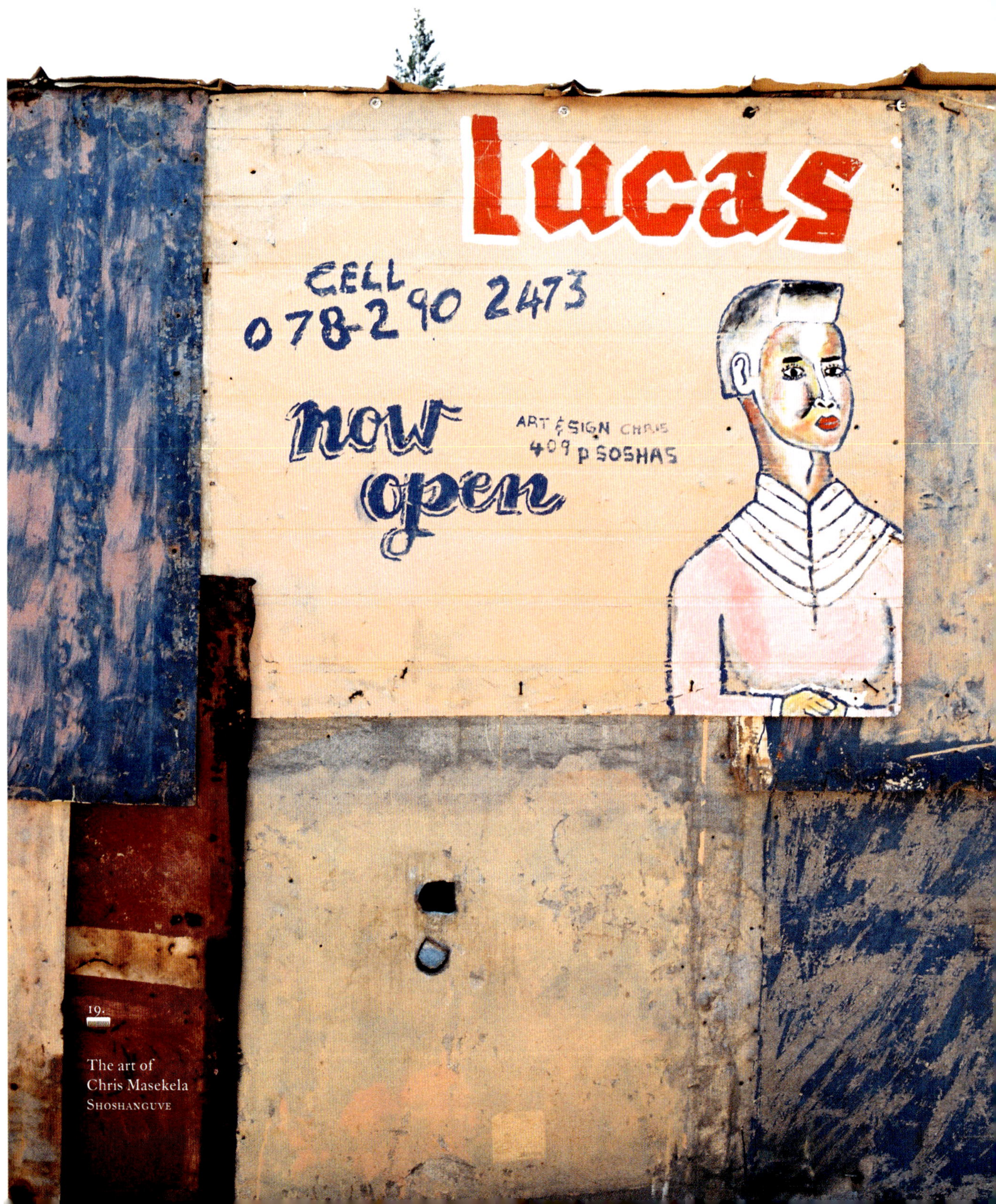

19.

The art of
Chris Masekela
Shoshanguve

2.2 Interview with CHRIS MASEKELA

How long have you been an artist?

Approximately twenty years.

Did you go to school for art?

I didn't go to school for art. I was inspired by an art gallery that I used to see when I came to town and became interested in white man's art. I like black man's art but I like white artists because they show real life and draw towns and people, for instance showing guys playing dice. Black art only shows traditional things like a black woman carrying a calabash on her head, going to fetch water from the river.

Do you only paint barbershops?

No, I do many different things. I like general art because it goes with general intelligence. If you have a specific intelligence it means you can't reach other areas, but general means you can cover the whole sphere. My stomach will remain empty if I only paint barbershops. South African people wouldn't understand it if a person only specialized in one thing. They don't know the meaning of art of the imagination. They just understand simple art, for a shop, like a label of Coca Cola or art for hair salon, they don't actually understand the meaning of art. Here artists just work in order to get money.

What kind of paint do you use?

Mainly acrylic but it depends on the surface I'm painting on, whether it's rough or smooth. When you do art on a textured material, it's very rough like crocodile skin and it has the feel of quality and it makes the picture come out very well.

Where do you produce the art?

People used to come to my apartment and I used to do the art there but I like moving. People used to ask me, "Why don't you build a shelter to do art?" I told them that I didn't want to be in just one place, I would become a lazy person. I'm like a mobile clinic, I'm interested in moving around. Unfortunately I don't have a motor car, I move on bare feet. I won't become old, I'll keep active. I'm fifty years old now and when I'm doing this kind of art, I move door-to-door, I like it, it gives me exercise.

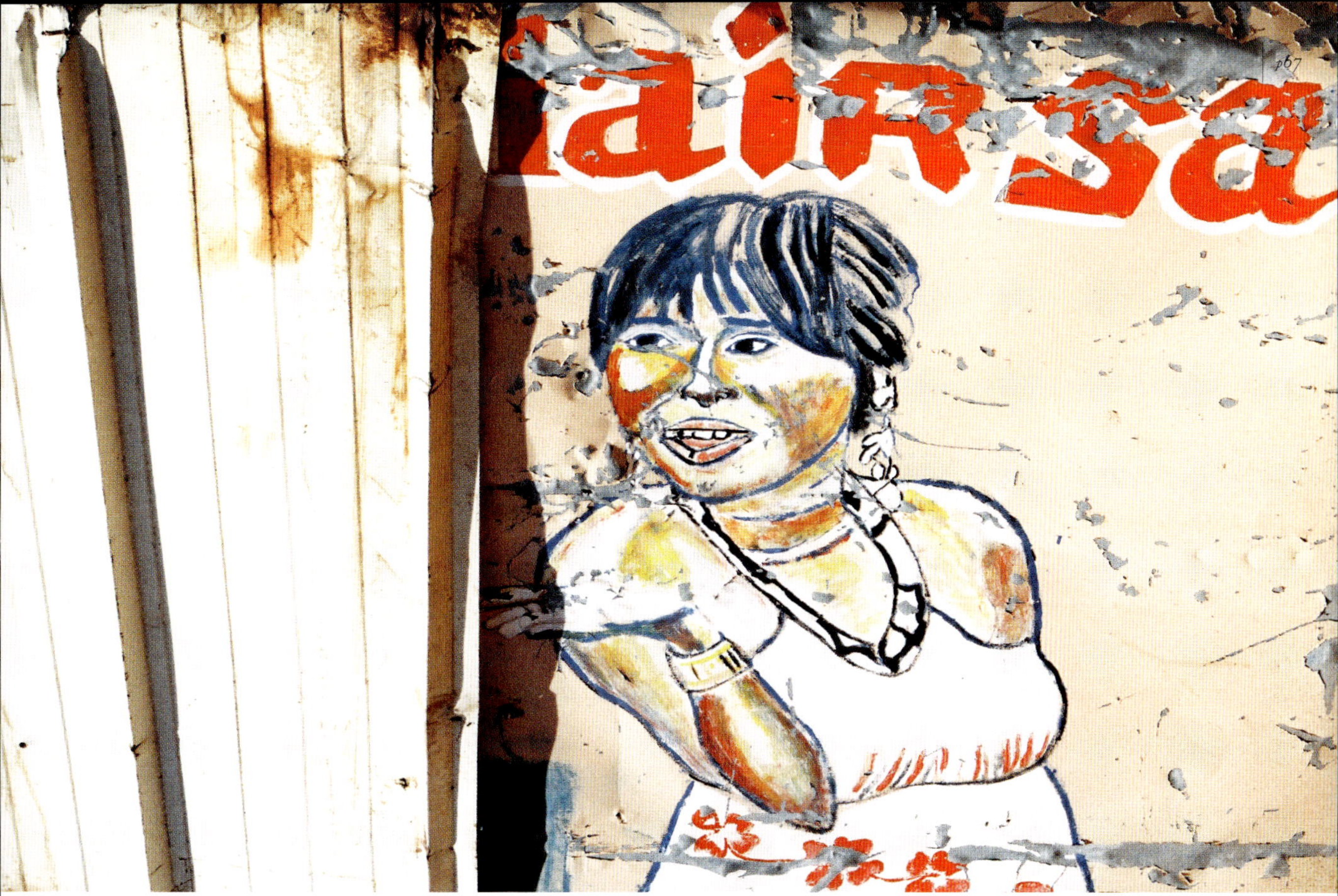

SETSWA
SE TSENA
CUT
HAIR CUT
ARTIST CHRIS

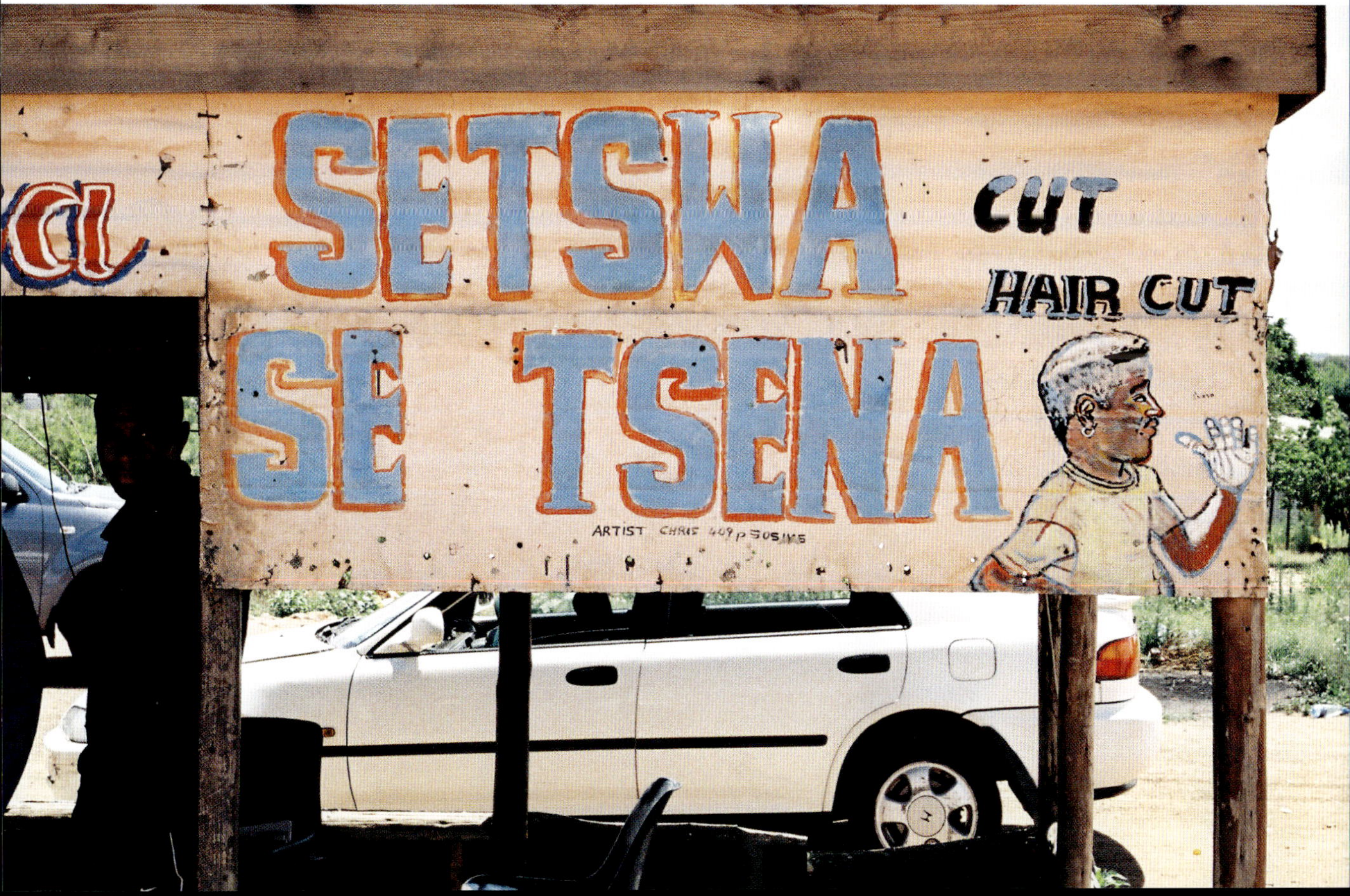

2.3 MPHAKANE

King Tiger's Hair Clinique is located in Dzanani, almost 300 miles north of Johannesburg. En route, Rudi and I pass through the small township of Mphakane. Noticing a number of salons we stop. The first barbershop is a shack full of people and no one speaks English. As the people stare I wish I had a trusty guide to translate for me. The owner eventually seems to understand what I want to do and allows me to photograph his business. Mphakane's barbershops all appear to have been painted by the same artist who specializes in portraits of cool looking guys wearing sunglasses.

The second barbershop I approach is far less intimidating. I decide to try and break the ice by showing the barber and customers my sunburned shoulders. The people burst out laughing at the sight of an Englishman who isn't used to the harsh African sun.

I have asked all of the barbers if anyone has ever taken a photograph of their salon before. Up until now, every single barber has answered no. When I ask this same question to the barber at T-Bone's Salon he answers yes. My heart sinks. Is there another photographer one step ahead of me? The barber explains that a white man had come the previous year to take photographs of the salon. He was from the town planning department and they wanted to demolish the shack so a pedestrian bridge could be constructed.

Rudi and I continue our journey toward the border of Zimbabwe. As we near the town of Polokwane we see a chilling sight; high on a hill stand hundreds of crosses, memorials to the farmers that have been murdered in recent years. Rudi tells me that since the end of Apartheid, in this province alone, over 3,500 people have been killed, both white and black.

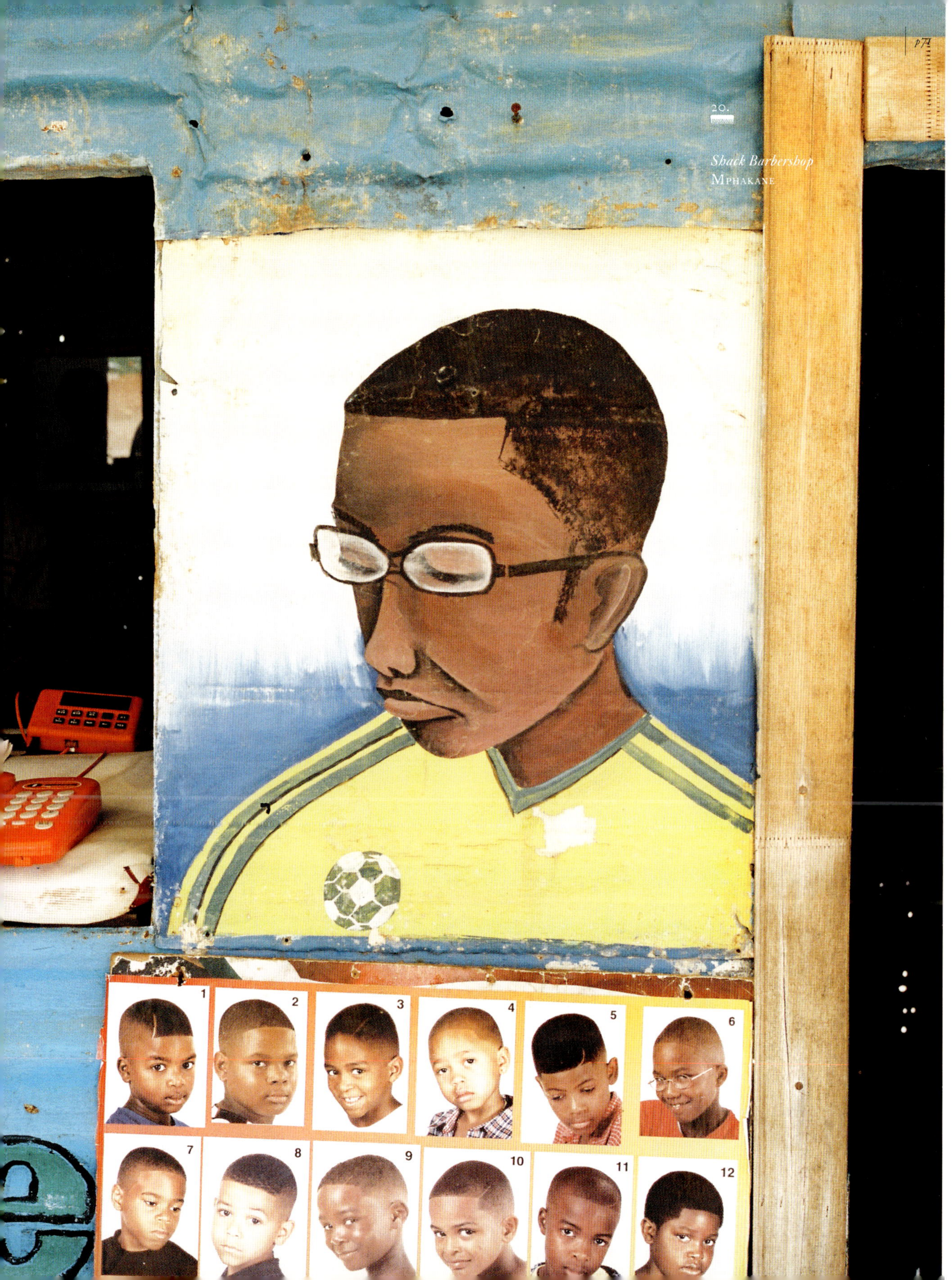

20.

Shack Barbershop
Mphakane

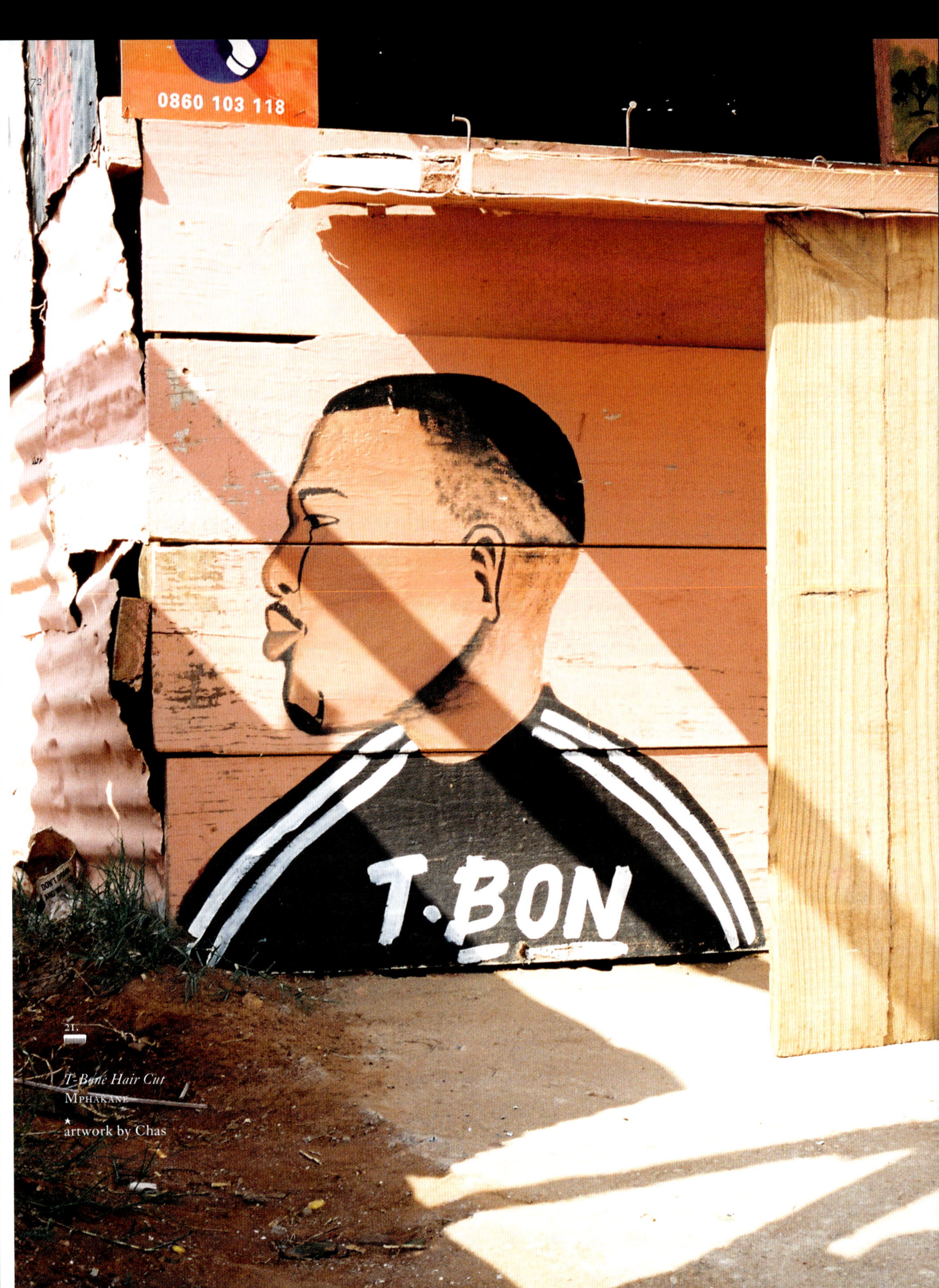

21.

T-Bone Hair Cut
Mphakane

★
artwork by Chas

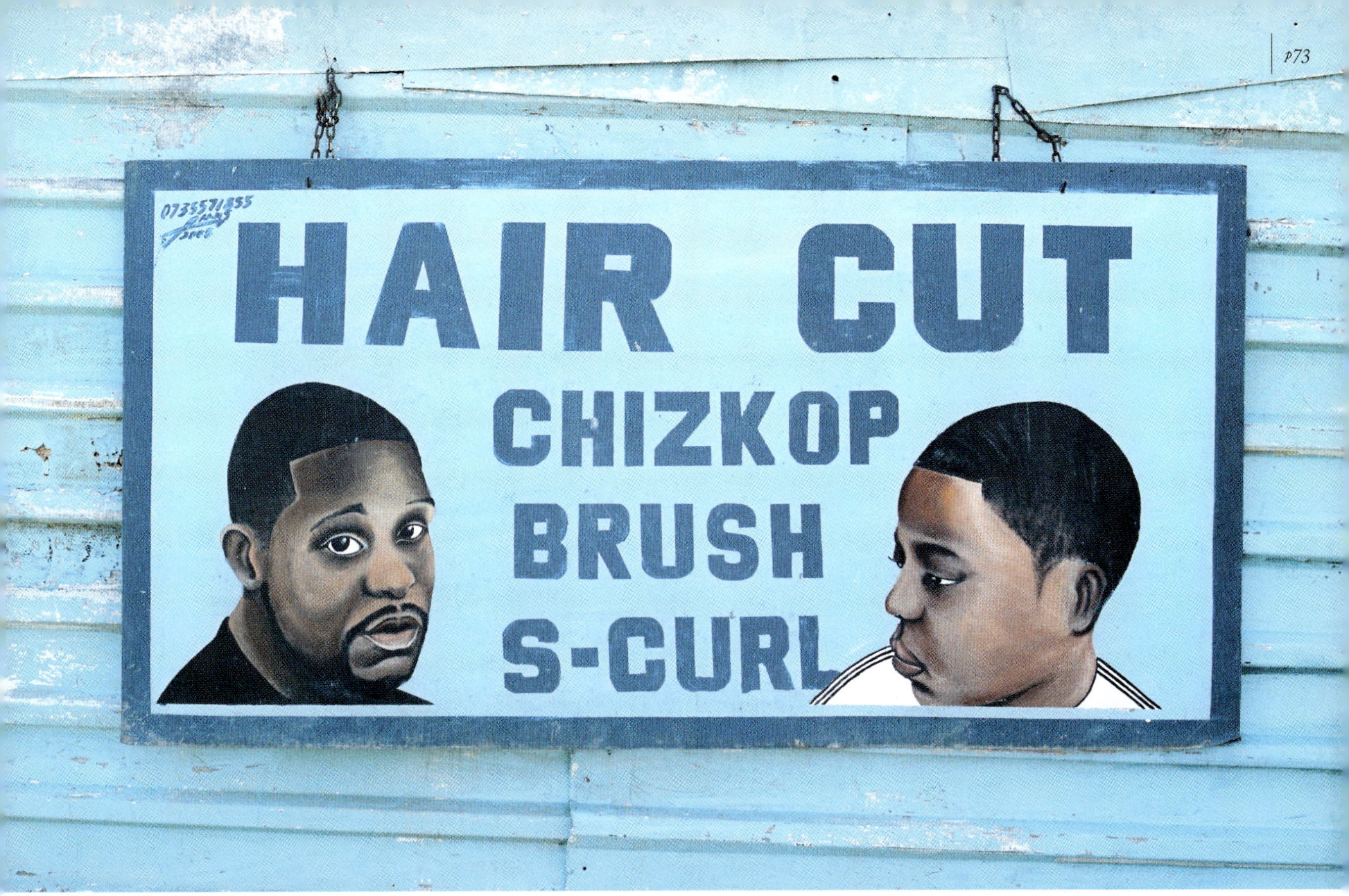

HAIR CUT
CHIZKOP
BRUSH
S-CURL

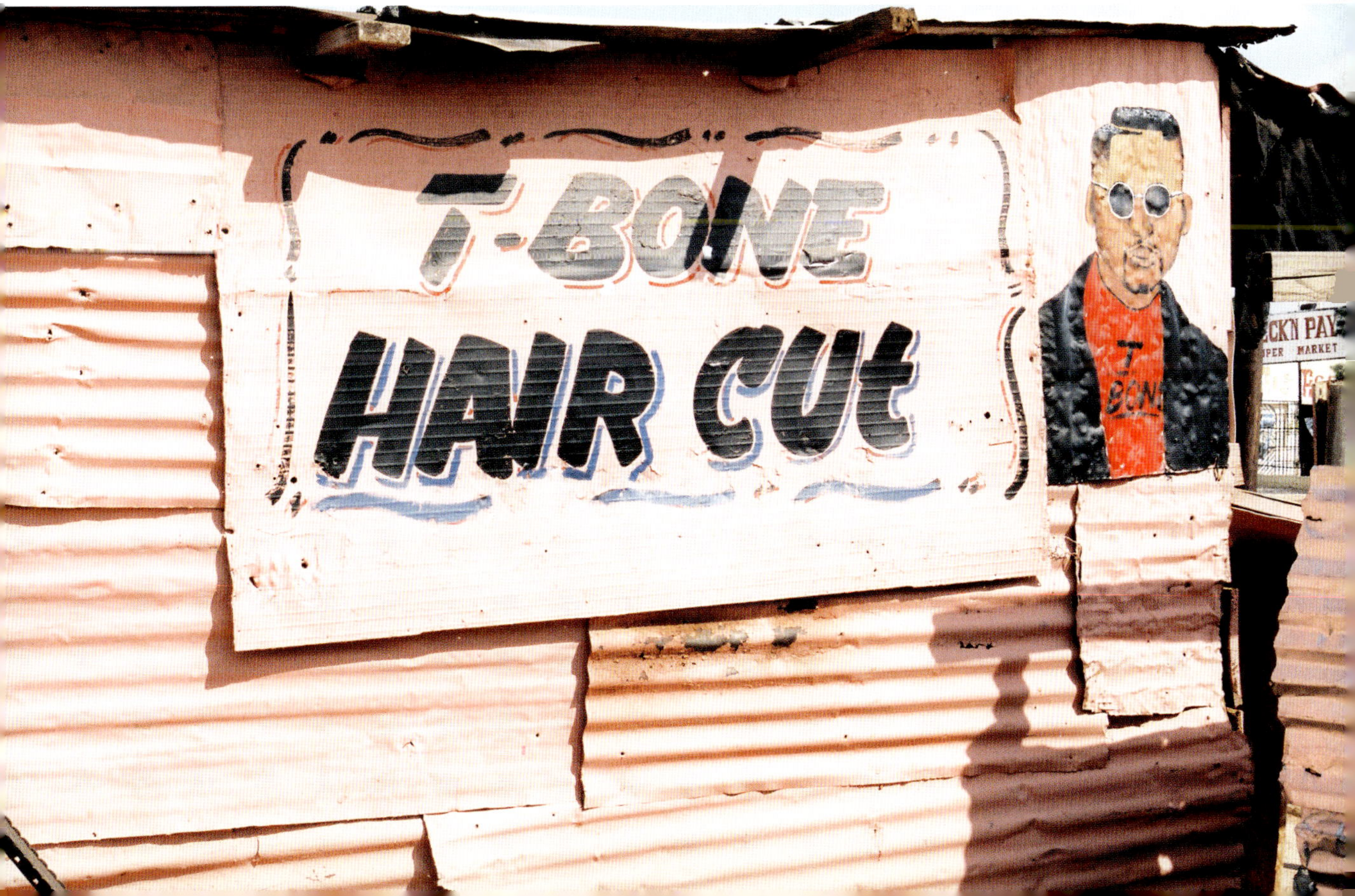

T-BONE
HAIR CUT

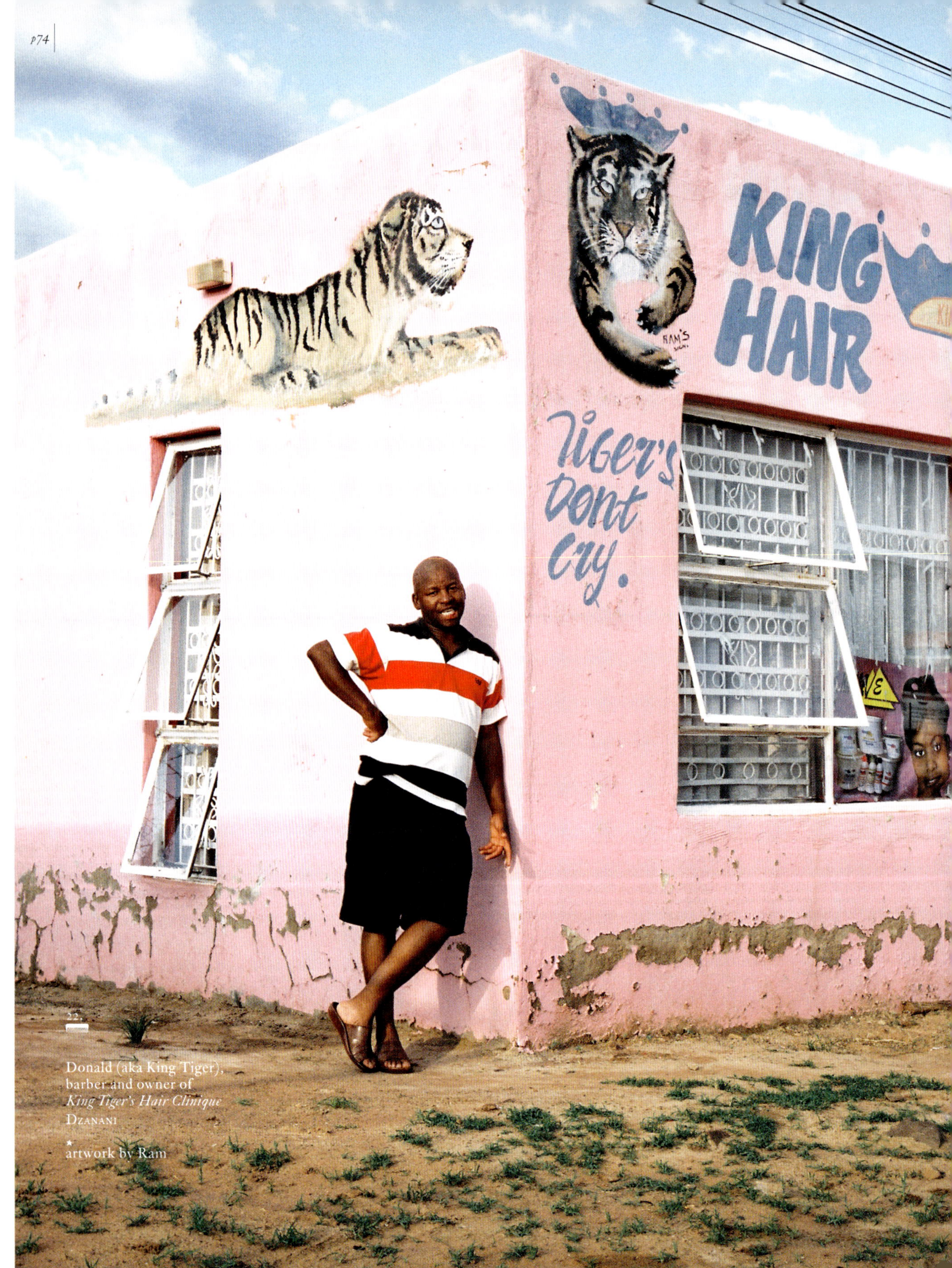

22

Donald (aka King Tiger), barber and owner of *King Tiger's Hair Clinique*
DZANANI

★
artwork by Ram

2.4 Dzanani

KING TIGER'S HAIR CLINIQUE

As we pull up at King Tiger's Hair Clinique I know that the long journey has been worthwhile. There in front of me is a small brick building, painted bright pink and emblazoned with a large illustration of a tiger; kitsch italic lettering announces, "Tigers Don't Cry."

A man walks out to greet us. It turns out to be King Tiger himself, a middle-aged man named Donald. A little wary of our intentions at first he breaks into a broad smile when I explain that we have driven all the way from Johannesburg to photograph his salon. King Tiger tells me that the salon is very famous in the area, not just for the building's façade but for the legendary haircuts that people travel many miles to receive.

Ram, a local artist, gets the credit for giving King Tiger's Hair Clinique a look that complements King Tiger's larger than life personality. The artwork took two days to complete and the business was re-launched with a big party, proving an instant hit with the community. Interestingly, not far from King Tiger's Hair Clinique is a salon with a huge leopard painted on one of the walls. This is big cat country.

After photographing the salon and chatting with King Tiger it seems like the perfect moment to get my first township haircut. King Tiger admits, "I've never cut a white man's hair before!" It is a source of great amusement for the other customers to watch. I ask Rudi how it looks, to which he replies, "It's definitely a haircut." What I end up with becomes my trademark for the rest of my stay in South Africa: a cross between a US marine and a cartoon character from *Beavis & Butthead*.

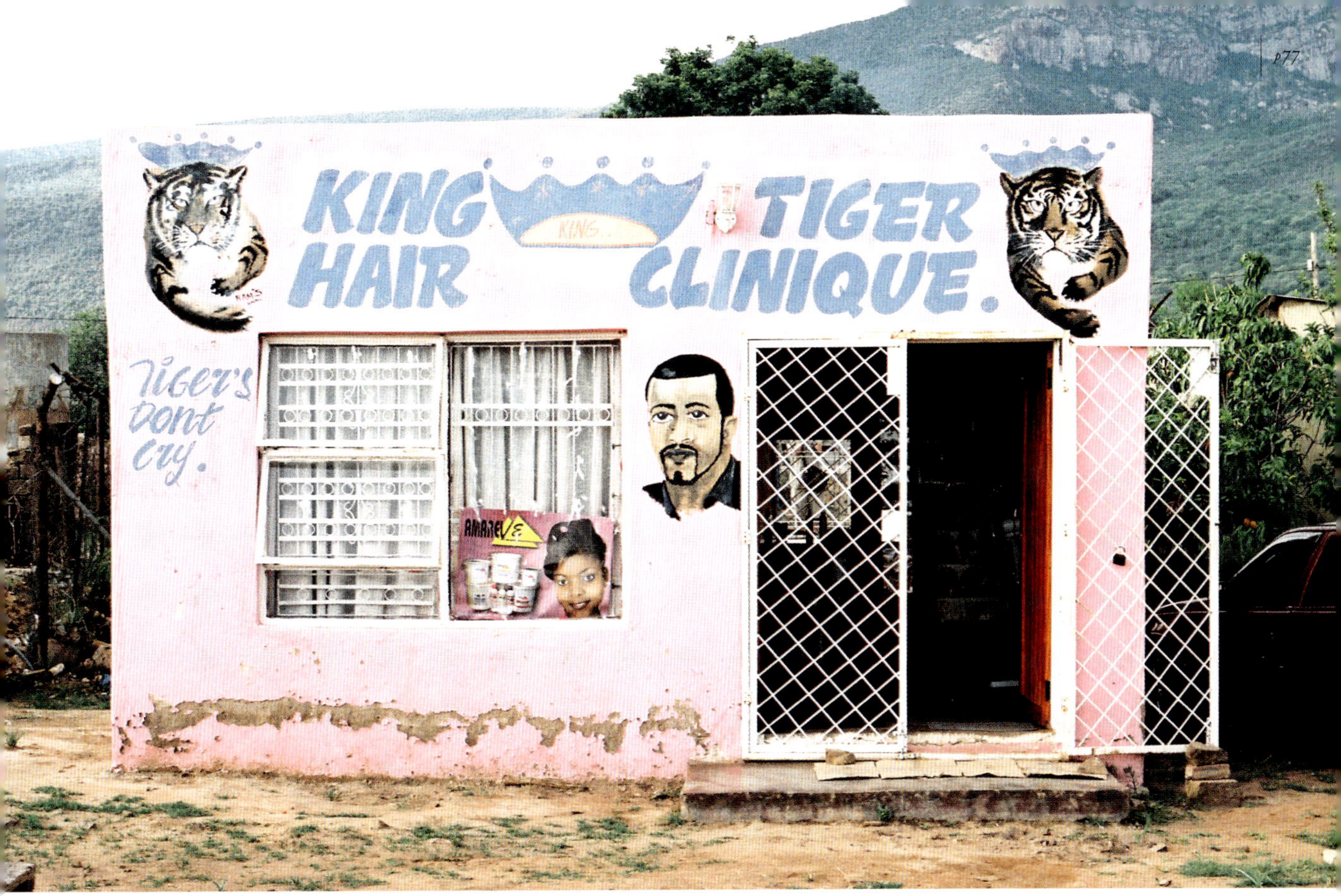

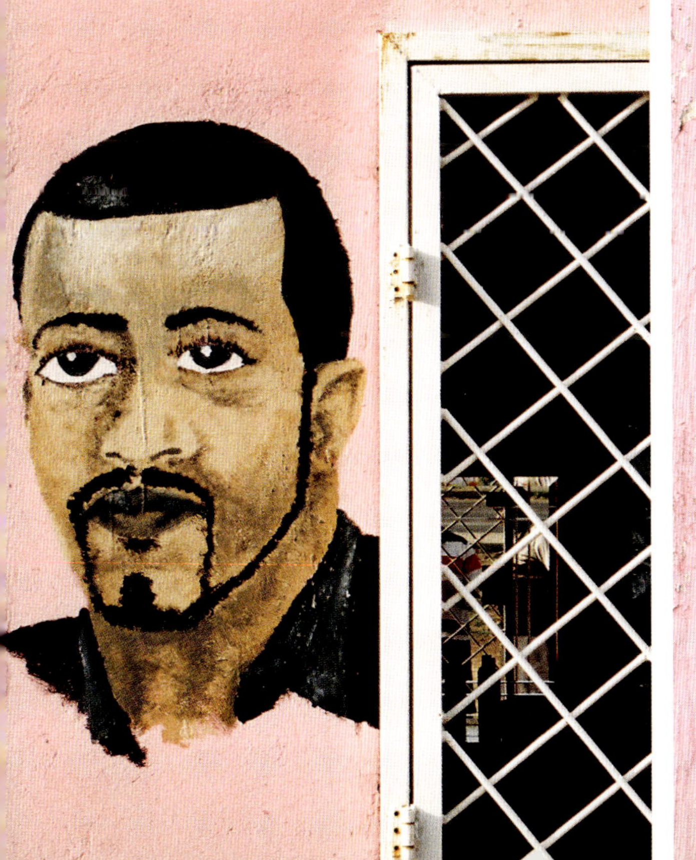

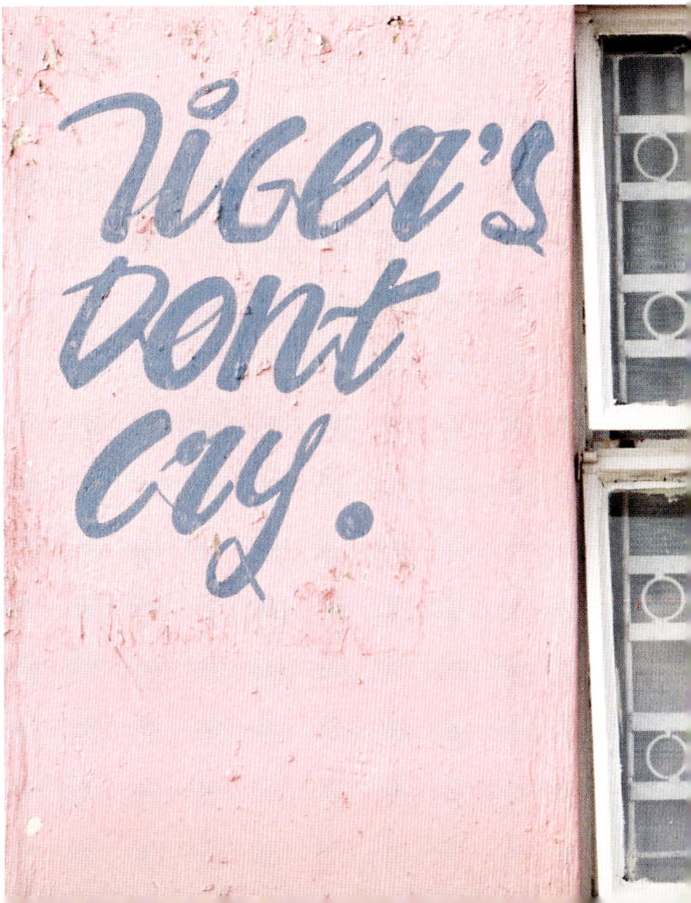

CHAPTER 3
DURBAN

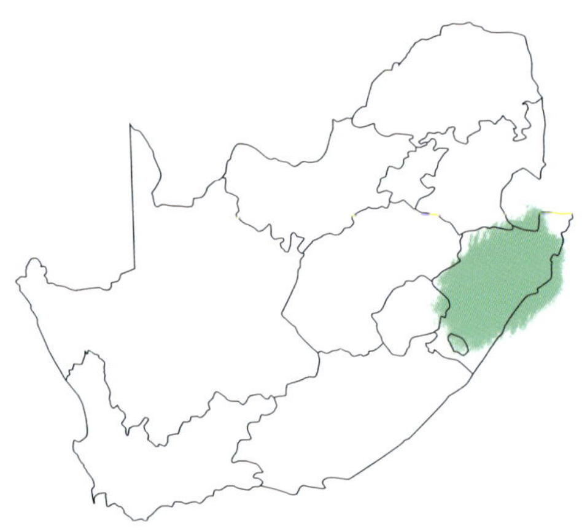

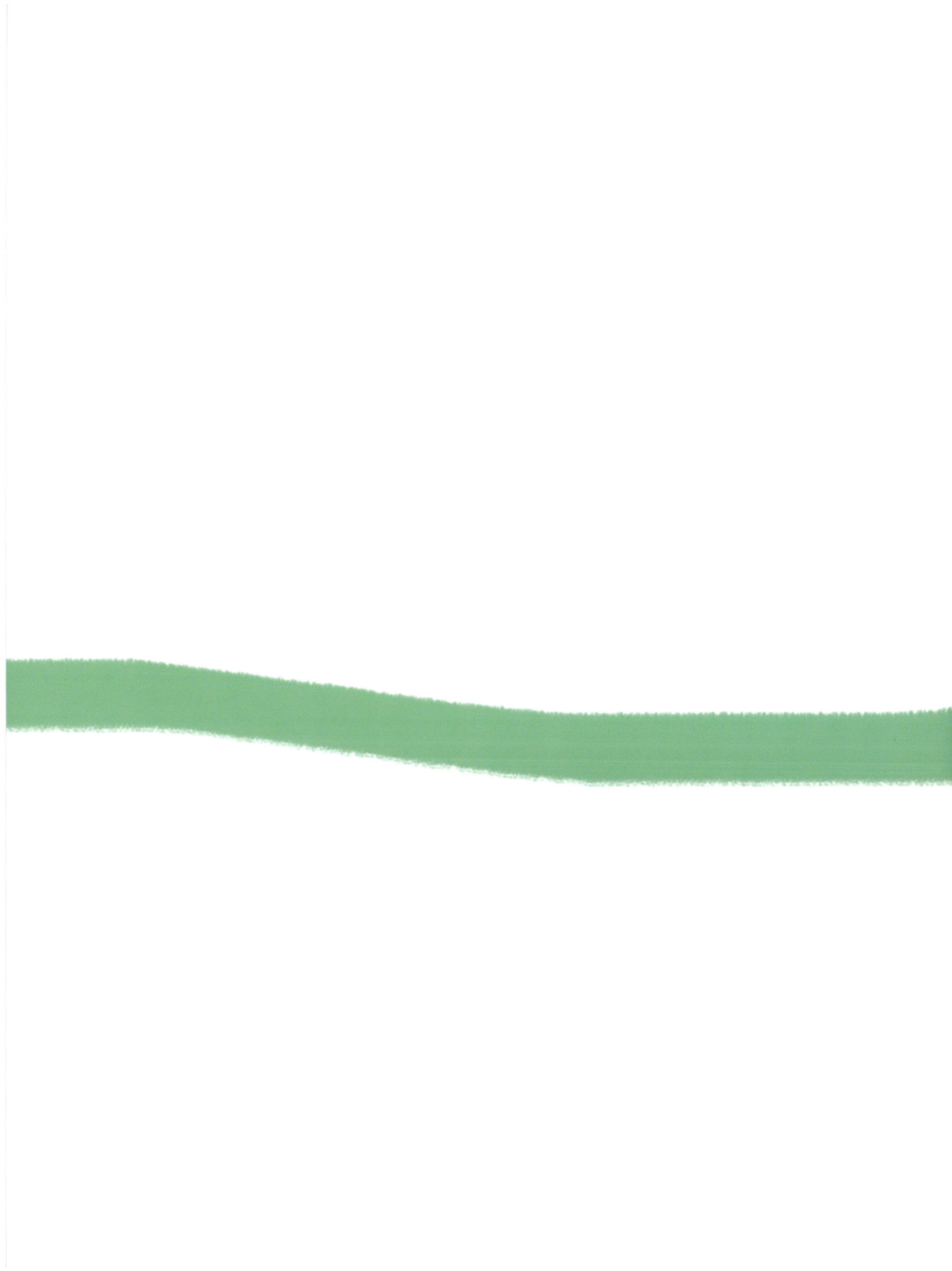

Attwood puts me in touch with Kennedy and I arrange to interview him at his apartment in the central business district area of downtown Durban. I book a cab and get chatting with the driver, Bongani. I explain that I am trying to find a guide to take me into the township Umlazi to photograph barbershops. Bongani offers to be my guide.

Since the end of Apartheid, the once desirable inner cities of South Africa are now plagued by crime. Bongani reaches the address and bids me farewell, arranging to pick me up later. As he drives away I look up and see a decaying apartment block, stewing in an air of real menace. This is just the kind of area that I have heard nightmarish stories of: high-rise residential buildings packed with immigrants, many illegal, with dozens of people crammed into small apartments. And here I am, on my own, weighed down with expensive camera gear. As I wait in the reception area of the crumbling apartment block my fears dissipate as I engage in a lively conversation with the security guard about English Premiere League Soccer and the World Cup. Kennedy eventually arrives and we make our way to his apartment.

Earlier, Attwood had told me about Kennedy's troubled background. A refugee from Burundi in central Africa, Kennedy had fled civil war. He and his family ended up in the Democratic Republic of Congo but later Kennedy set off alone and traveled to Tanzania, eventually settling in South Africa. Despite so much suffering and upheaval Kennedy had become a successful barbershop artist in Durban, but sadly was one of the many immigrants who faced persecution during the xenophobic riots in 2008. Eventually the situation in the city calmed and he was able to rebuild his business, continuing to make his mark on the barbershop industry and, more recently, in fine art and the world of commercial illustration.

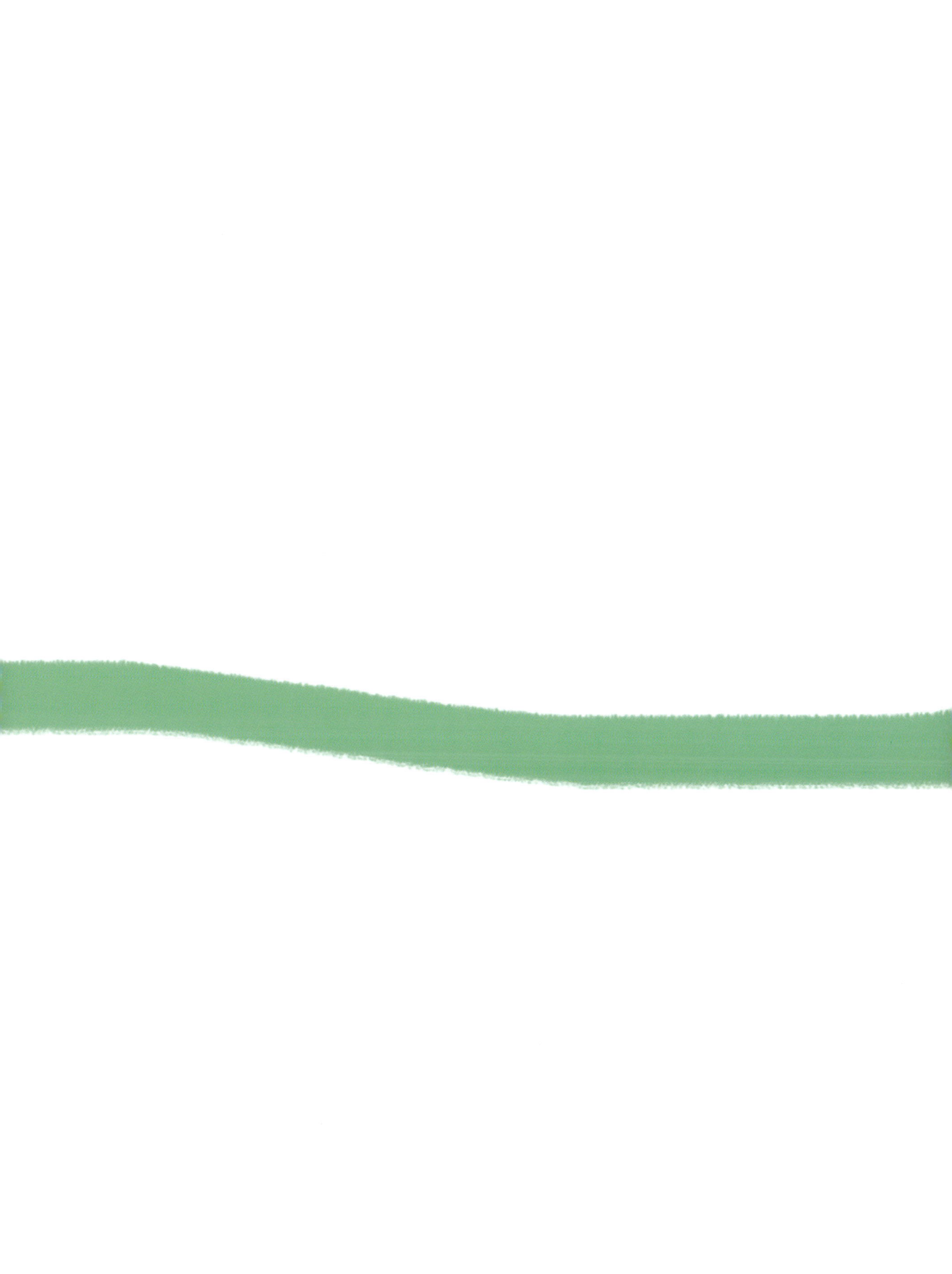

3.1 DOWNTOWN

Durban, South Africa's third largest city, is situated on the country's east coast on the Indian Ocean and boasts a tropical climate. But, for me it is freezing cold and pouring rain.

Frustratingly, my first two days in the city are a complete washout and I'm left stuck on the hostel's *stoep* (veranda) putting the world to rights with the other guests while the rain continues. On the third day there is a break in the weather and I head to an internet cafe on Florida Road, a tourist friendly bohemian area. I notice a number of township barbershop portraits in a contemporary art gallery. I learn that the work is done by local artist Espoir Kennedy. He produced the prints with Artists' Press, a small studio that specializes in producing limited edition lithographic prints by South African artists. I phone Mark Attwood, who runs the studio. He first noticed Kennedy's barbershop signs on a roadside salon in the town of Carolina.

Attwood puts me in touch with Kennedy and I arrange to interview him at his apartment in the central business district area of downtown Durban. I book a cab and get chatting with the driver, Bongani. I explain that I am trying to find a guide to take me into the township Umlazi to photograph barbershops. Bongani offers to be my guide.

Since the end of Apartheid, the once desirable inner cities of South Africa are now plagued by crime. Bongani reaches the address and bids me farewell, arranging to pick me up later. As he drives away I look up and see a decaying apartment block, stewing in an air of real menace. This is just the kind of area that I have heard nightmarish stories of: high-rise residential buildings packed with immigrants, many illegal, with dozens of people crammed into small apartments. And here I am, on my own, weighed down with expensive camera gear. As I wait in the reception area of the crumbling apartment block my fears dissipate as I engage in a lively conversation with the security guard about English Premiere League Soccer and the World Cup. Kennedy eventually arrives and we make our way to his apartment.

Earlier, Attwood had told me about Kennedy's troubled background. A refugee from Burundi in central Africa, Kennedy had fled civil war. He and his family ended up in the Democratic Republic of Congo but later Kennedy set off alone and traveled to Tanzania, eventually settling in South Africa. Despite so much suffering and upheaval Kennedy had become a successful barbershop artist in Durban, but sadly was one of the many immigrants who faced persecution during the xenophobic riots in 2008. Eventually the situation in the city calmed and he was able to rebuild his business, continuing to make his mark on the barbershop industry and, more recently, in fine art and the world of commercial illustration.

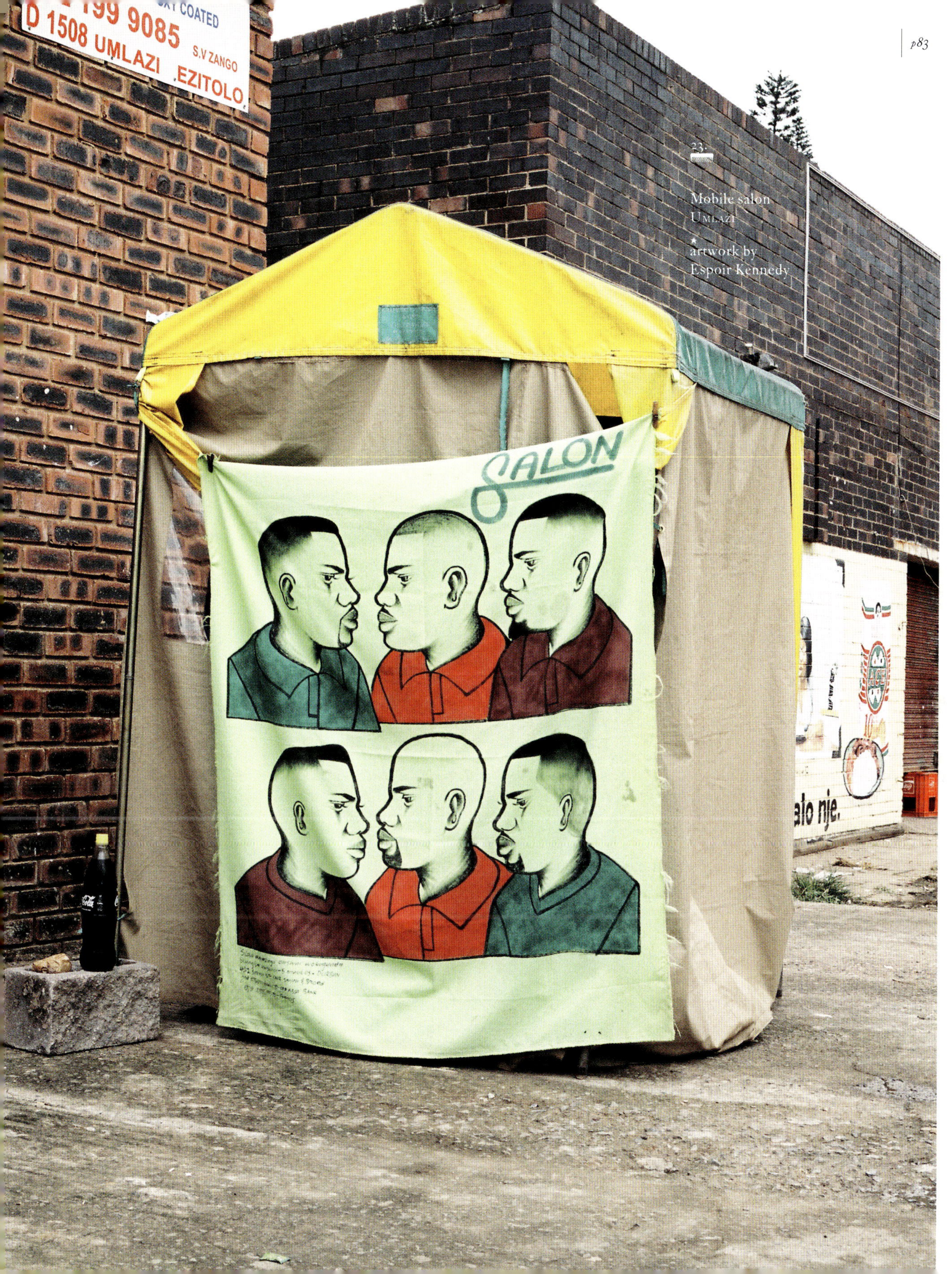

23.

Mobile salon
UMLAZI

★

artwork by
Espoir Kennedy

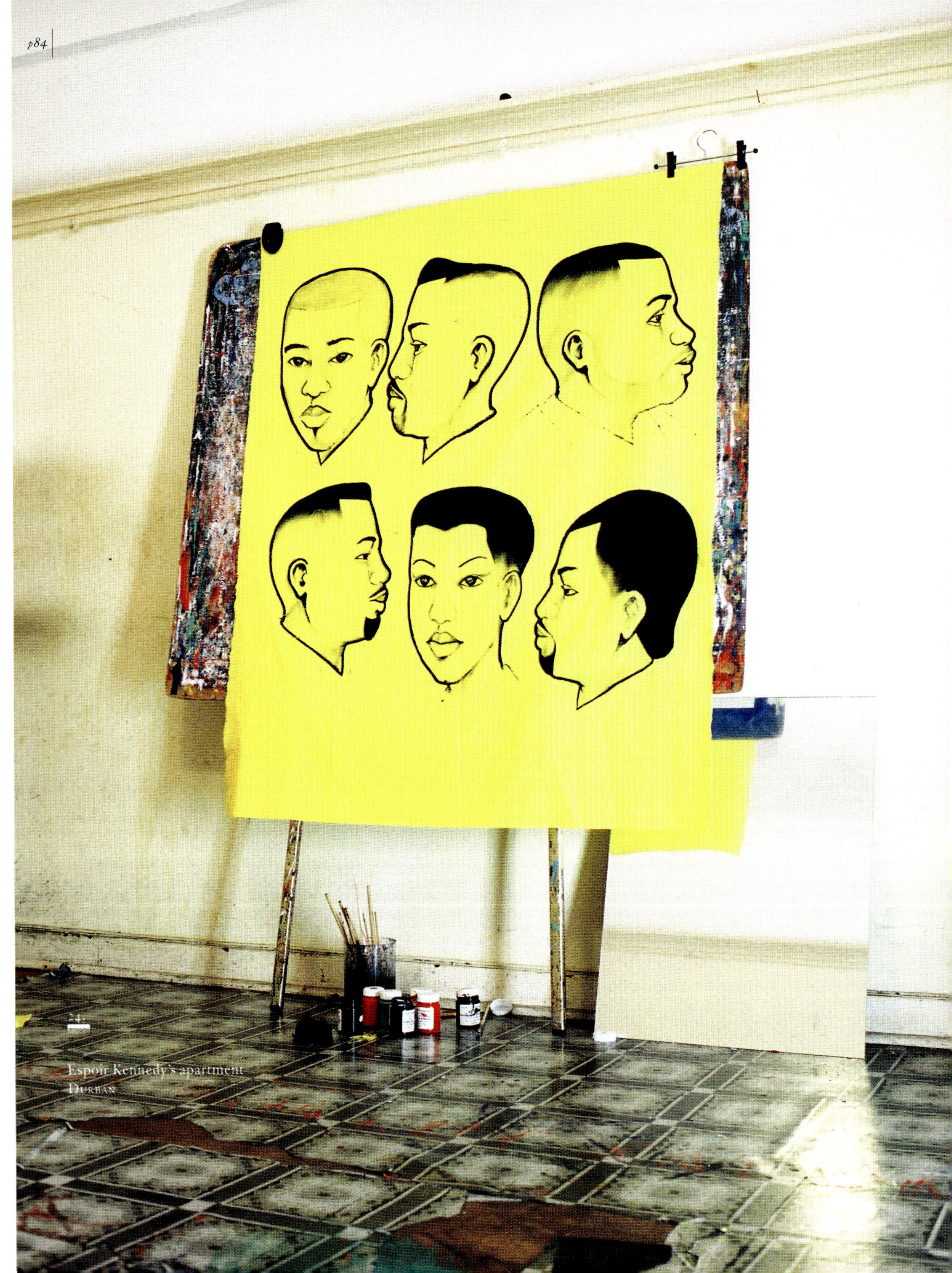

24.

Espoir Kennedy's apartment
Durban

After hanging out in the apartment looking at Kennedy's work, he takes me on a tour of downtown Durban, showing me examples of his work hanging on numerous barbershops and salons. Like in the townships, American celebrities figure heavily into these signs. Over the years Kennedy has been asked to paint everyone from Tupac and Barack Obama to David Beckham, Enrique Iglesias, Madonna and even Marilyn Monroe.

Kennedy likes his work but having gotten a taste for the high prices gallery work can fetch, he recognizes the difference: "When I make art like a barbershop banner it's small money but when it's in a gallery it's very expensive. The ones for sale in the gallery are something like R700 each (approx $95 US) but for my barbershop banners I will only charge R300 (approx $40 US) and it takes me a lot of time."

Before we part ways Kennedy gives me names of businesses in Umlazi that feature his work, and reminds me that his work is also on view in Cape Town and Johannesburg.

p86

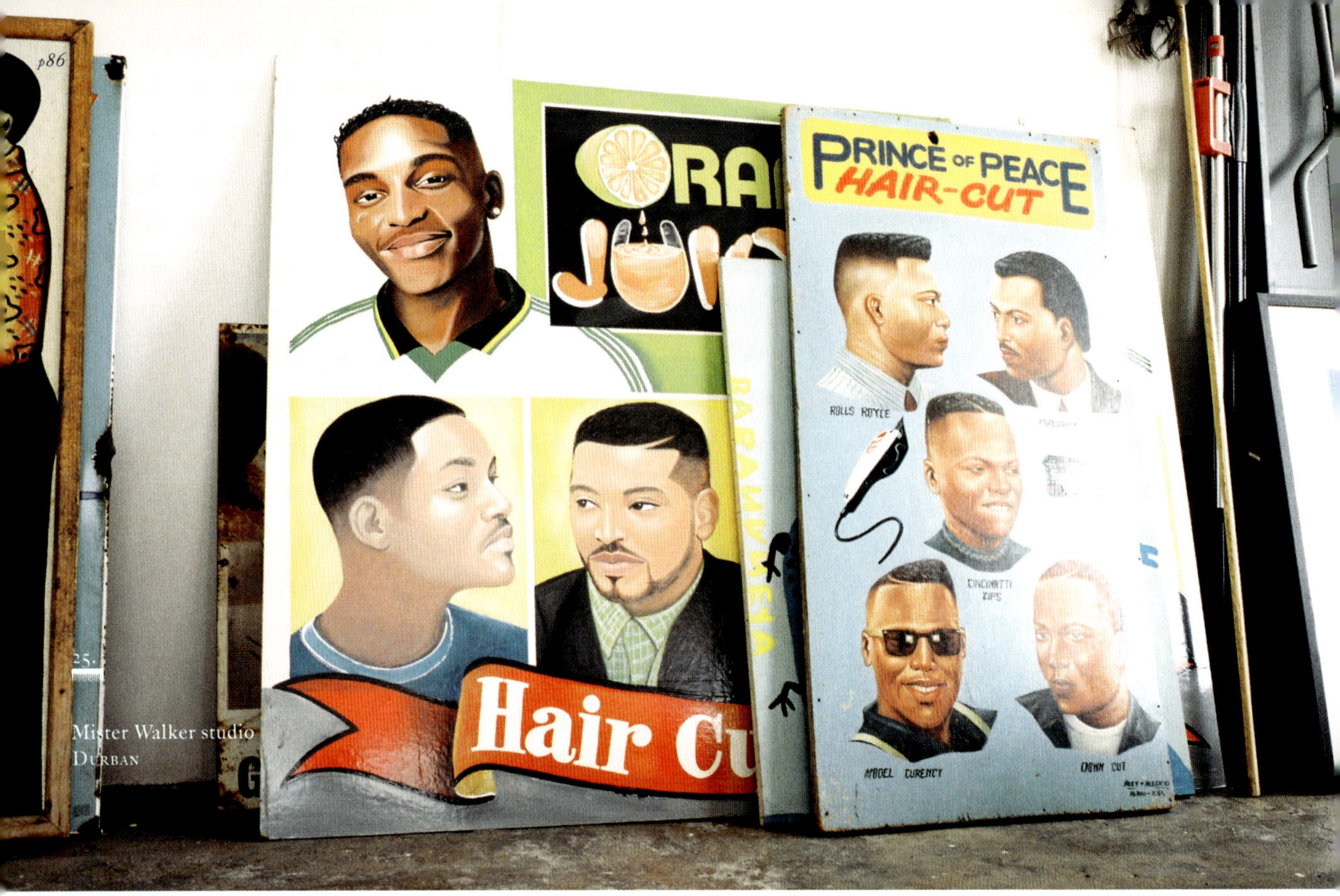

25.

Mister Walker studio
Durban

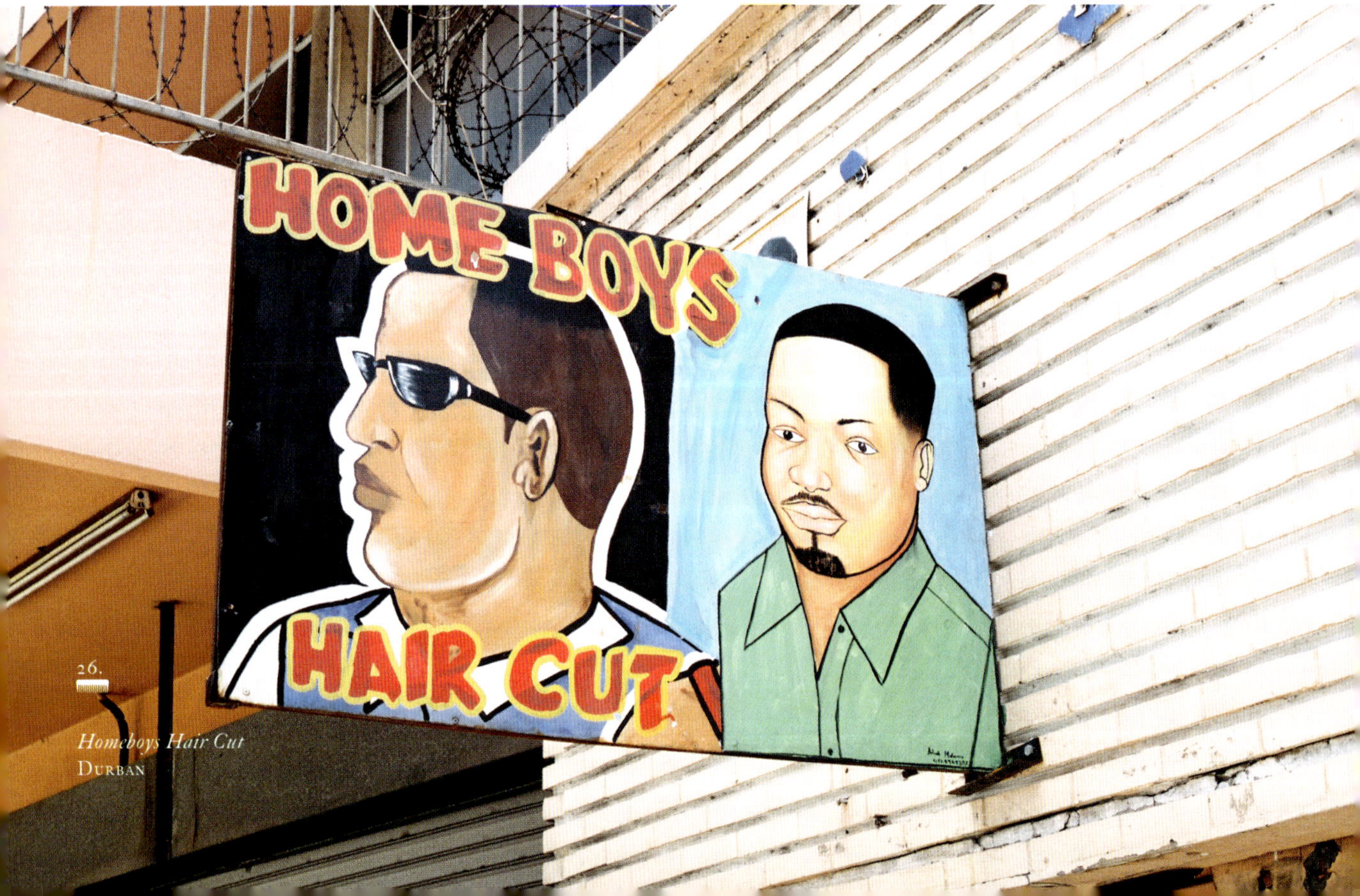

26.

Homeboys Hair Cut
Durban

3.2 Interview with GARTH WALKER

Working as a designer since 1976, South African Garth Walker has garnered international acclaim working for clients large and small, earning 100 creative awards and features in countless magazines and books. In 1995 he opened Orange Juice Design, which was later acquired by Ogilvy South Africa. In 2008 Walker opened a new studio, Mister Walker. He publishes *i'Jusi*, South Africa's only experimental design magazine, which draws heavily from street culture and folk art, including barbershop and salon signage.

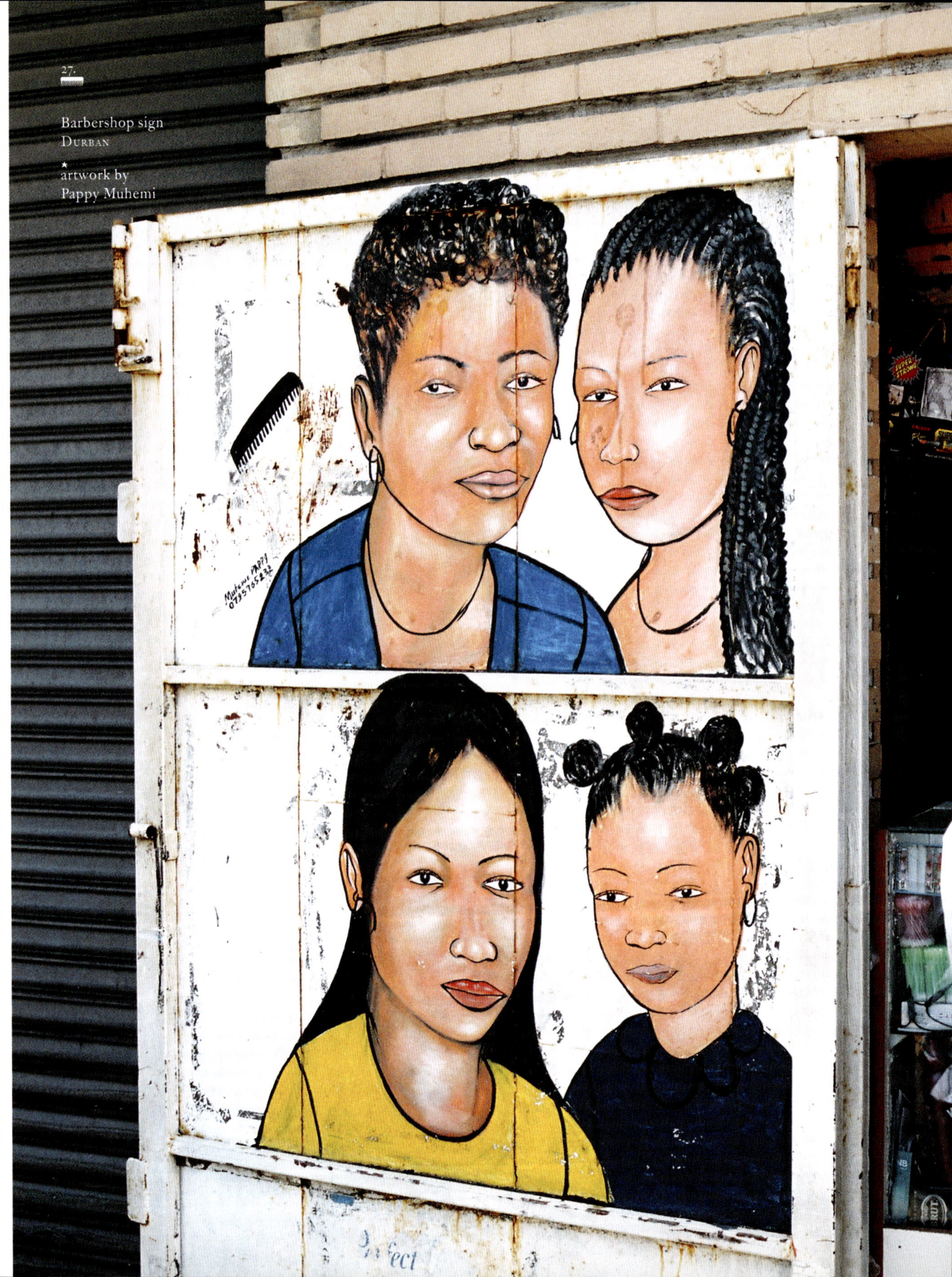

27.

Barbershop sign
Durban

★

artwork by
Pappy Muhemi

How did iJusi *begin and what were your aims with the magazine?*

iJusi began in 1995 when I started Orange Juice Design and needed to keep myself busy. The aim was to design a design magazine and as there were many better-designed mags around, I felt I needed to design in a style that no one was using. So that was African, and following the 1994 elections we, as a nation, were more Afrocentric.

When did you first feature barbershop art in iJusi*?*

In one of early issues we interviewed Bruno, a legal refugee from the Democratic Republic of Congo (DRC), who pioneered barber graphics in Durban in the 1990s. He brought the skills down from the DRC and developed this platform on yellow or orange fabric and then a very graphic head with a white outline and then these very elaborate names for the barbershops. He was the master. He went to London. He started the genre that was then adopted by local guys.

Were you aware of these vernacular township styles and designs during Apartheid?

During Apartheid, the Group Areas Act meant that blacks could not live in the city, but could commute from the townships, so there was little vernacular to see.

Can you see an influence of American culture here?

Here American culture is supreme. A lot of the icons are contrasted with locals; it's very simplistic. They will have Robert Mugabe, Malcolm X and Nelson Mandela on some salons and then American athletes and TV and music stars.

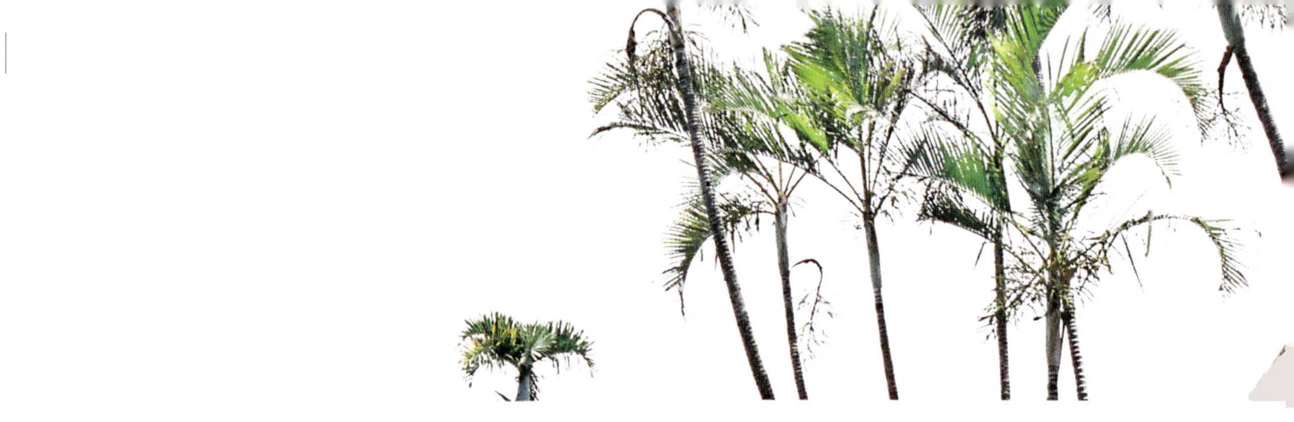

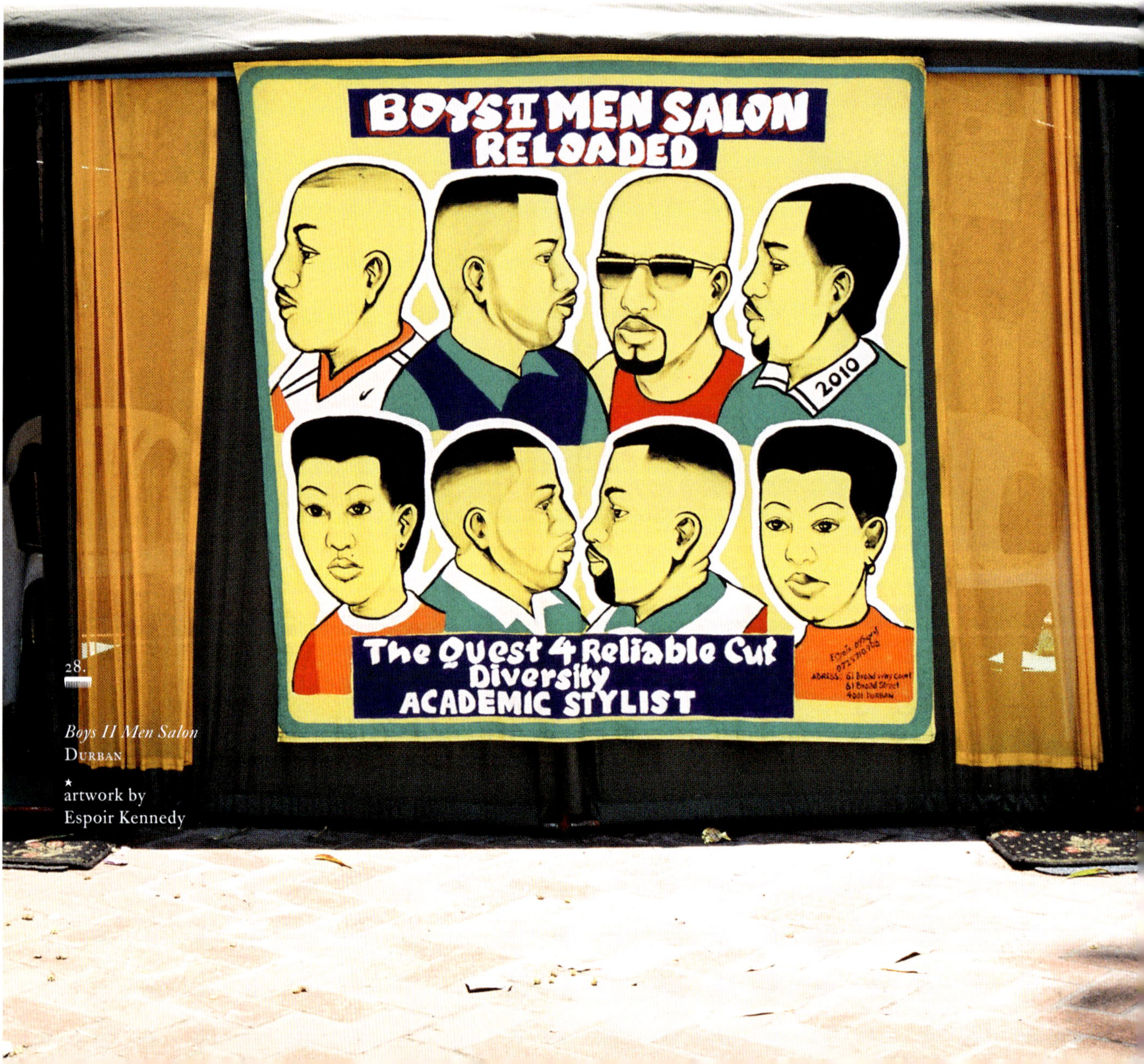

28.

Boys II Men Salon
Durban

★
artwork by
Espoir Kennedy

Do you think there is a future for hand-painted sign writing in the digital age?

Yes, as we Africans aren't as in love with the computer as the rest of the world, especially in light of costs and connectivity. Eventually the digital graphic printer will replace the sign painter, and that's happening already, but it's not going to happen overnight.

Why is vernacular sign writing and folk art so appealing to Western artists and designers?

Because it's joyful, handmade and looks good. We have lost the way in "professional design" as we are now slaves to clients, design dogma and what London or New York designers are doing. Here on the street it's just have fun and make it look great! It's fresh, it's got energy and it works. We like it because it looks good and it makes you feel good and that's what graphic design is supposed to do. There is no concept, it's just joyous. That is the bedrock of the African approach to just about everything: if you like it, do it! We don't formalize things to do or not to do, it's kind of new world, new money, new everything. If you've got it, flaunt it. Helvetica and Swiss typography are a no-no because Africans don't like reductive, pared down anything. One is not discreet, one is a show-off.

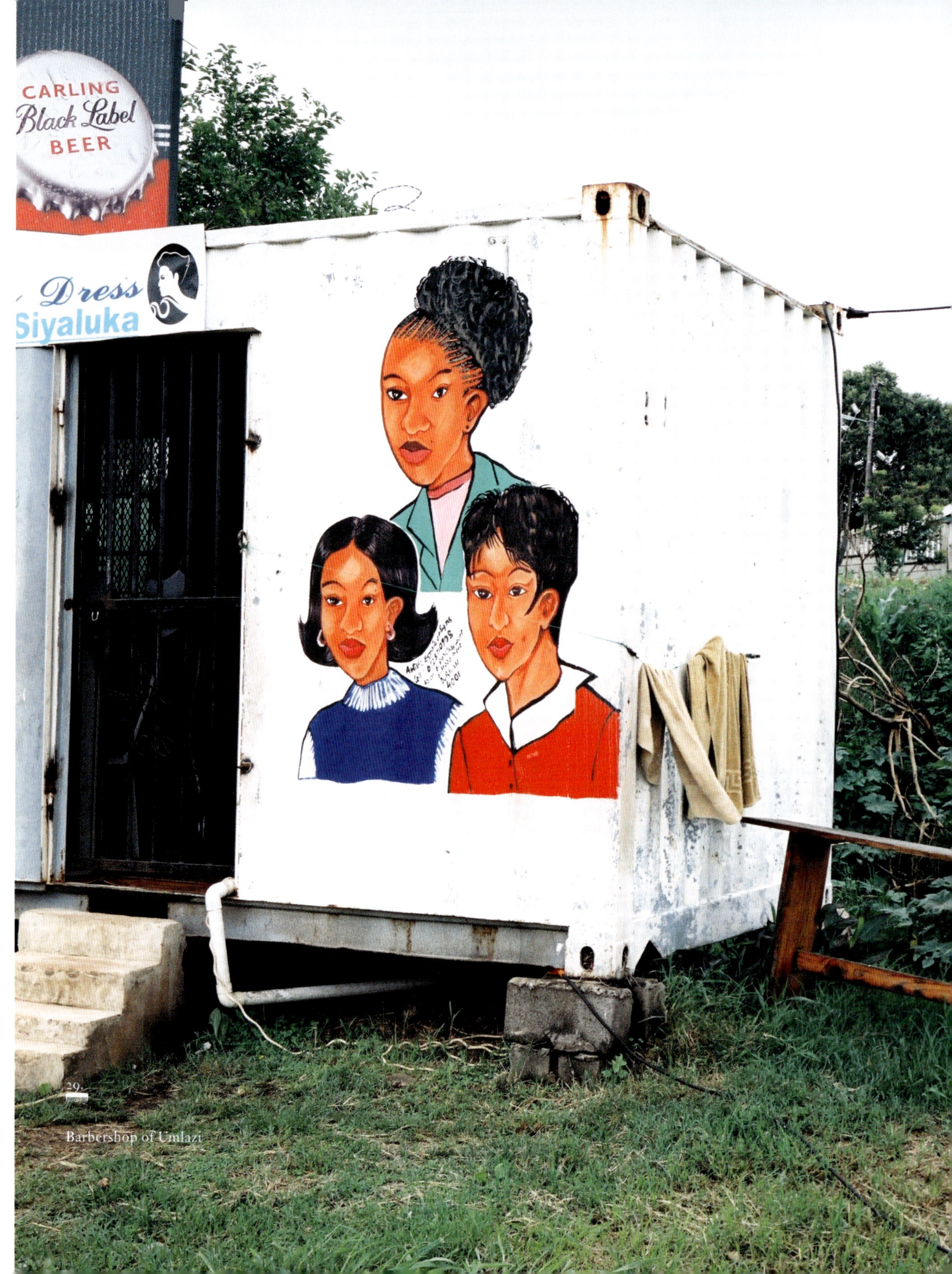

Barbershop of Umlazi

3.3 UMLAZI

Umlazi feels different compared to the Johannesburg townships. Firstly, many of the salons and barbershops are housed in old shipping containers, due to Durban's massive port, the busiest in Africa. The containers are perfect structures in which to house a small business. Barbers here also use small gazebos, not unlike tents used for outdoor parties. I am told that these are actually preferred by many due to the tropical temperatures and humidity.

Espoir Kennedy is the artist of choice in Umlazi. His banners hang from almost every barbershop. As Kennedy had explained, owners request the same artwork or sign already used by another business. Unsurprisingly, every salon and barbershop in Umlazi looks identical. While Johannesburg offers hundreds of quirky one-off barbershop signs and paintings, this is not the case in Durban. The crude hand-painted Boyz & Girlz Salon sign stands out because Kennedy didn't paint it. Of course, I am viewing the barbershop signage in a completely different way than potential customers who would rather see a professional, welcoming sign.

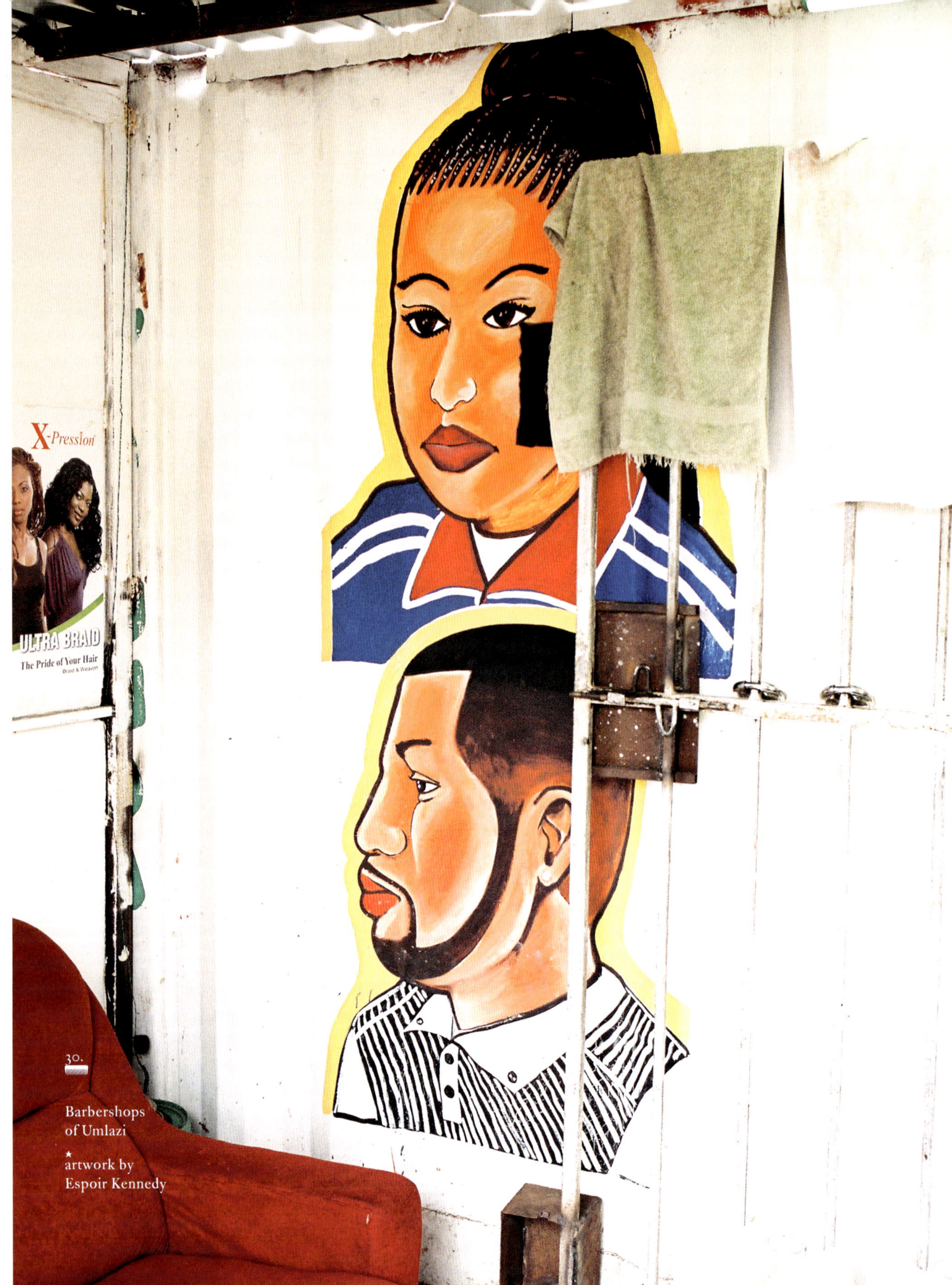

30.

Barbershops of Umlazi

★ artwork by Espoir Kennedy

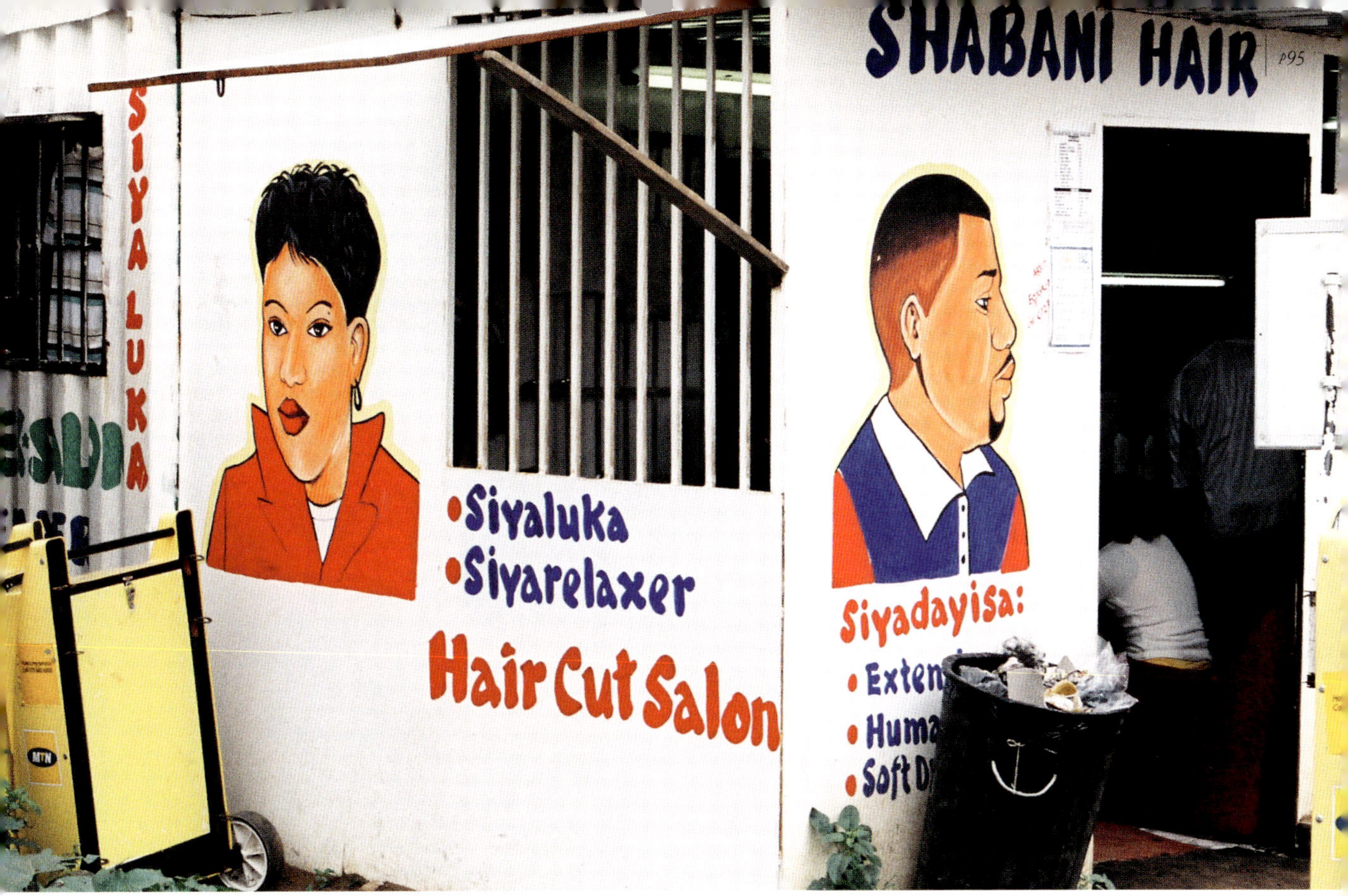

SHABANI HAIR
SIYALUKA
•Siyaluka
•Siyarelaxer
Hair Cut Salon
Siyadayisa:
CEMENT & TILES 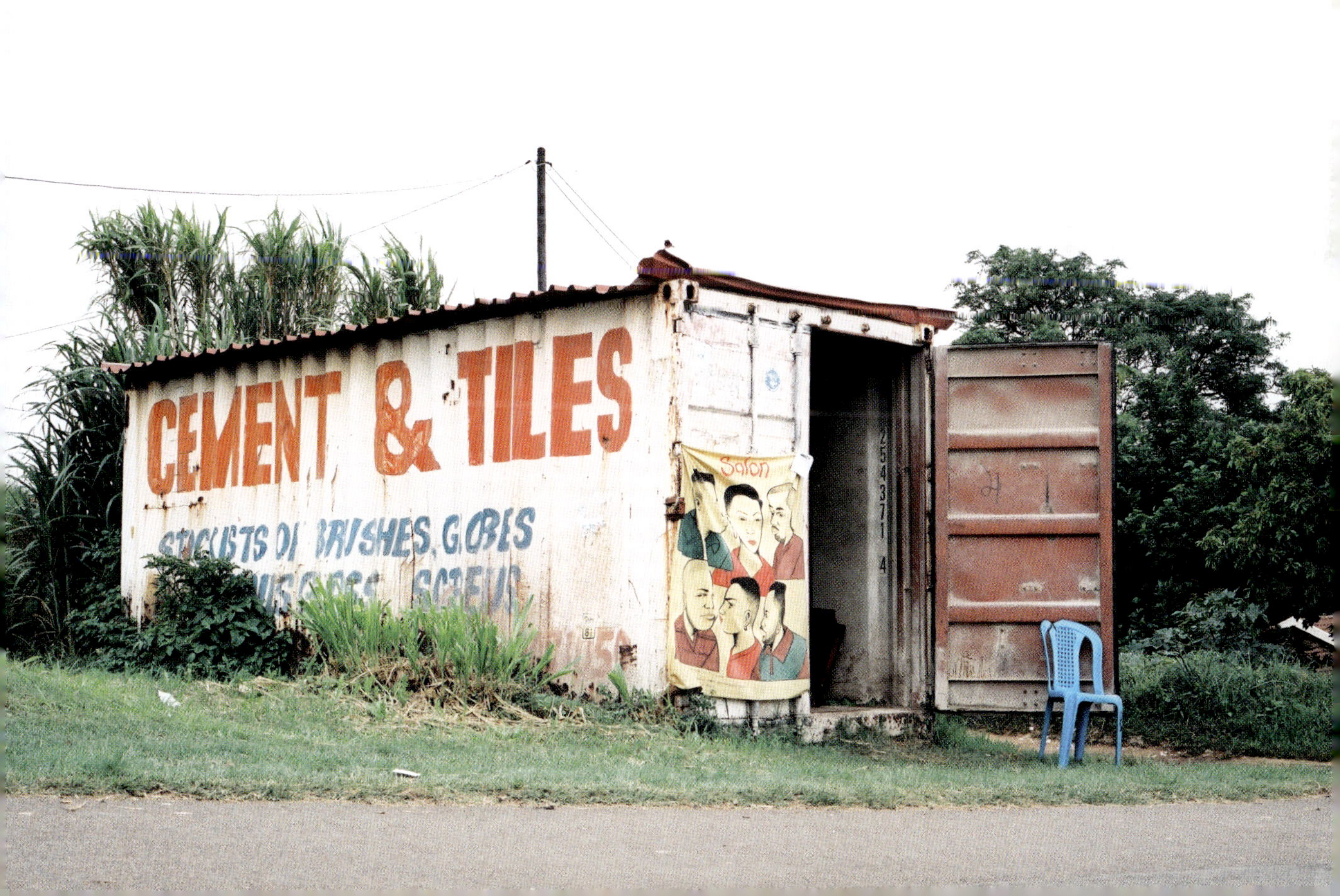
Salon

CHAPTER 4
CAPE TOWN

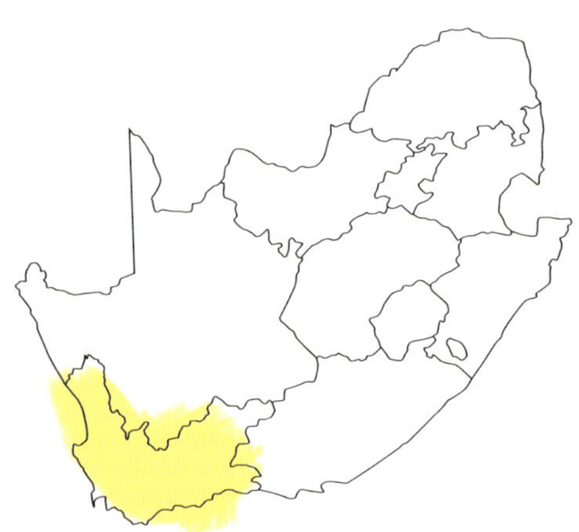

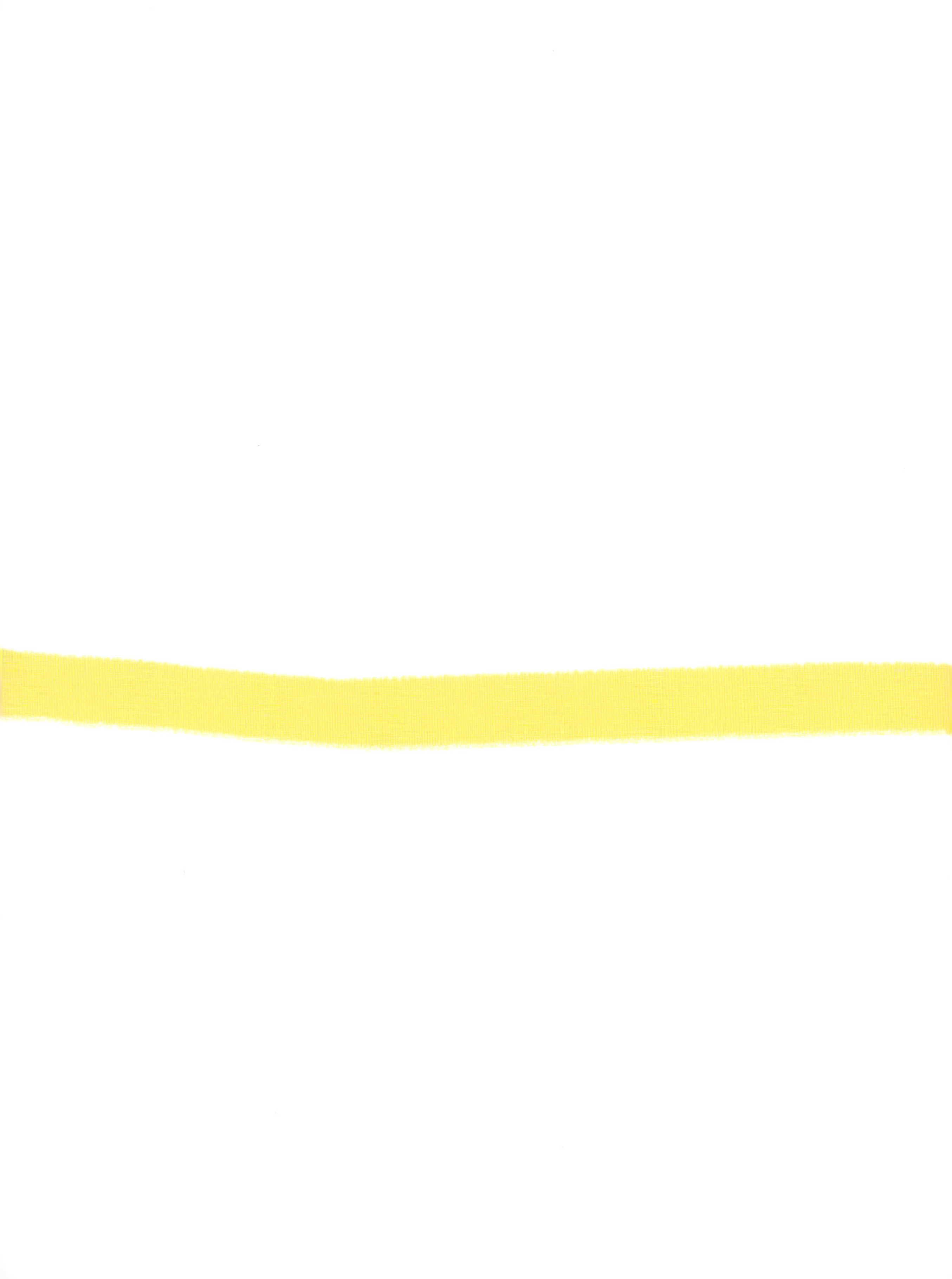

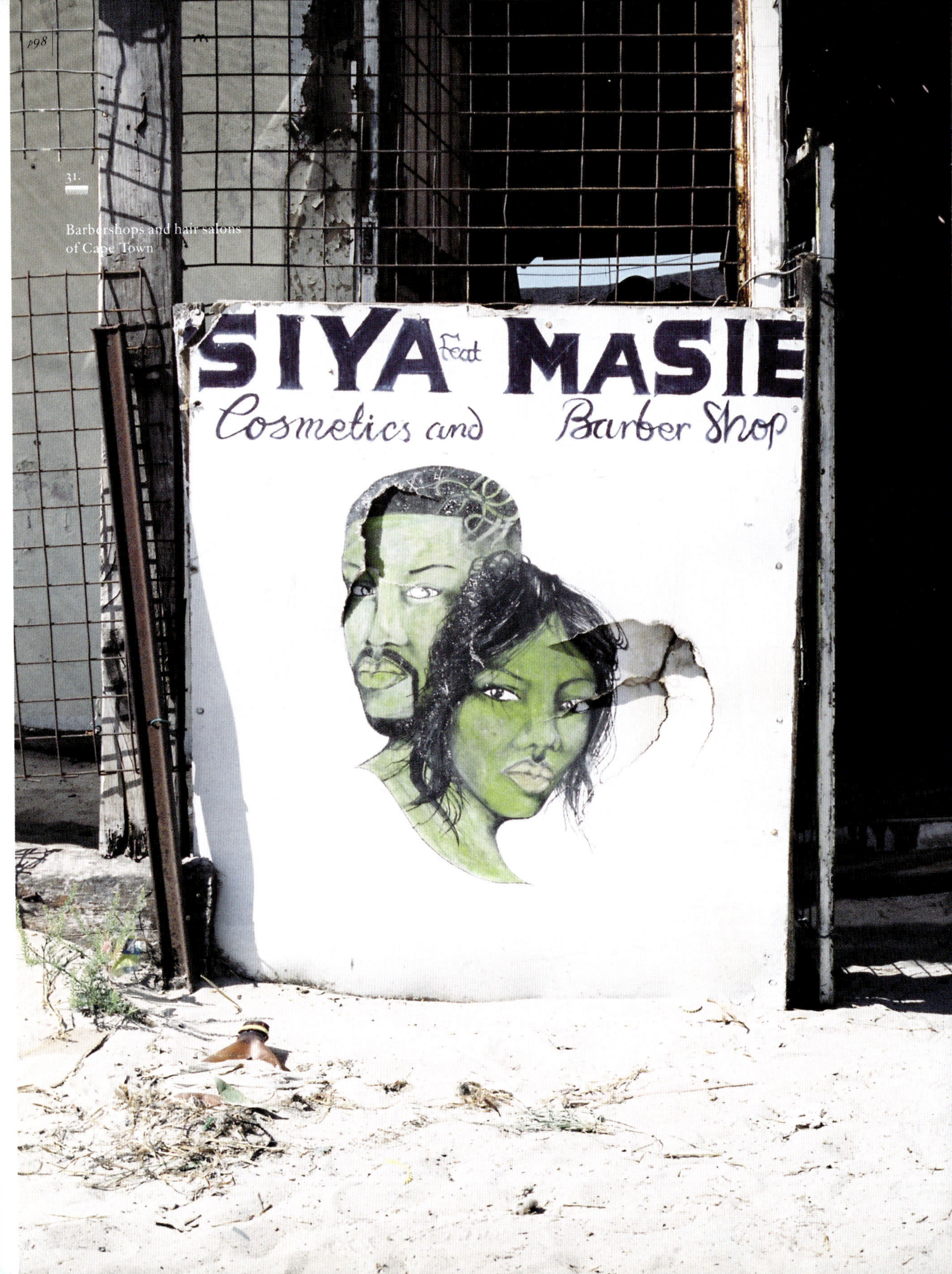

31.

Barbershops and hair salons of Cape Town

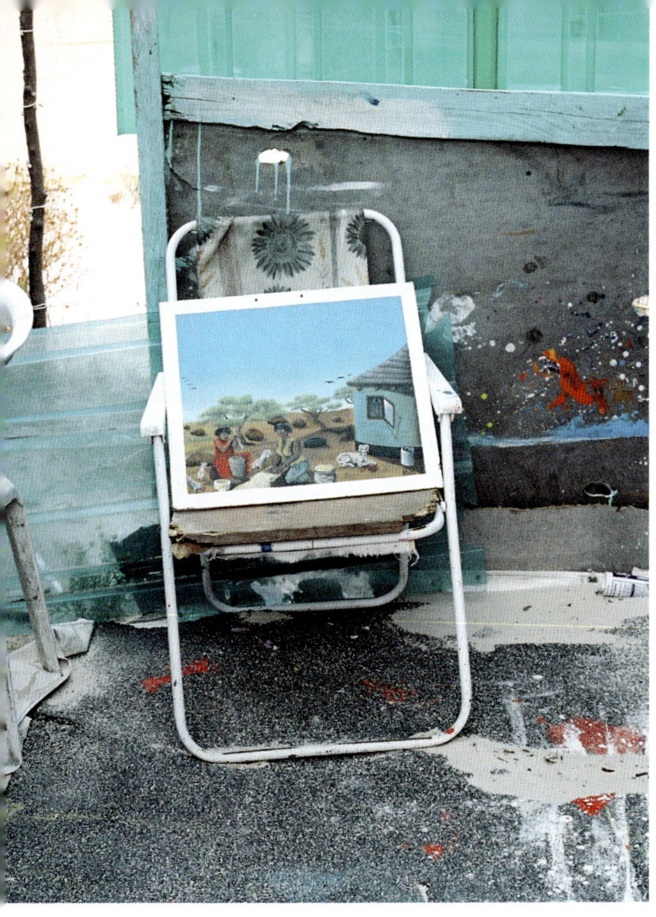
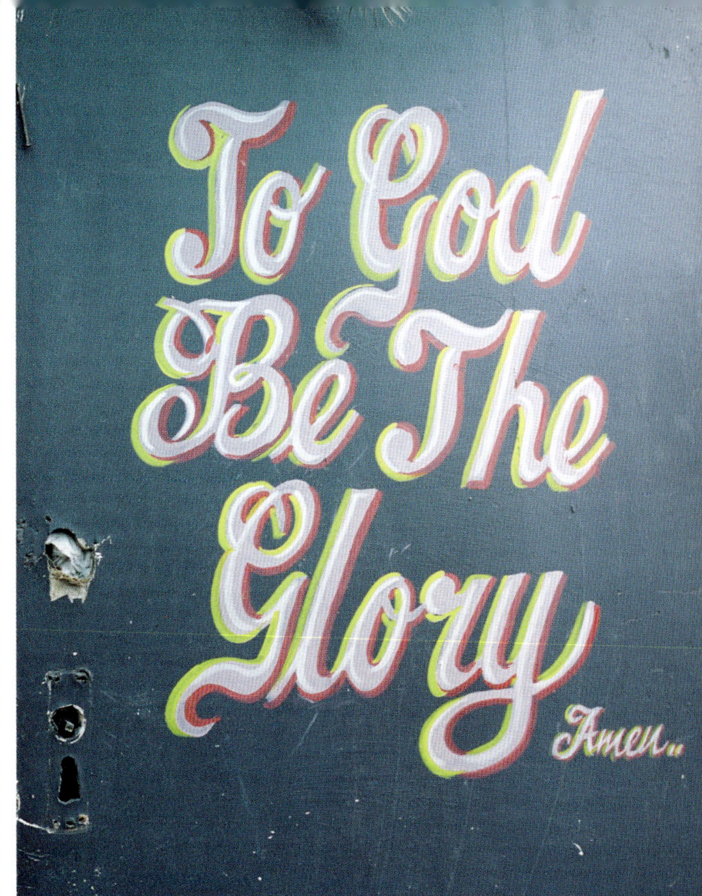
To God
Be The
Glory
Amen..
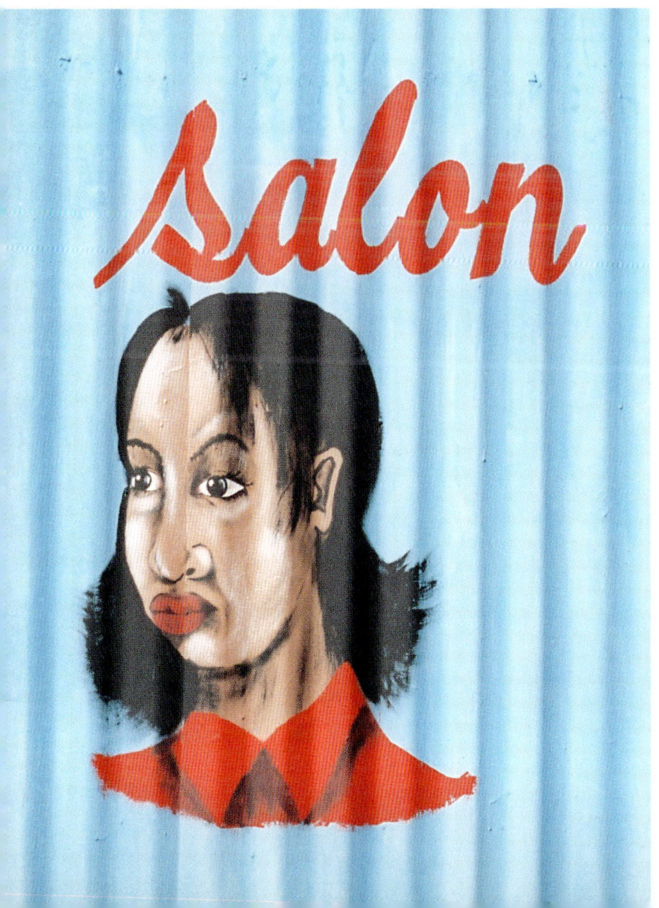
Salon
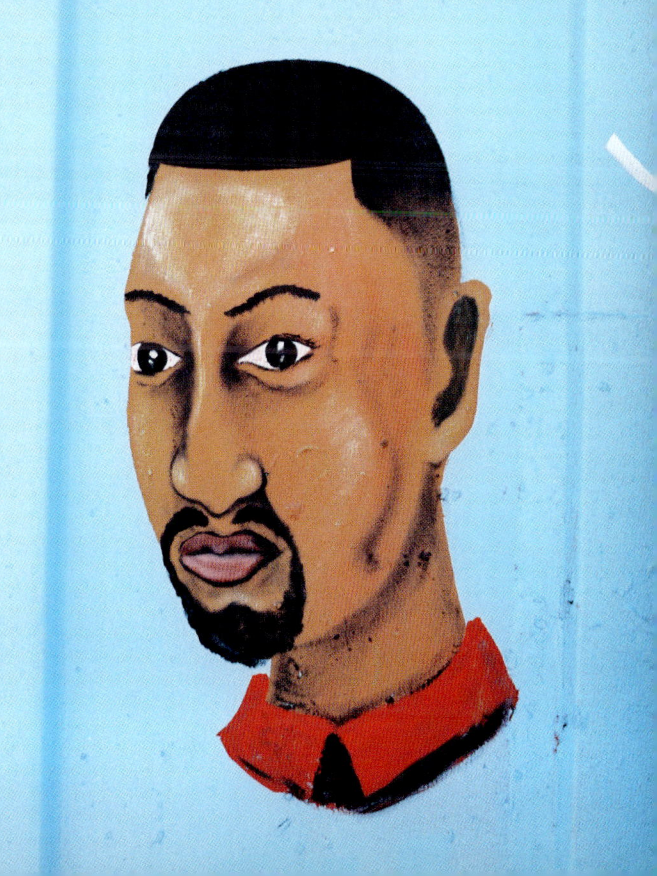

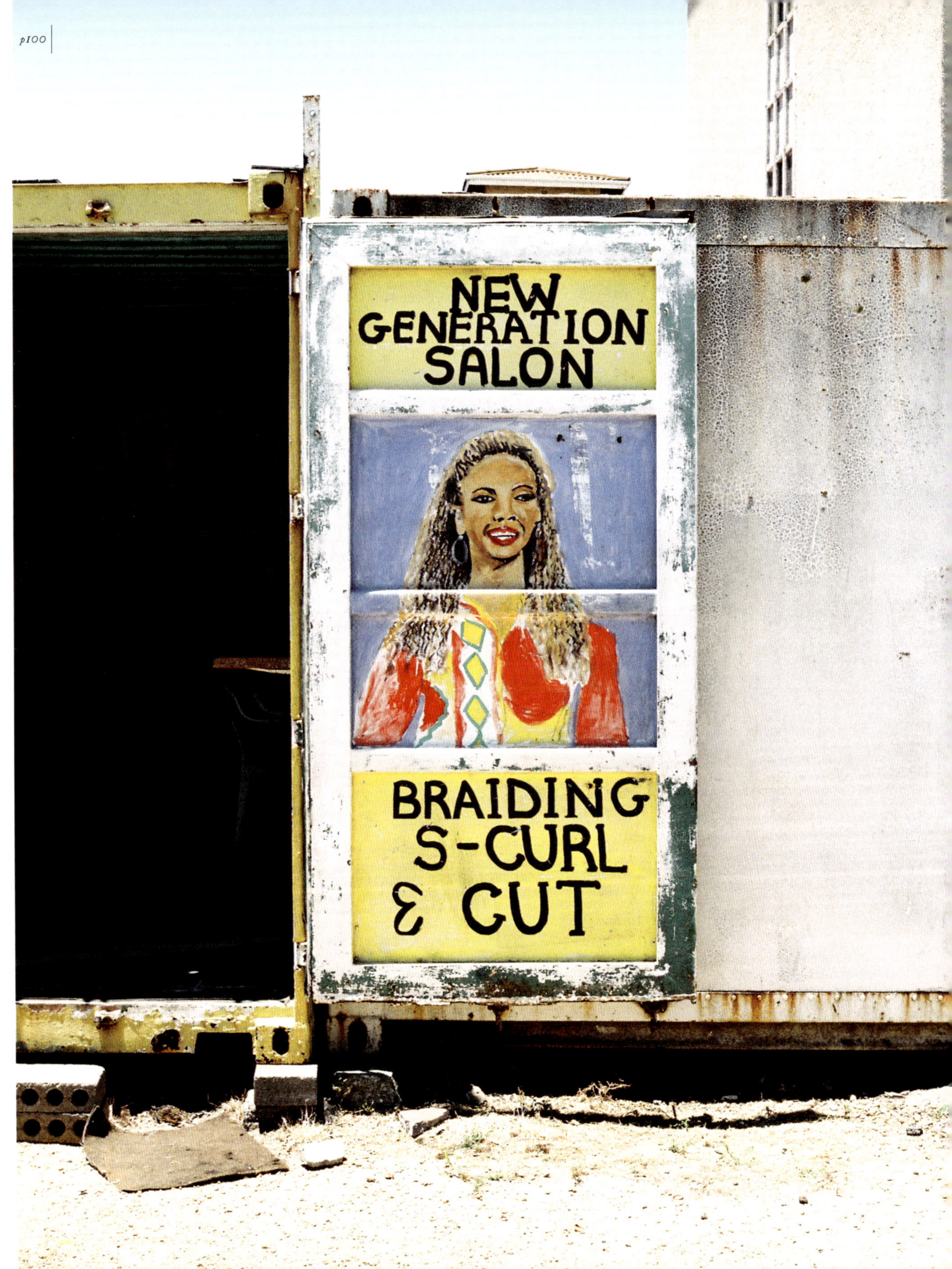
NEW GENERATION SALON
BRAIDING S-CURL & CUT

4.1 LANGA

With the breath-taking backdrop of Table Mountain, Cape Town, South Africa's second largest city, is widely regarded as one of the most beautiful cities in the world. International visitors flock here to enjoy sandy beaches, adventure sports, wineries and world-class dining. Yet a visit to the District Six Museum in the city center reveals a dark and painful history. Here, a once thriving multi-ethnic neighborhood was destroyed when the Group Areas Act designated the area for "whites only," forcibly evicting residents. Thousands of families were driven from their homes and relocated to the barren scrublands of the Cape Flats, forming the sprawling and impoverished townships in the southeast of the city.

Through the staff at my hostel I meet Sam, a black South African who offers township tours. Langa, the oldest township in the city, is the first stop on most of these tours. Despite concerns that the tours exploit poverty they actually play a huge role in eroding the bad reputations that the townships have earned.

Sam introduces me to Abosh, a local man who has agreed to show me the area's barbershops. We begin at the Joe Slovo squatter camp, where many of the residents have been lured by the promise of work. The majority of the township is actually made up of brick houses and dilapidated apartment blocks. Like in Durban, many of Langa's salons and barbershops are housed in used shipping containers thanks to Cape Town's massive port.

Many of the salons here also offer other services like shoe mending and cell phone repair. I return to Langa a number of times with Abosh and also document a staggering number of barbershops in the neighboring townships of Gugulethu and Philippi.

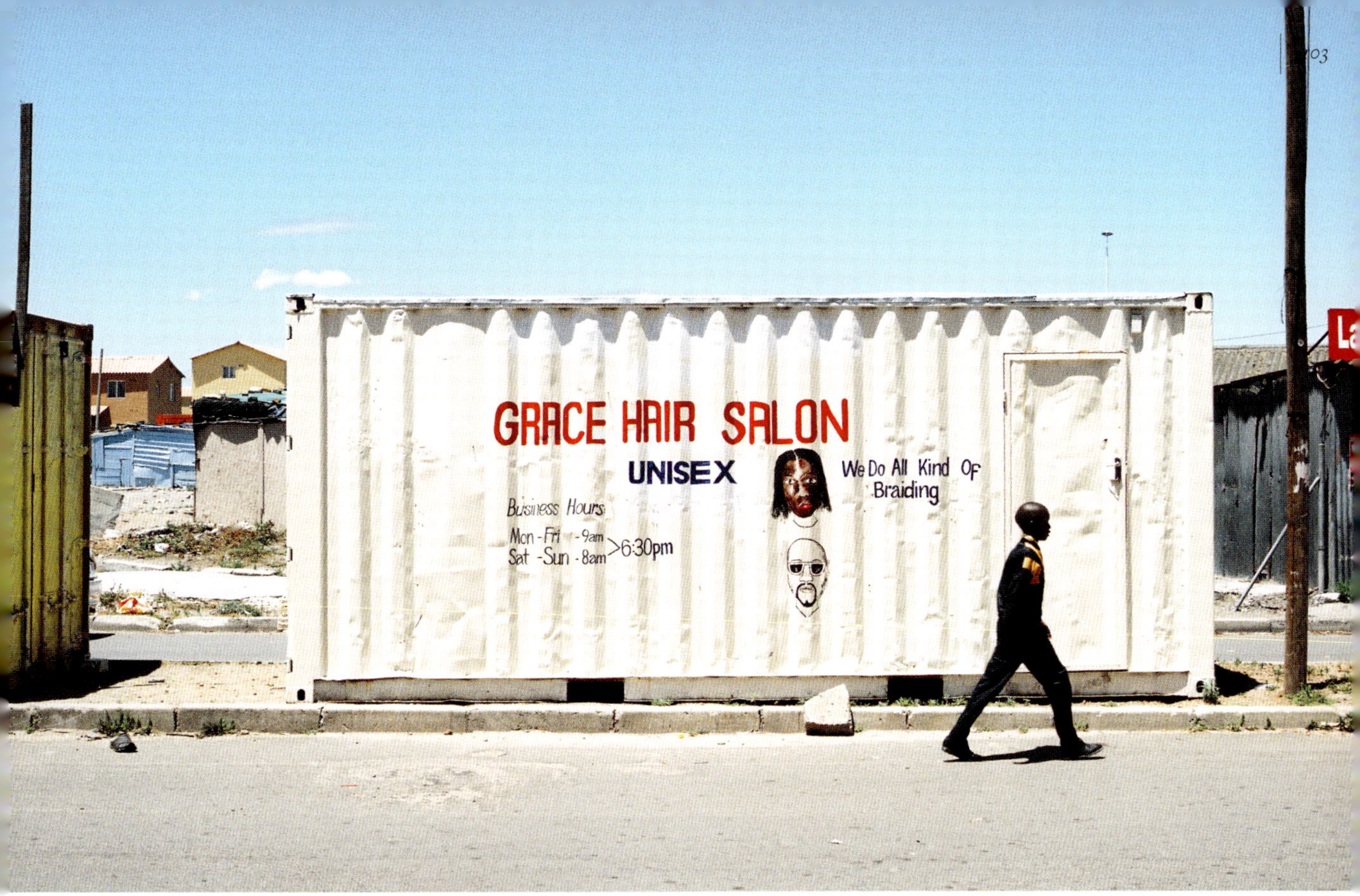

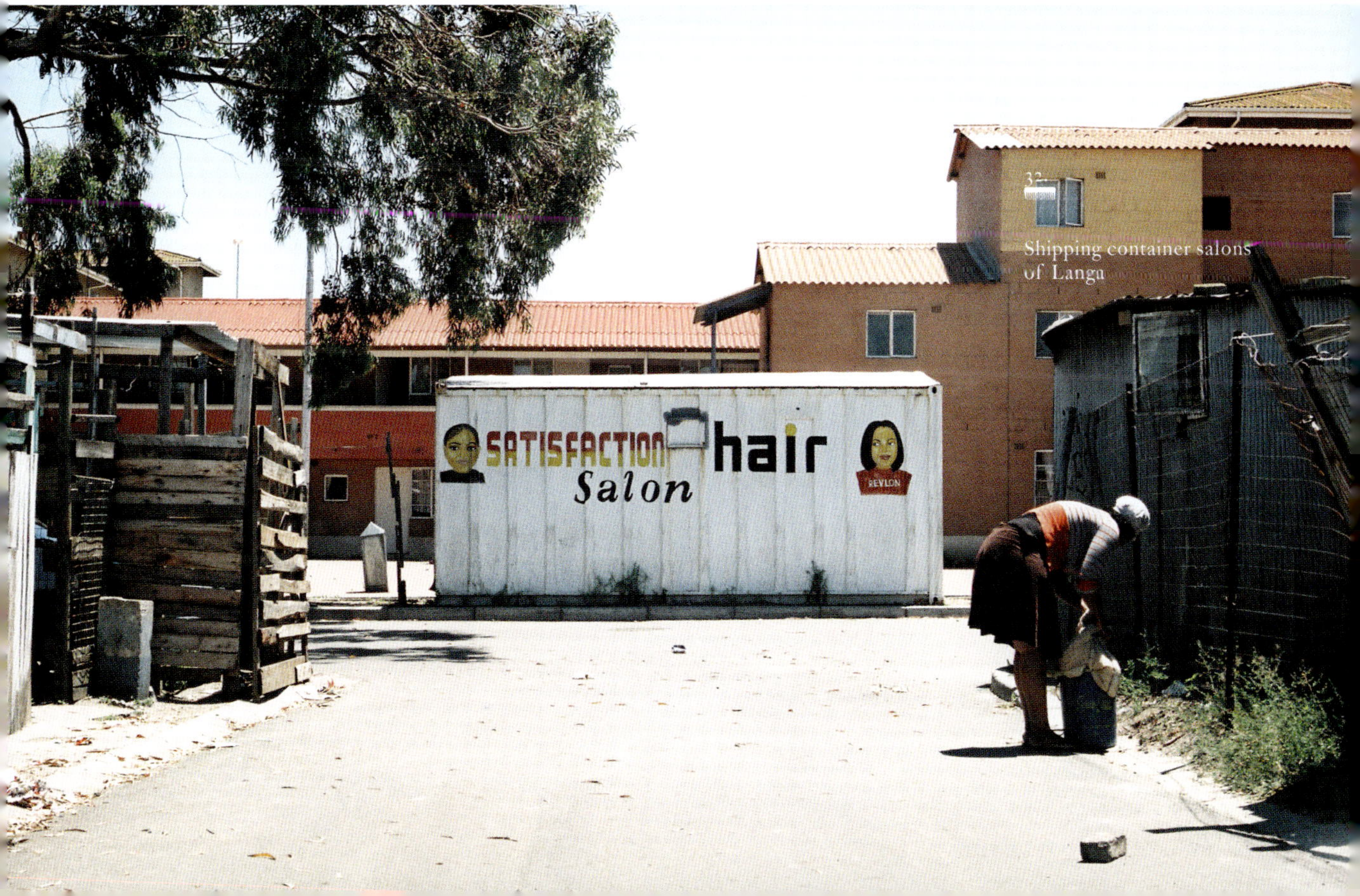

32

Shipping container salons of Langa

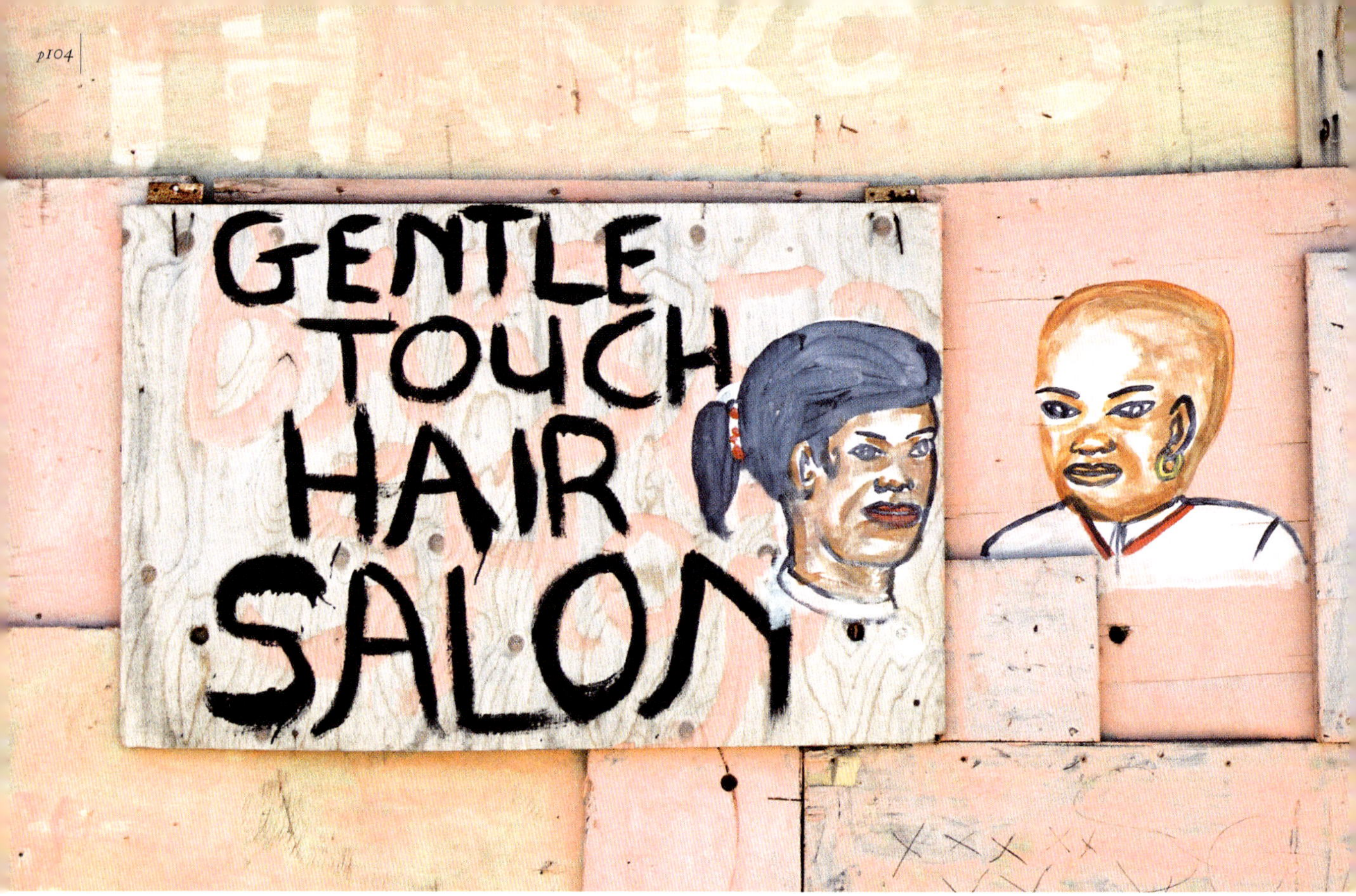

GENTLE TOUCH HAIR SALON

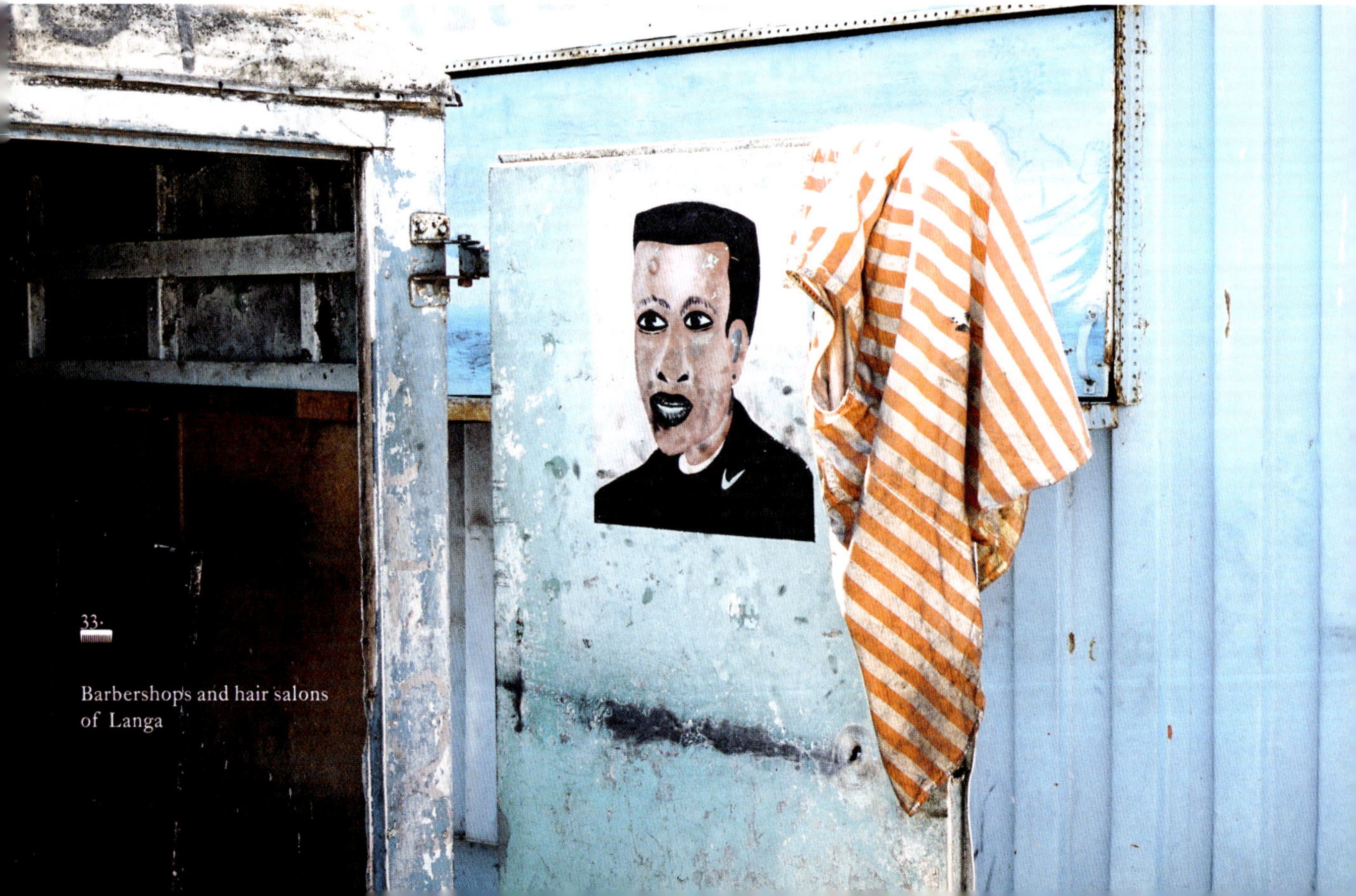

33.

Barbershops and hair salons of Langa

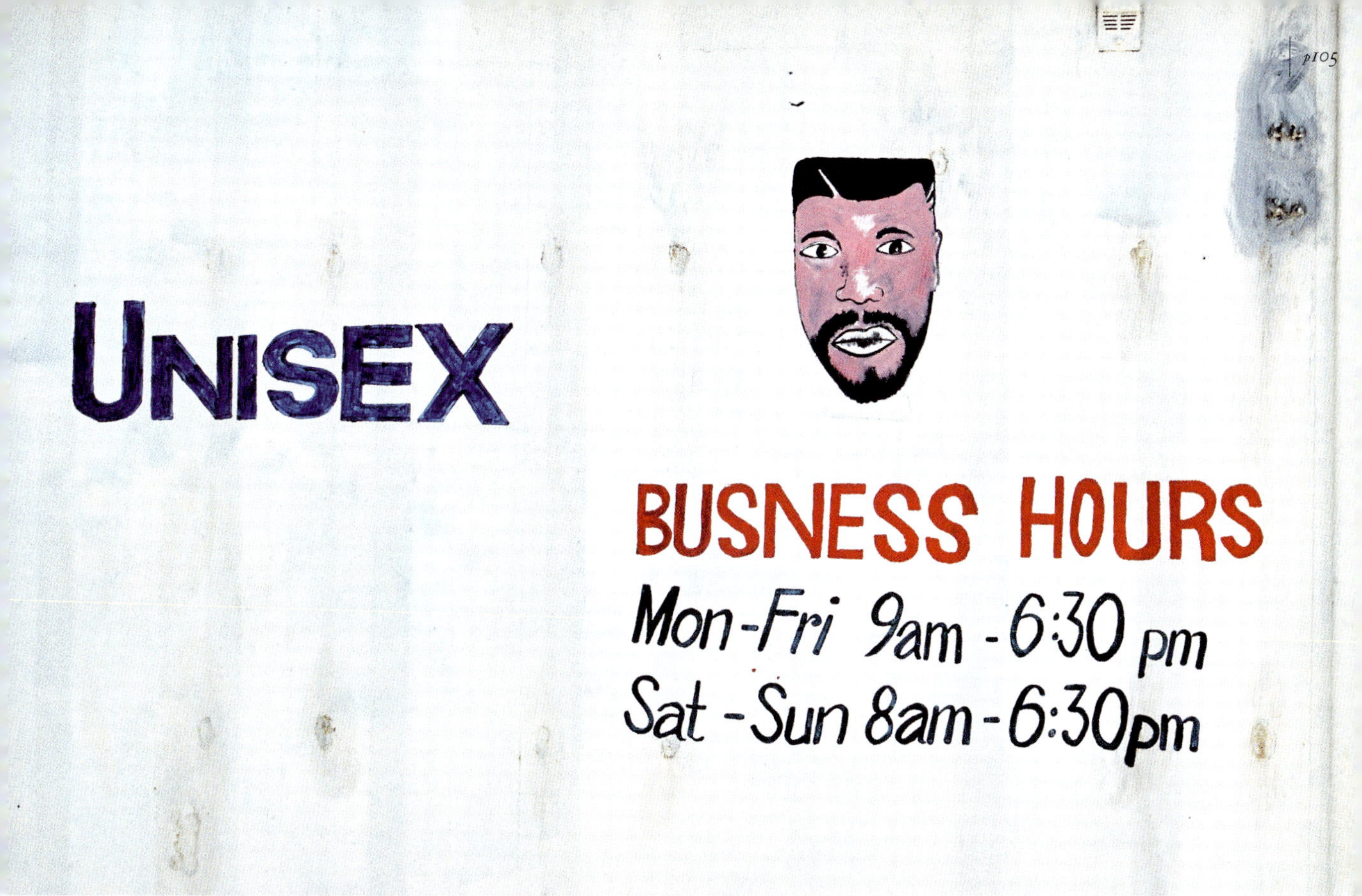

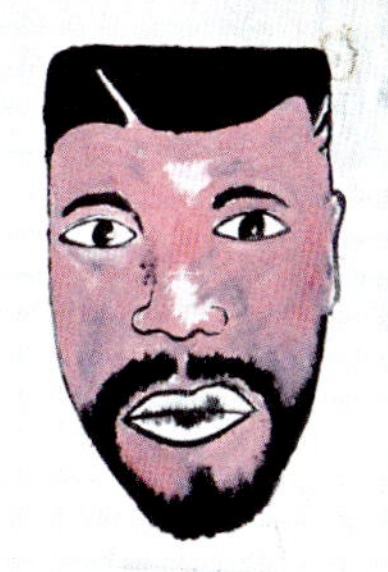
UNISEX
BUSNESS HOURS
Mon-Fri 9am -6:30 pm
Sat -Sun 8am -6:30pm

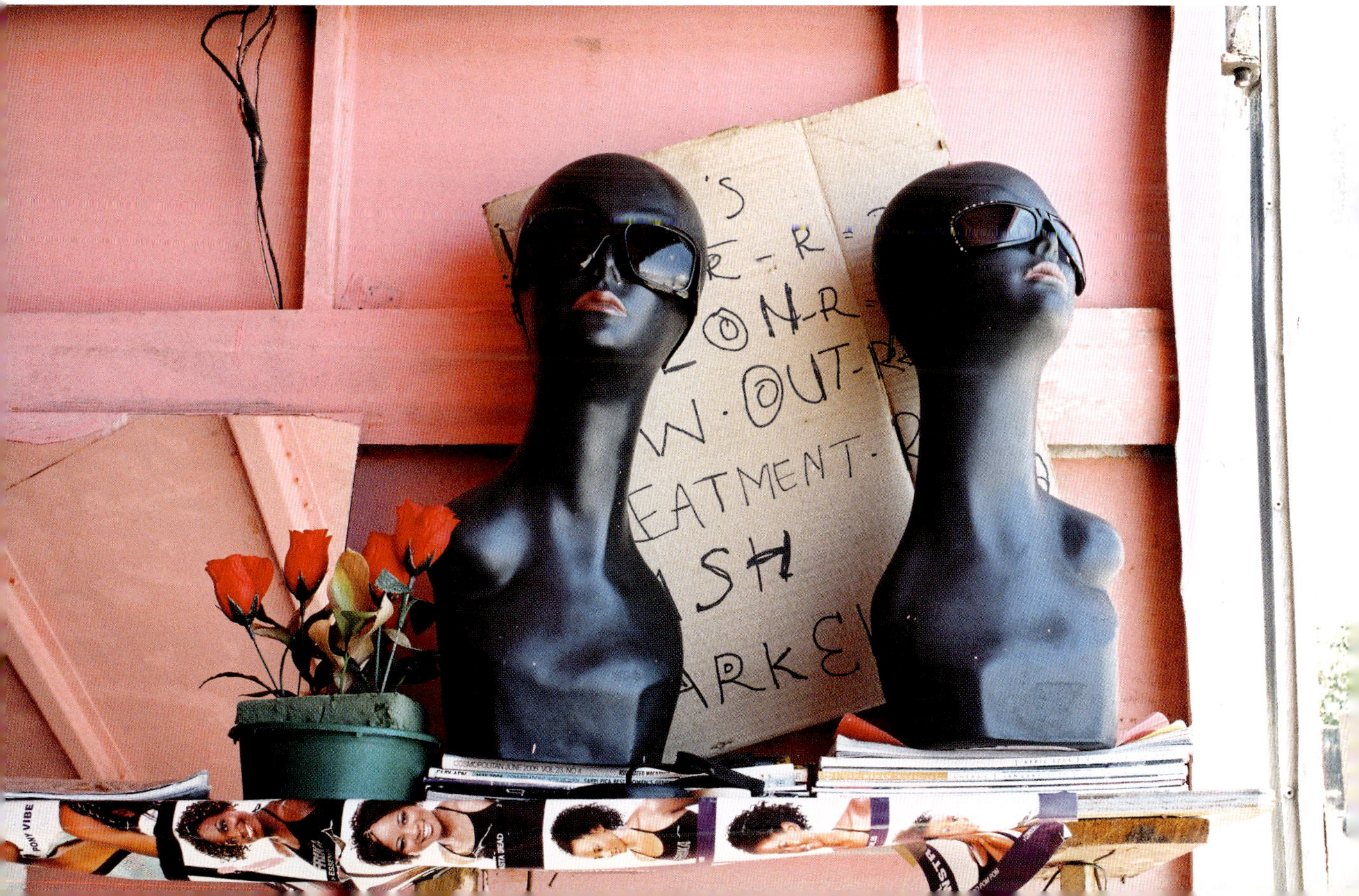

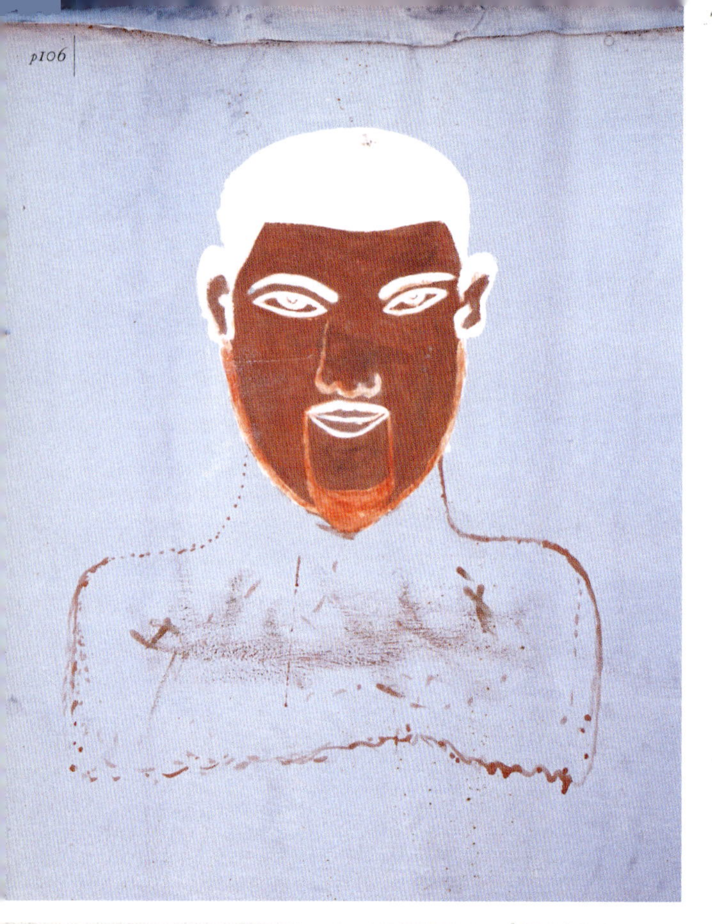

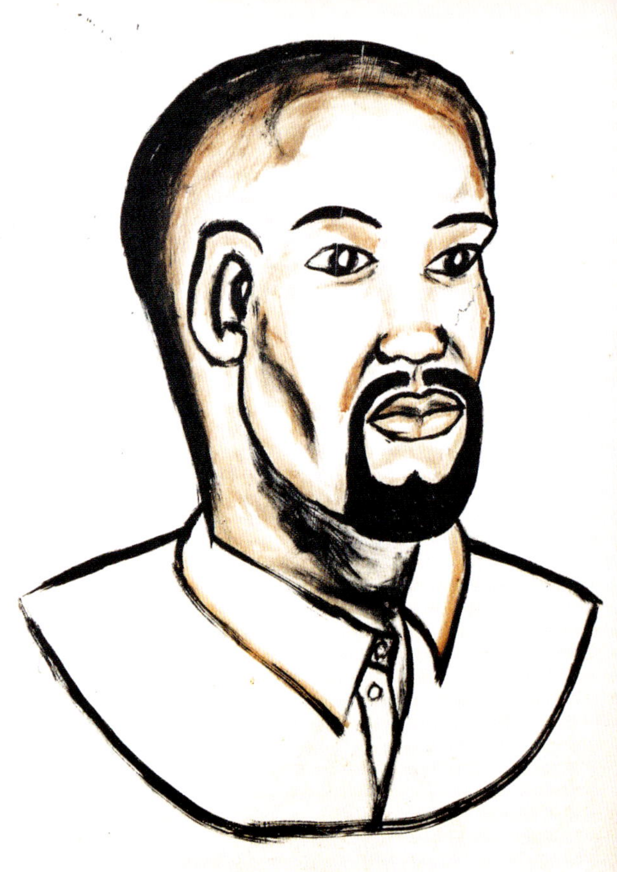

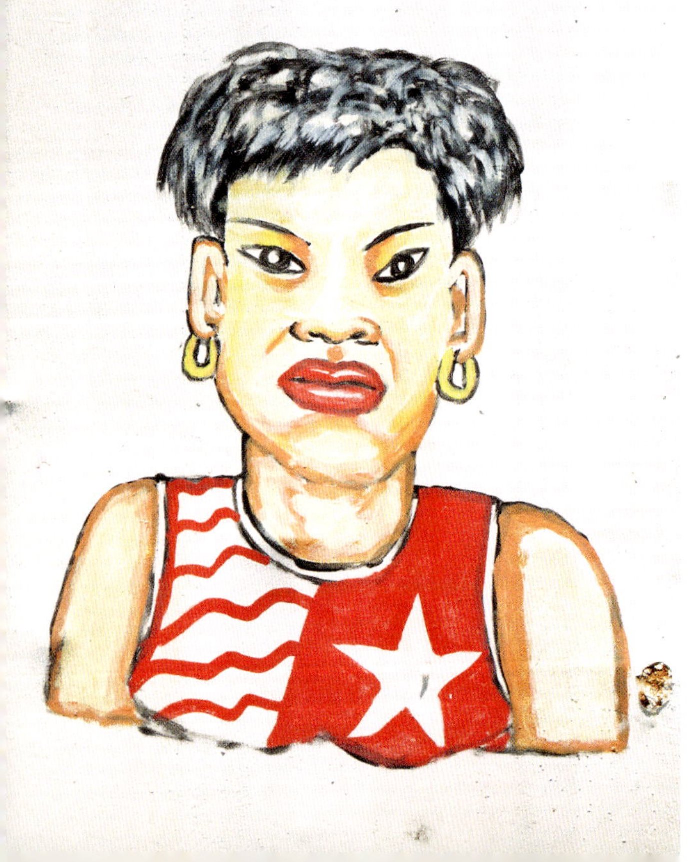

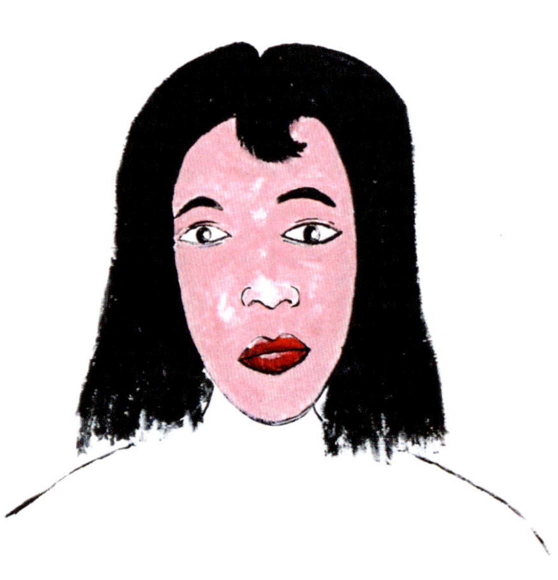

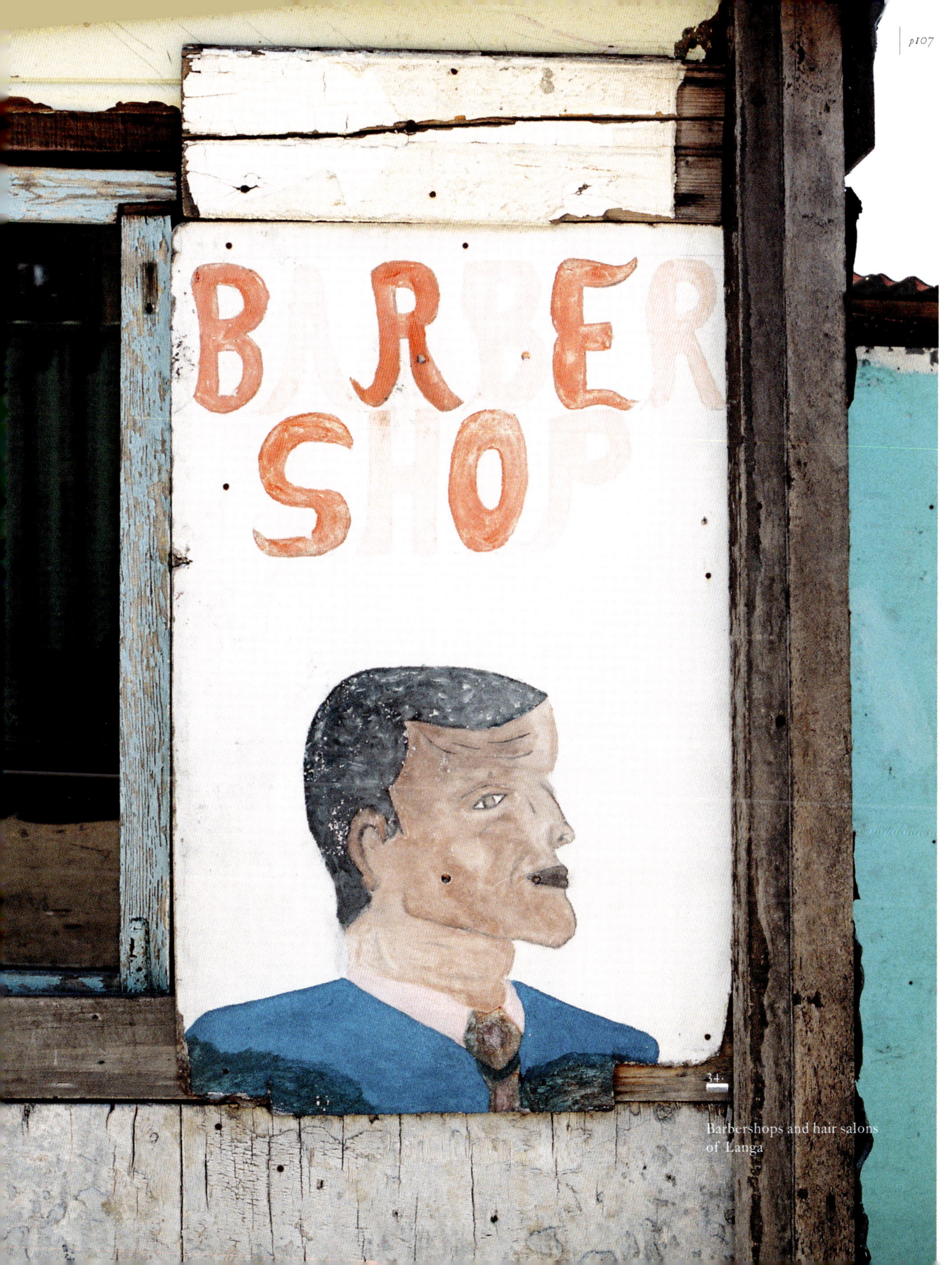

34.

Barbershops and hair salons of Langa

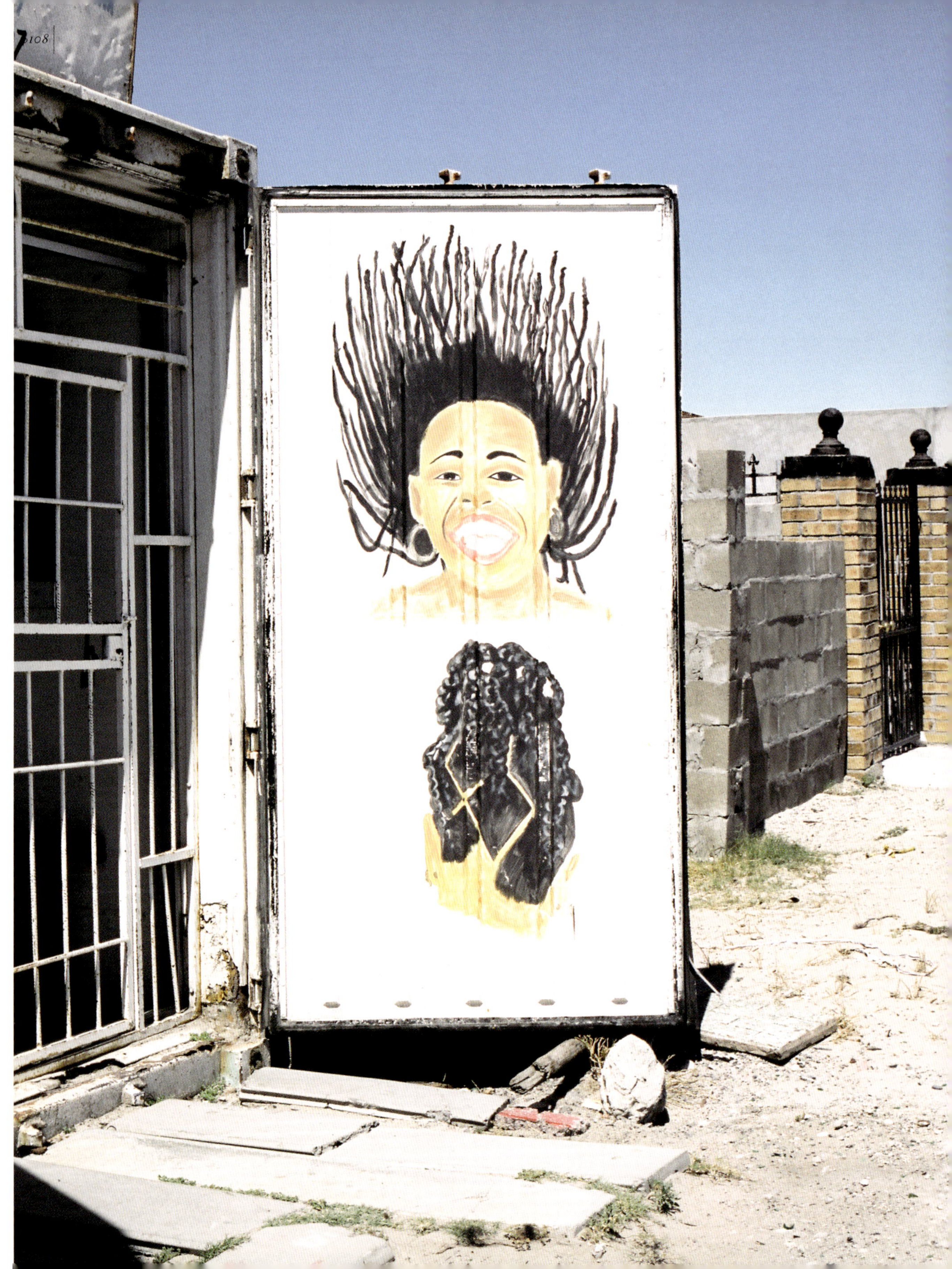

4.2 GUGULETHU

After we explore Langa for a number of days, Abosh agrees to take me into the neighboring township of Gugulethu. Formed in the 1960s as Langa became dangerously overcrowded, Gugulethu was the first township I had visited earlier in the year so I was keen to revisit the area that had sparked this project.

I was lucky enough to meet the area's resident artist Moses, a Rastafarian immigrant from Tanzania, and possibly the sweetest and most gracious man I have ever met. He talks to me about the struggles of making a living painting signs in the townships. During our conversation Moses agrees to paint my author portrait (see page 127), a welcome commission on an otherwise quiet day.

After parting ways with Moses, Abosh and I cross into the nearby township of Philippi, which feels noticeably poorer than Gugulethu. It is in Philippi where I experience my only really uncomfortable moment of the trip. As I photograph a salon dozens of people shout *mlungu* at me. Abosh tells me not to worry as this is just the word for "white man" and I shouldn't be offended. Later on I discover that the word is actually a racial slur. It is a reality check for me. Despite the friendly welcome I have almost always received, some people are not happy to see a white man in their community.

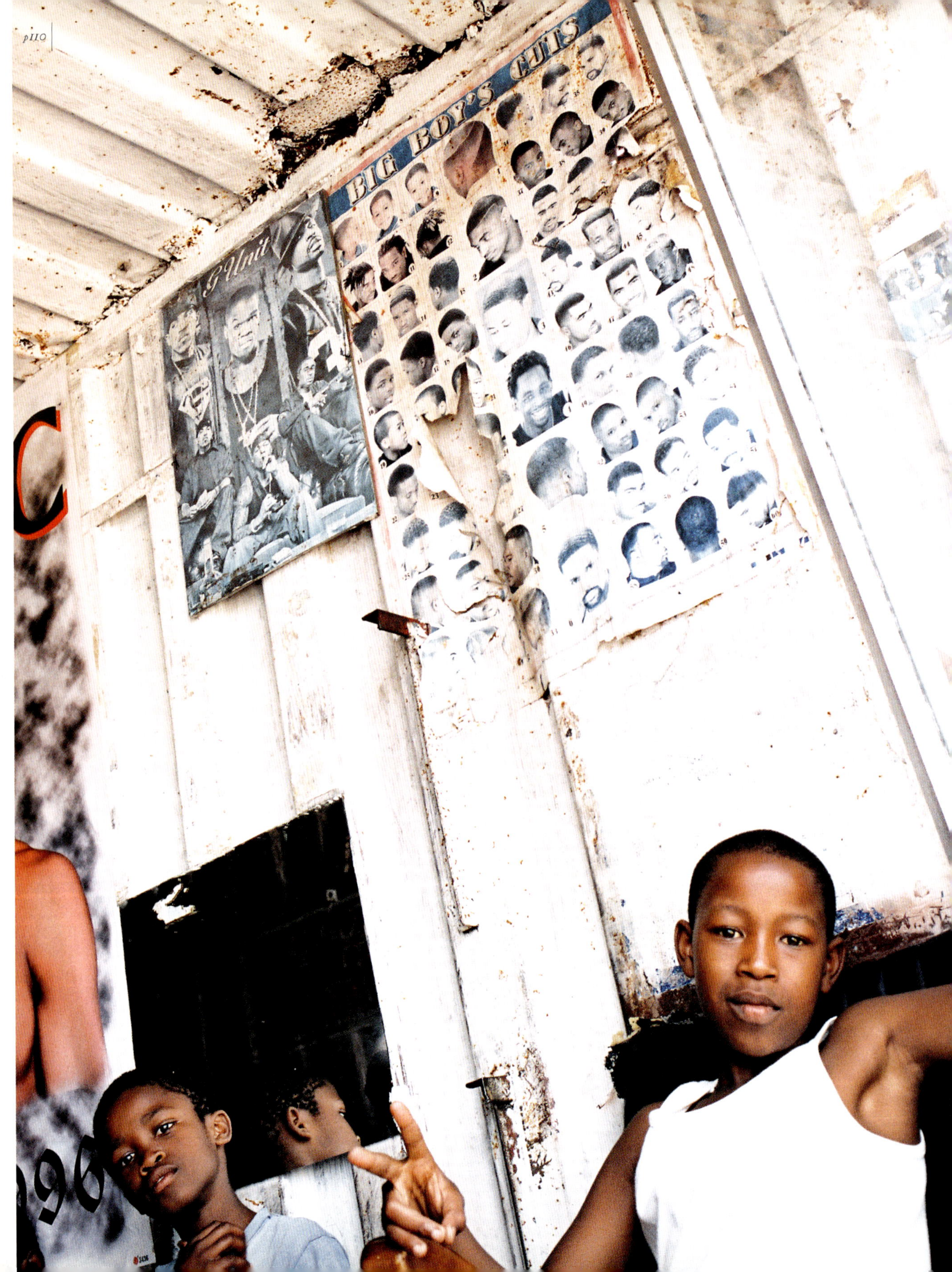
BIG BOY'S CUTS
G-Unit

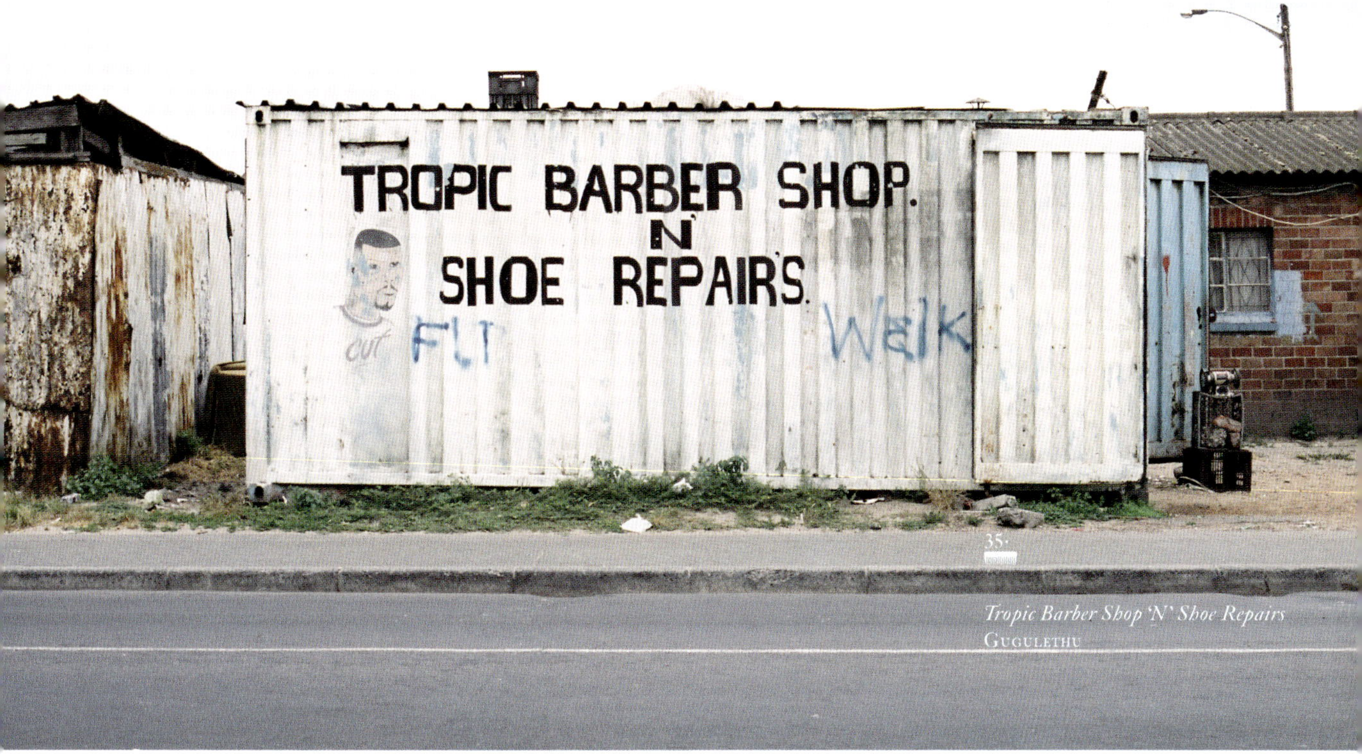

35.

Tropic Barber Shop 'N' Shoe Repairs
Gugulethu

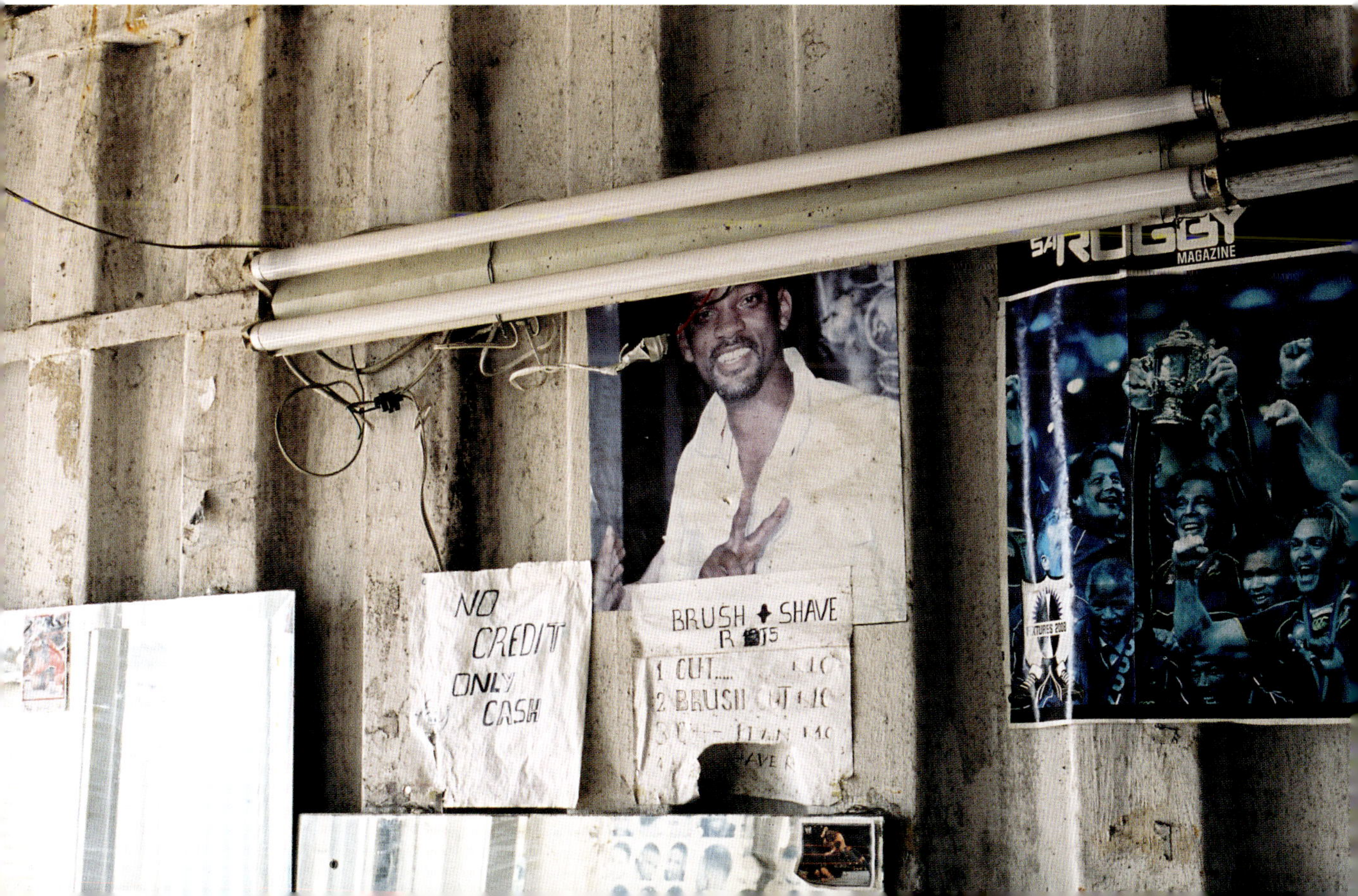

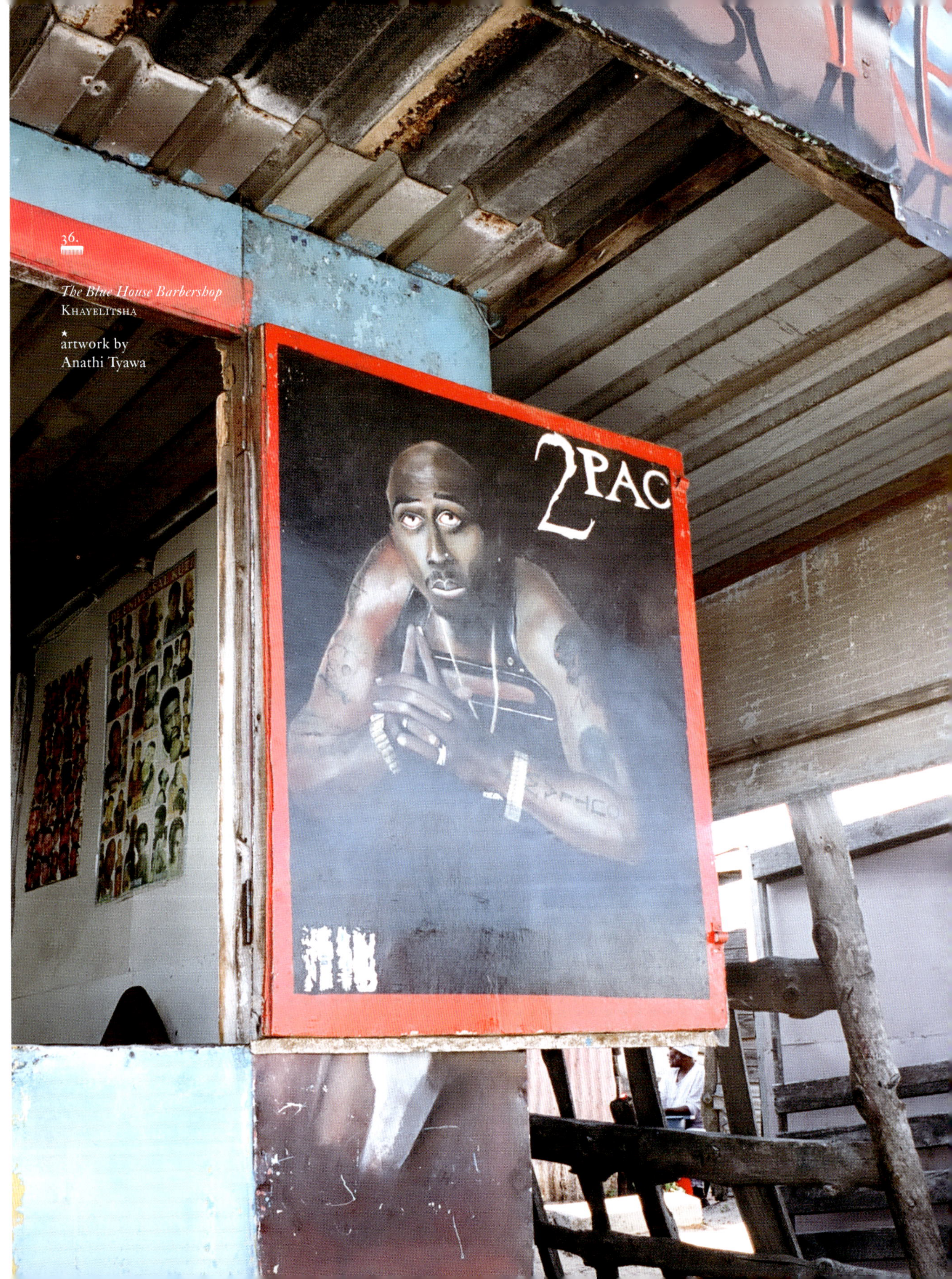

36.

The Blue House Barbershop
Khayelitsha

★
artwork by
Anathi Tyawa

4.3 KHAYELITSHA

I decide that it is time to extend my time in townships beyond day trips. I find a place to stay in Khayelitsha, eKasie Backpackers, which boasts the slogan "Come and feel the township vibe." When I arrive, after a harrowing drive, I learn that I am the sole guest. The young girl at reception tells me I have just missed a busy period and the guest book confirms this.

I am introduced to Victor, a local guide in his mid thirties, who agrees to show me the area's barbershops and salons. We visit the Blue House Barbershop, a shrine to the African American entertainment industry. The business is decorated with paintings and photographs of Usher, Kanye West, 50 Cent, P Diddy and Tupac Shakur (a hugely popular figure for black South Africans, but nowhere more than in Khayelitsha). What does it say about many of these young men that a Los Angeles rapper murdered in a hail of bullets in 1996 serves as an iconic figure for these townships? Victor assures me that a huge part of Tupac's appeal is simply the combination of his clean-shaved head, or Chizkop, and well kempt goatee, one of the most popular barbershop styles.

The Hollywood Barbershop is another business influenced by American culture. A beautifully painted portrait of what looks to me like the actor Will Smith hangs above the entrance to the shack. I start talking to Lucky, the owner and head barber, and compliment him on the artwork. "This is not Will Smith," he protests. "It is Martin Lawrence!"

I apologize and Lucky forgives my indiscretion. I ask him about the inspiration for the business's theme. "We saw the barbershops in the Hollywood movies," he explains, "and we try and take that style and bring it to South Africa. Here too the barbershop is a place where you can discuss the game that was played last night while you are waiting. We talk about a mixture of things that happen in our lives – politics, girls, cars, soccer and movies." Lucky goes on to talk about the importance of good artwork for his business. "It really helps to attract people. Anyone that walks past can see that it's a good barbershop. We attract the people from the outside, then when they come inside they just trust us."

A number of the informal township barbershops and salons have traded their unique signs for professional banners or billboards, advertising hair care products, soft drinks or cell phone companies. I ask Lucky if he would ever consider a commercial sponsor for his barbershop. He answers, "No, we don't promote Vodacom or Coca Cola. We promote ourselves. We don't need anybody's logo here. We wanted a different style from others as there are so many barbershops and salons here."

How is it possible for such a large number of barbershops and salons to survive when there are literally hundreds of businesses offering almost exactly the same service? In Khayelitsha it doesn't take long to see that the market is completely saturated and for every thriving business there is often another just down the street that has ceased operating.

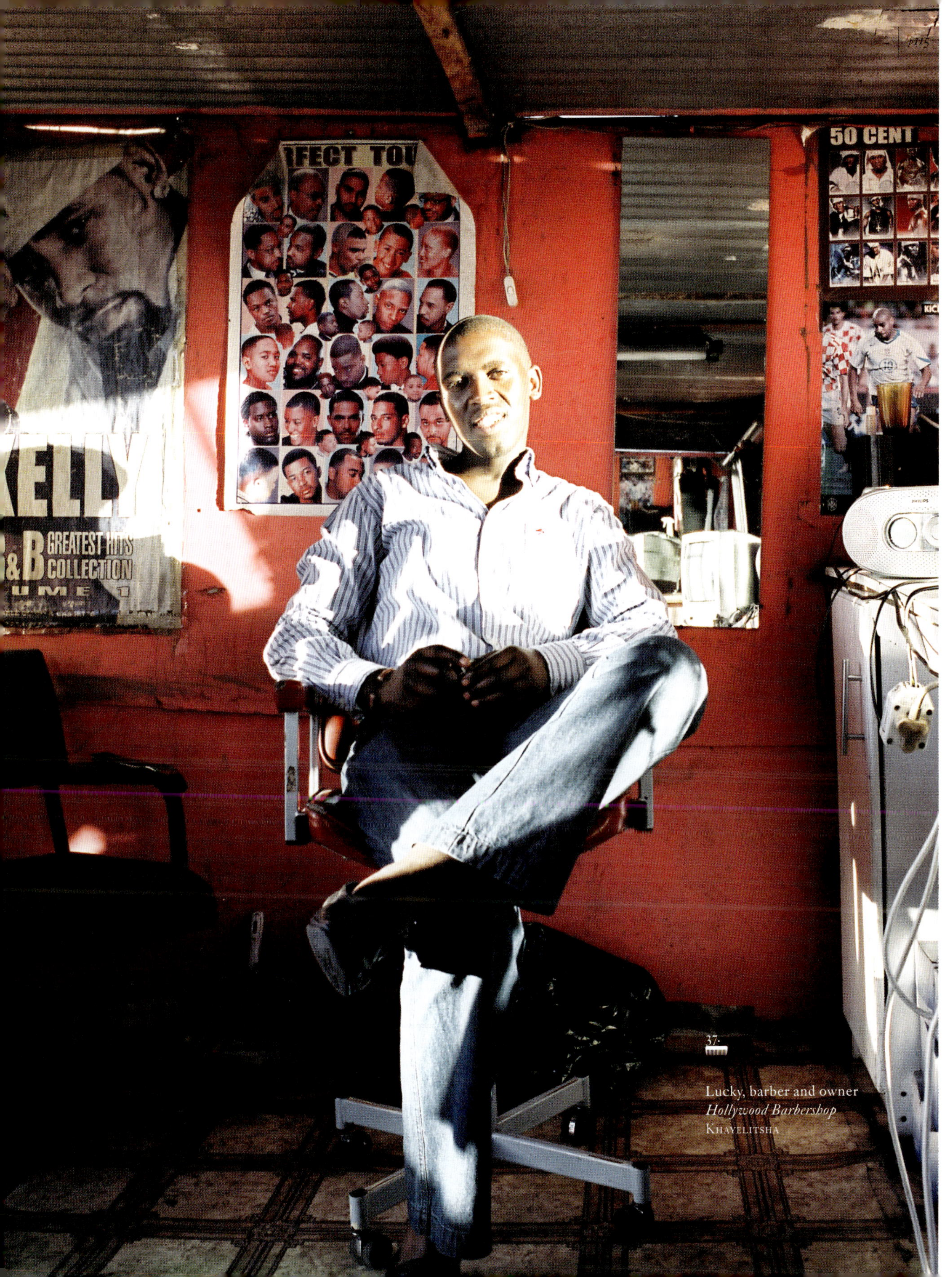

37.

Lucky, barber and owner
Hollywood Barbershop
Khayelitsha

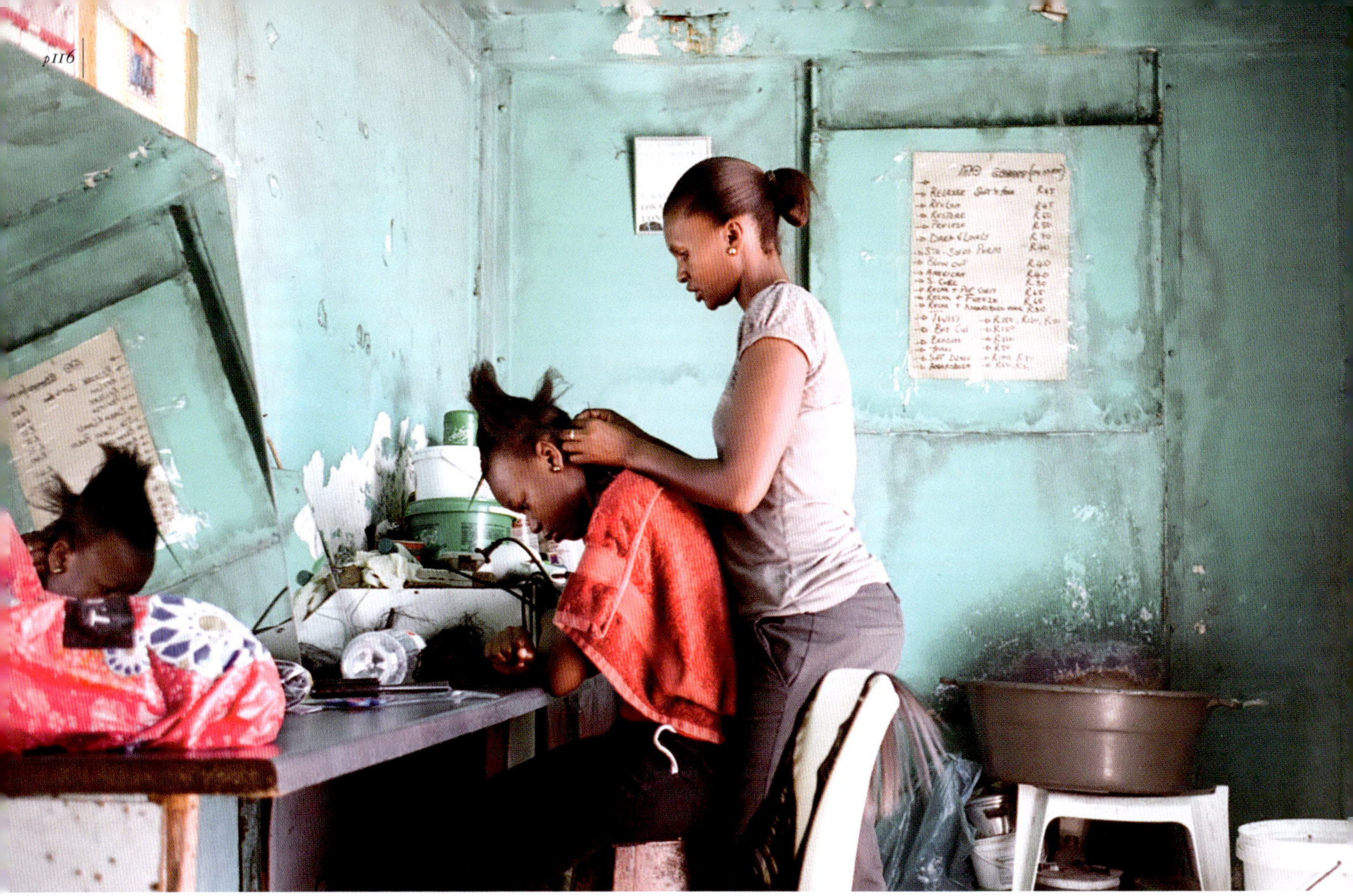

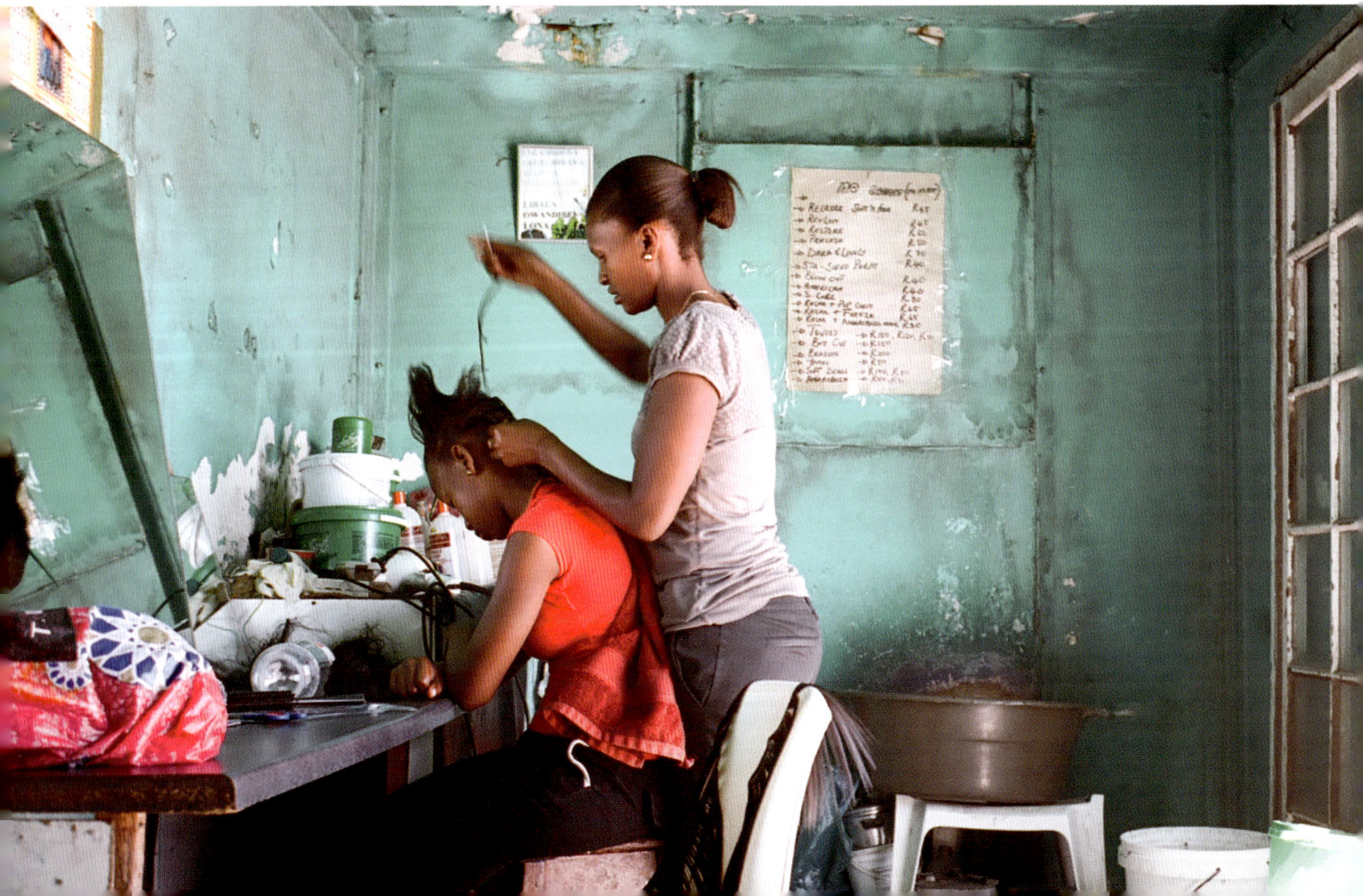

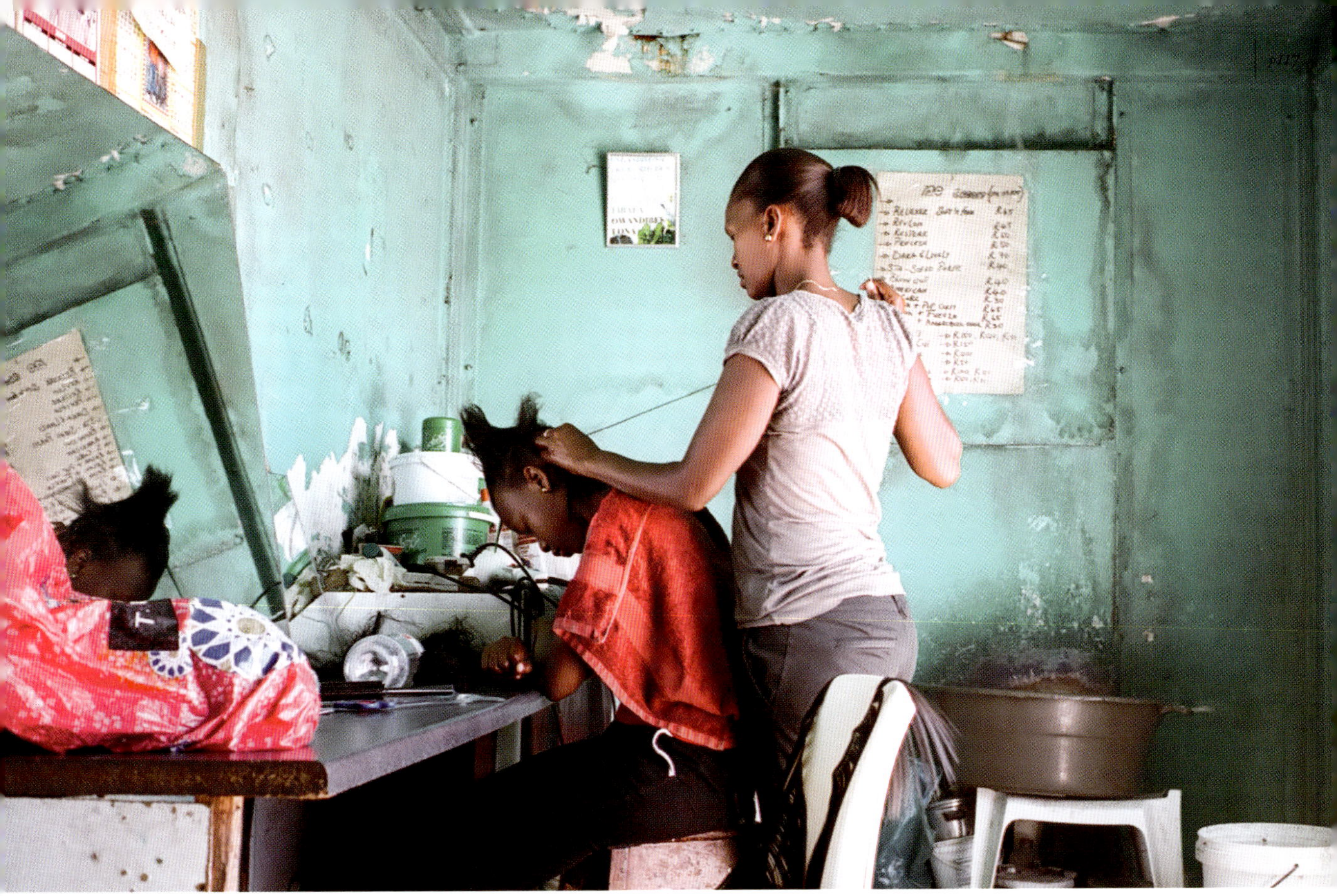

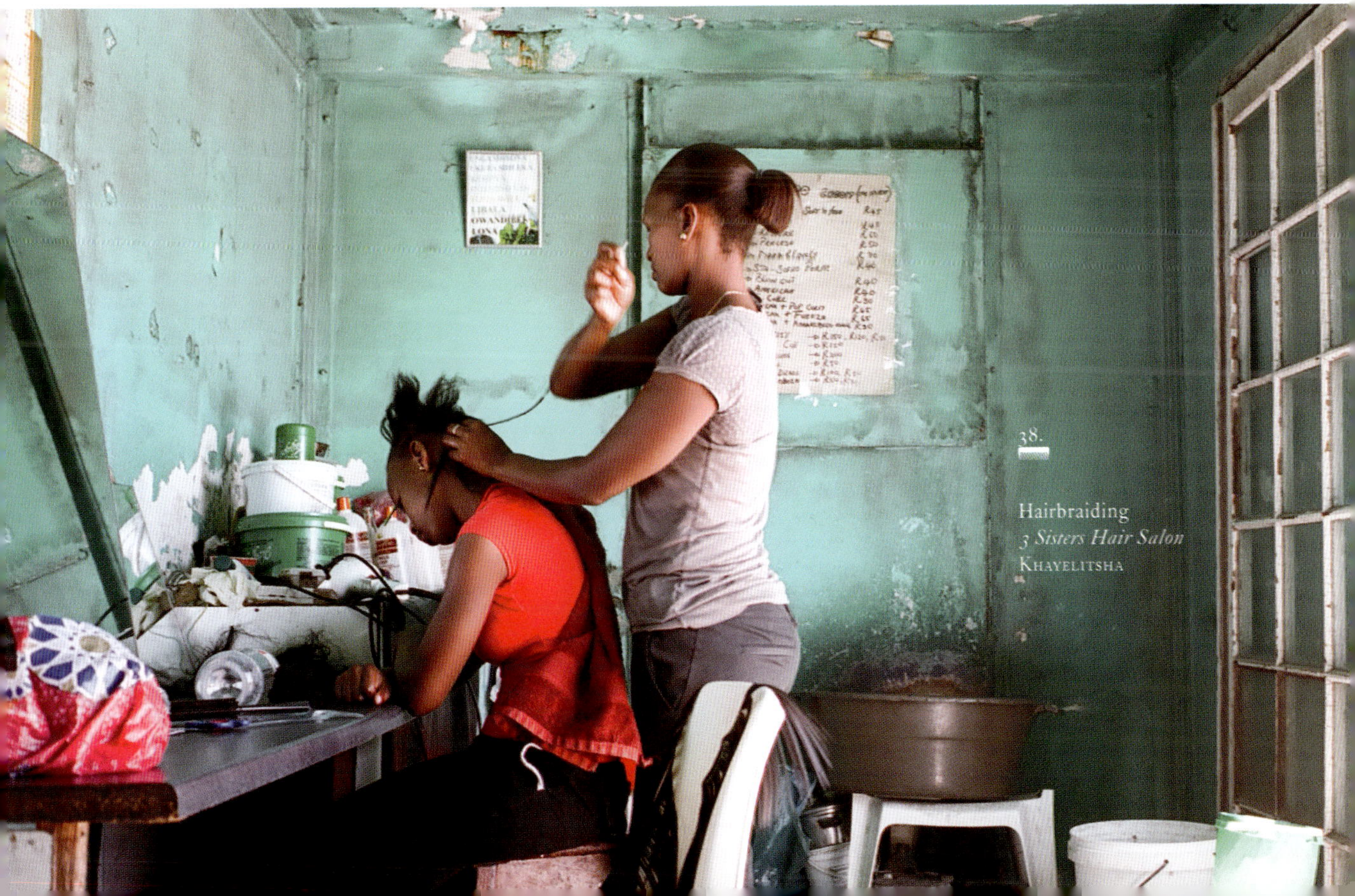

38.

Hairbraiding
3 Sisters Hair Salon
Khayelitsha

39.

3rd Class Hair Shop
Khayelitsha

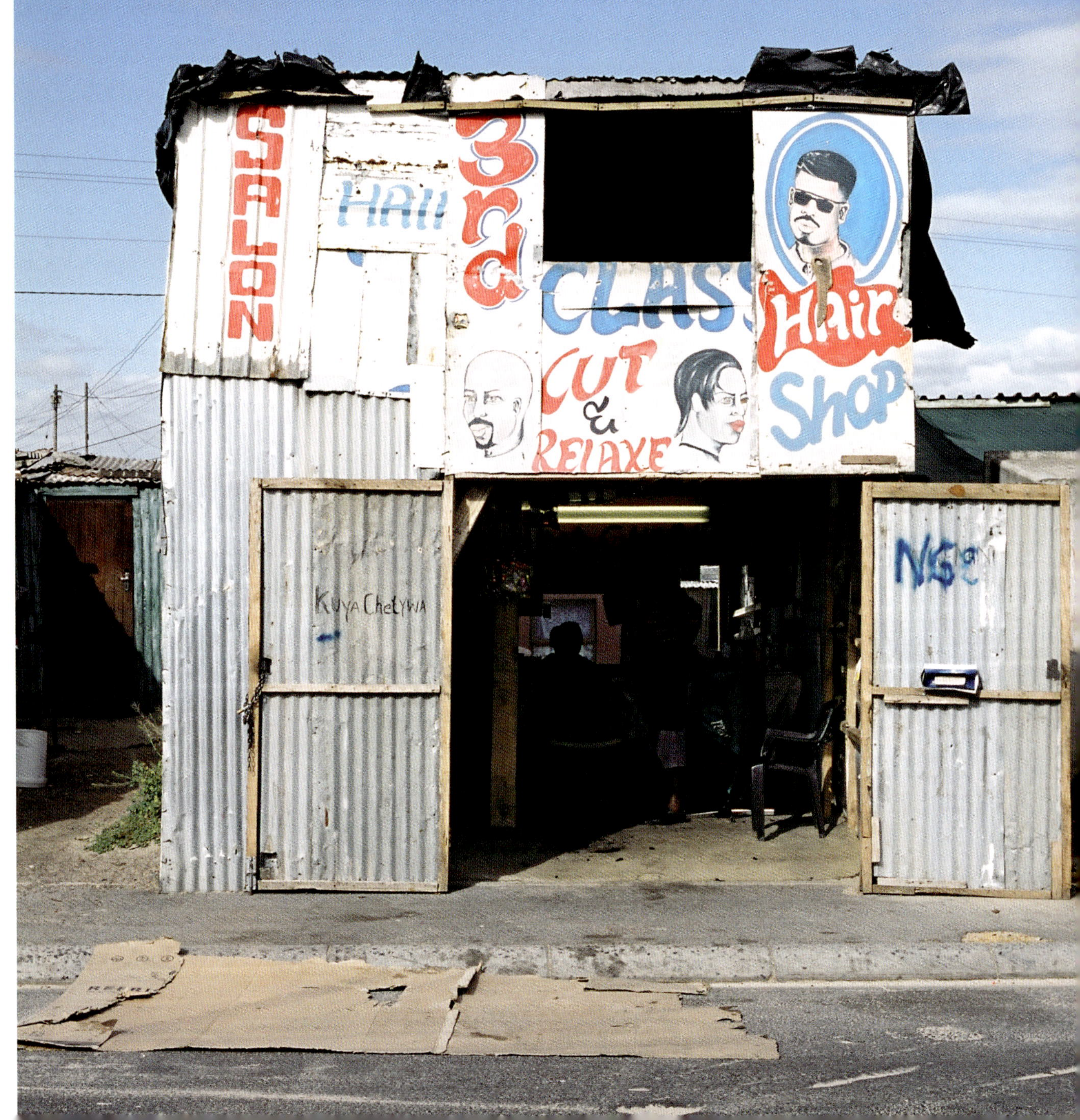

Later on I discover 3rd Class Hair Shop, which occupies a two-storey tin shack. As Lenox, the owner, shaves a grid style into a customer's hair he explains to me the significance of the shop's name: "It is because we are third-class citizens in our own country." While the Ghetto Hair Salon seems to derive from a similar political stance, Thabisa, the owner, informs me that the word "ghetto" is a source of pride in the townships. "The ghetto is a place that everybody loves," she says, "it's not a terrible word here."

My journey ends in Khayelitsha. On my last day I happen upon three of the best shipping container salons I have seen – one has a huge, rusting portrait of the controversial American R&B star R Kelly; just up the street the Serious Hair Saloon is open for business; and, finally, the salon with the most epic misspelling of the trip, Jugdement Day.

Victor and I decide to celebrate the end of my project with a visit to Mzoli's BBQ, the restaurant in Gugulethu where months before I had enjoyed my first township experience. When we arrive the place is buzzing. There is a diverse crowd of Cape Town locals, both black and white, as well as many tourists, everyone enjoying the beer, the televised soccer and the famous food. It is a glimpse of how perhaps things should be everywhere in the Rainbow Nation, an amazingly multicultural but divided country.

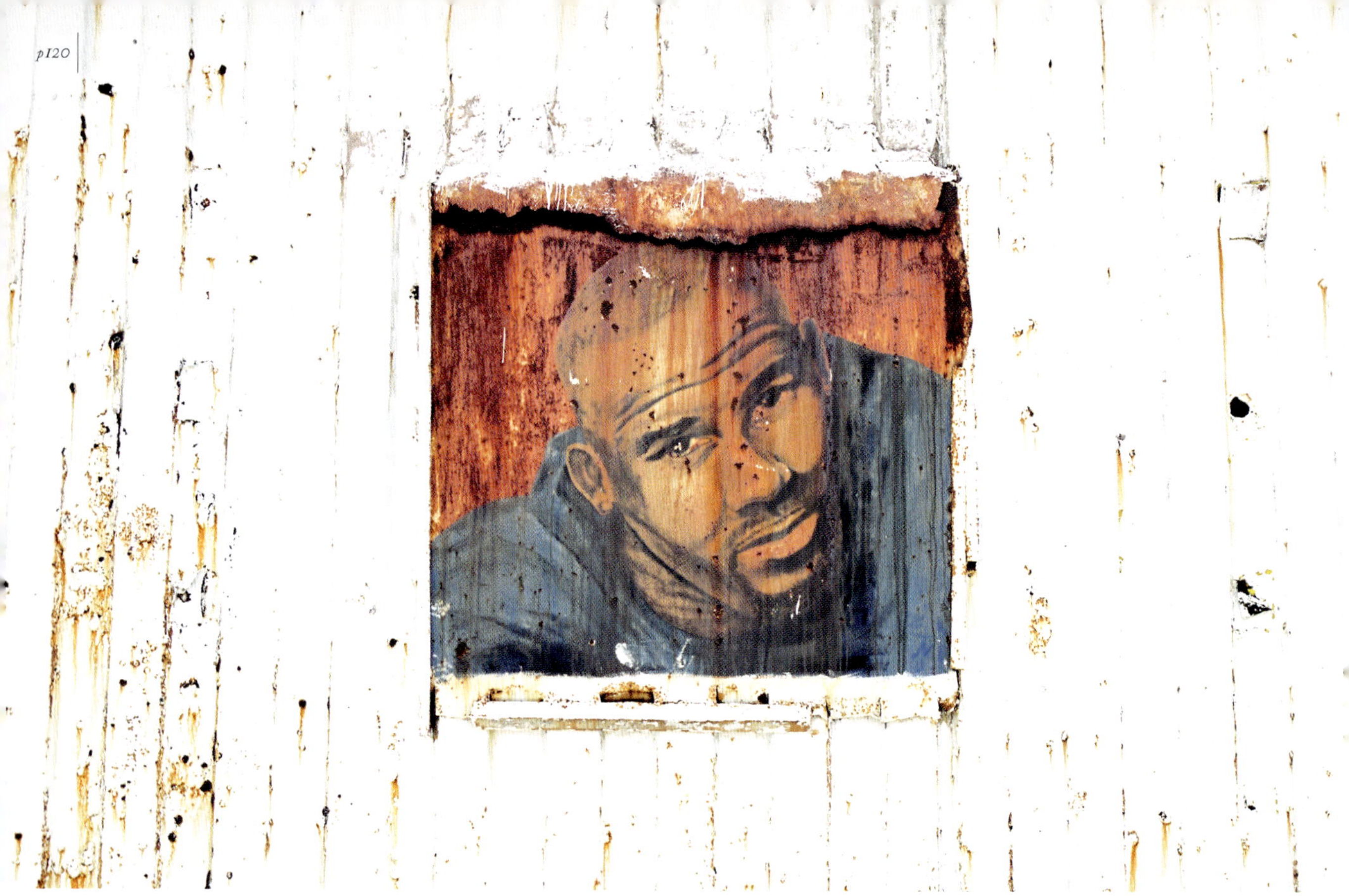

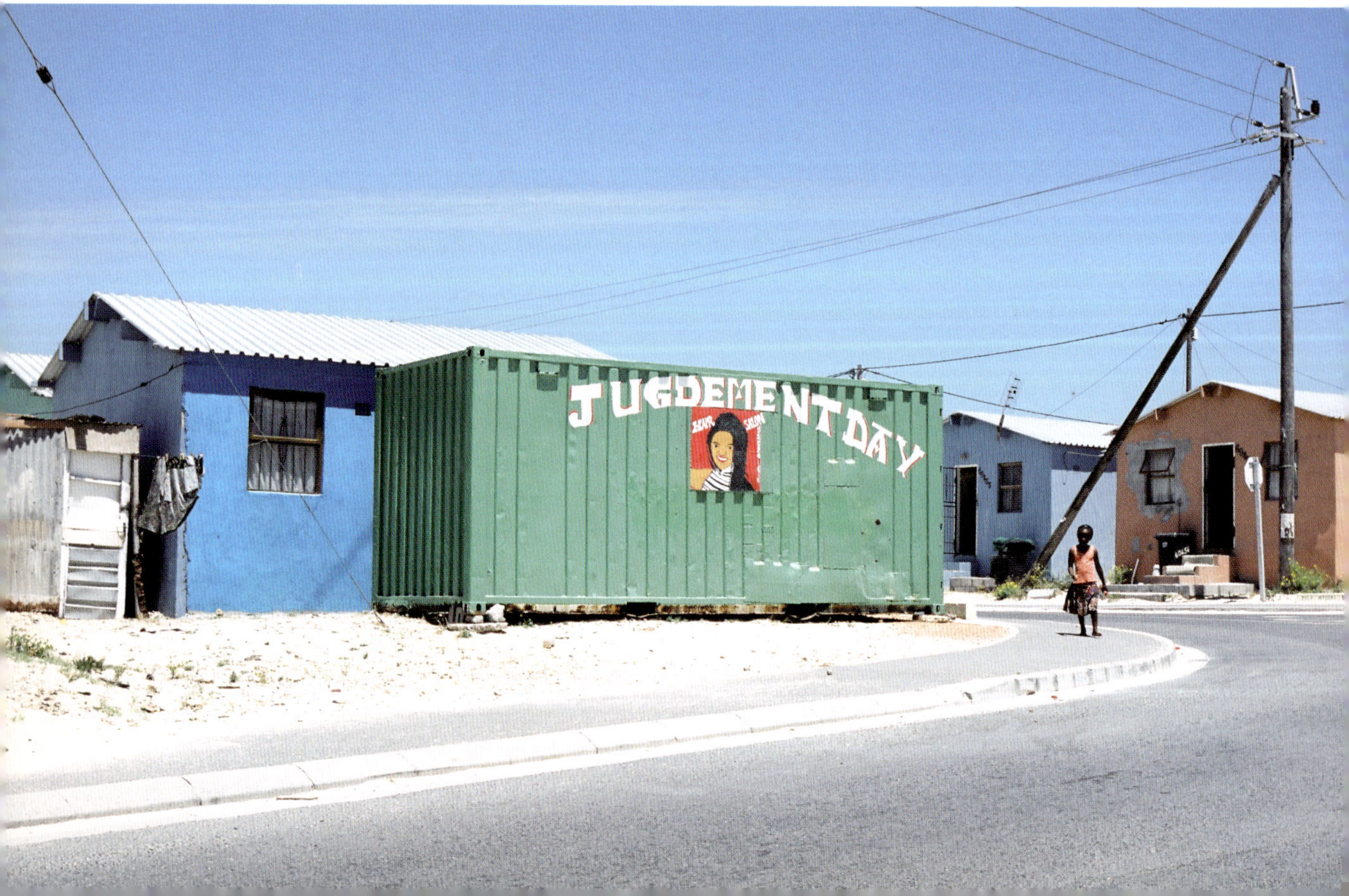

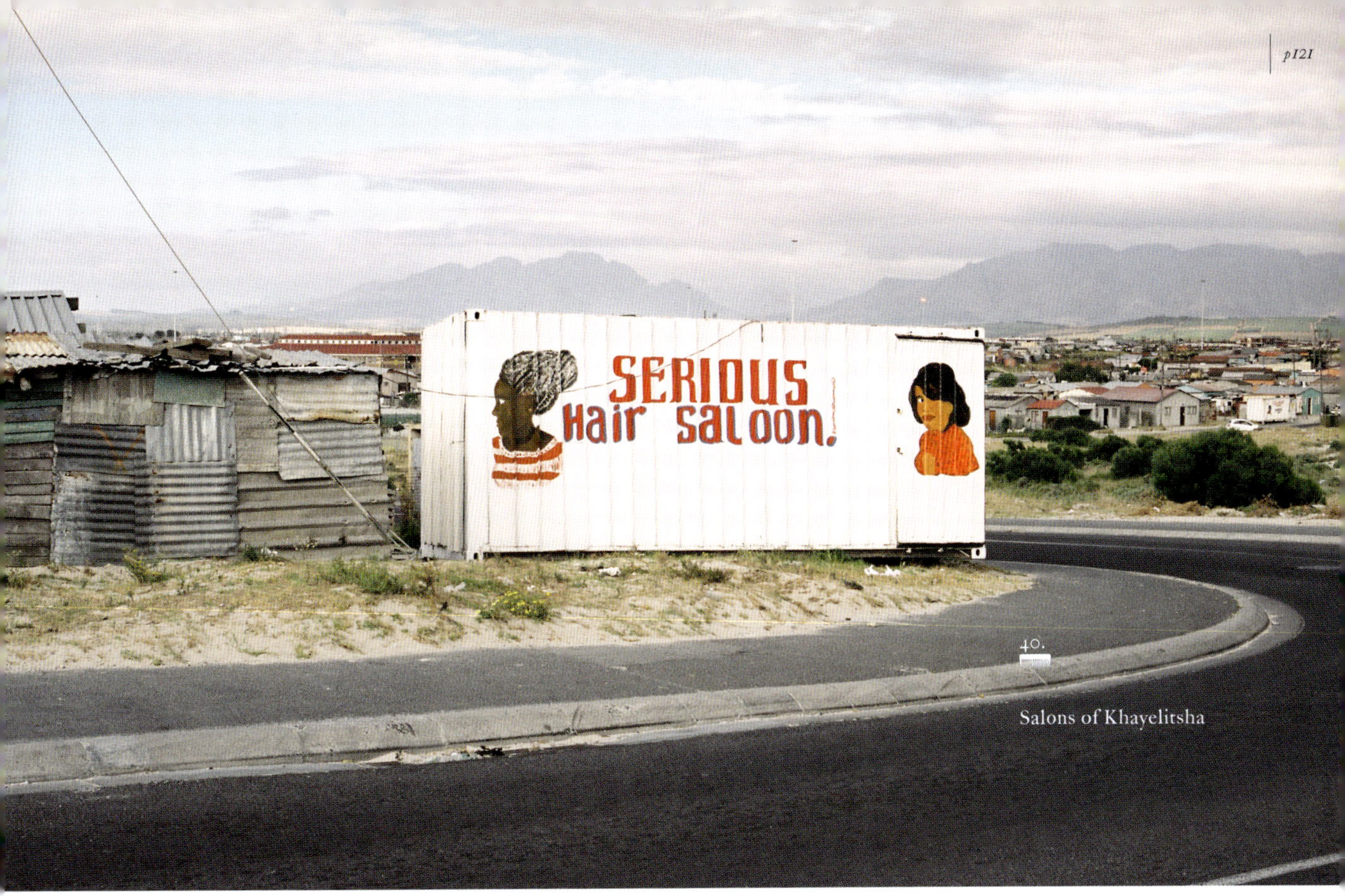

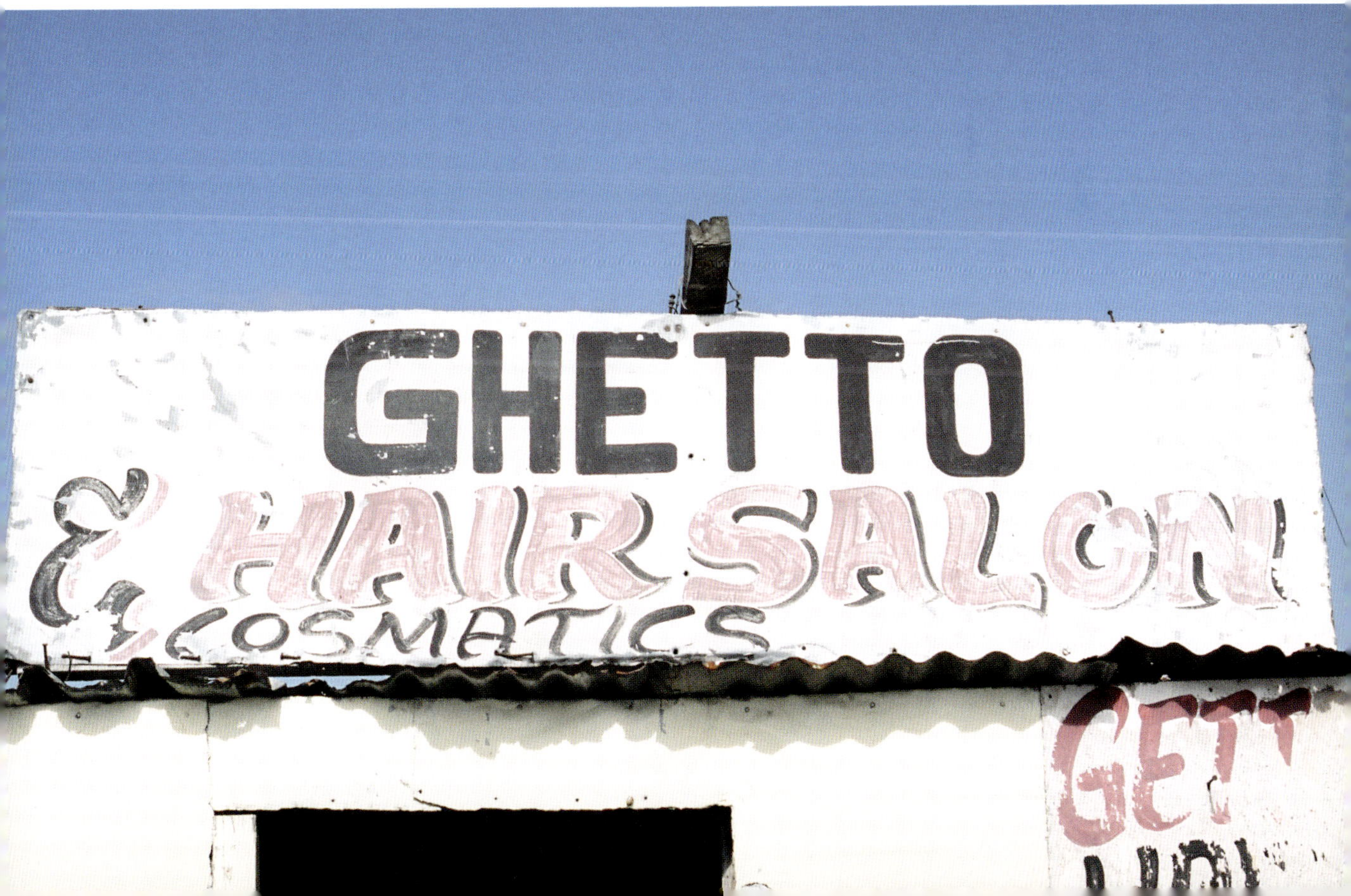

40.

Salons of Khayelitsha

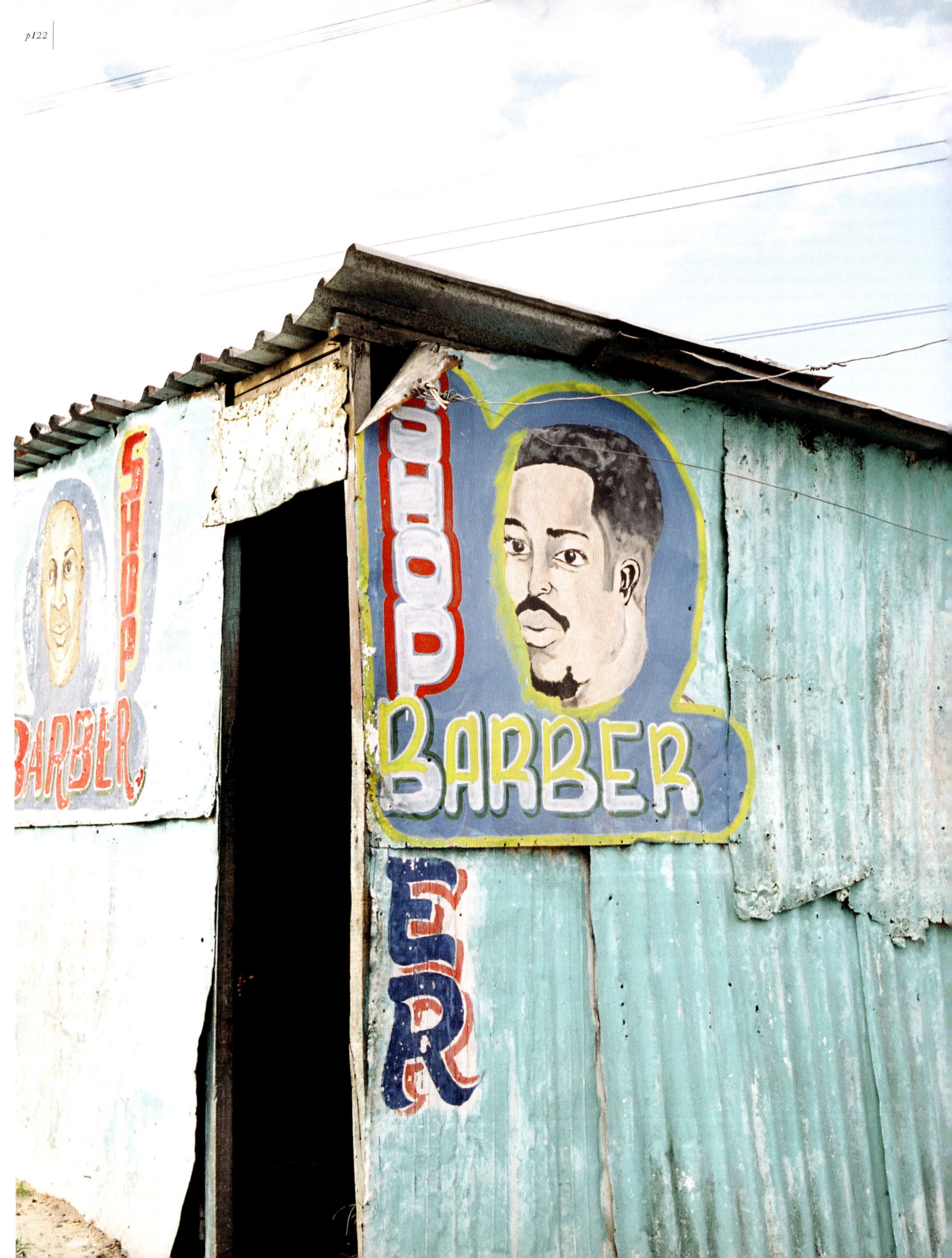
SHOP
BARBER
SHOP
BARBER
ER

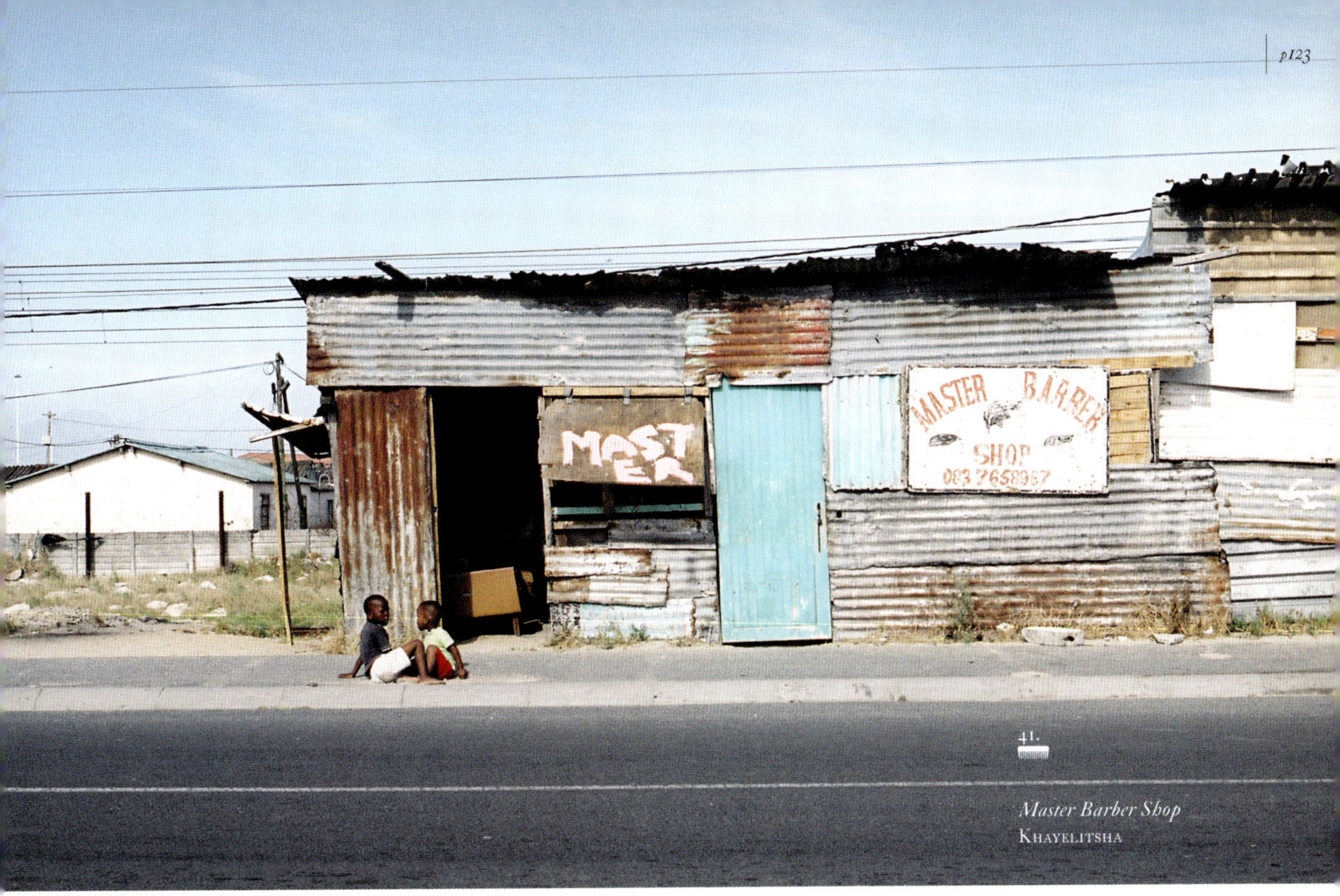

41.

Master Barber Shop
Khayelitsha

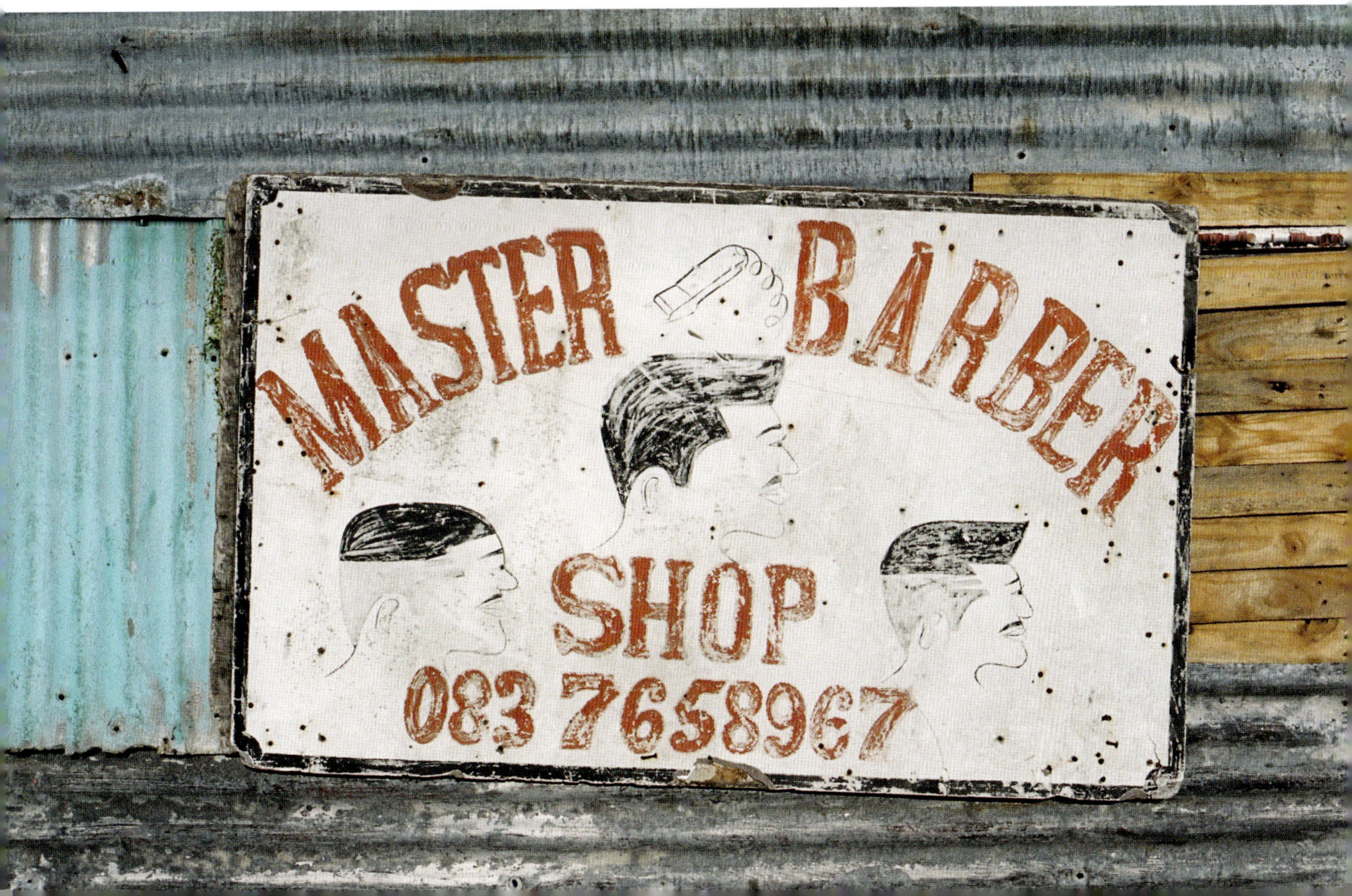

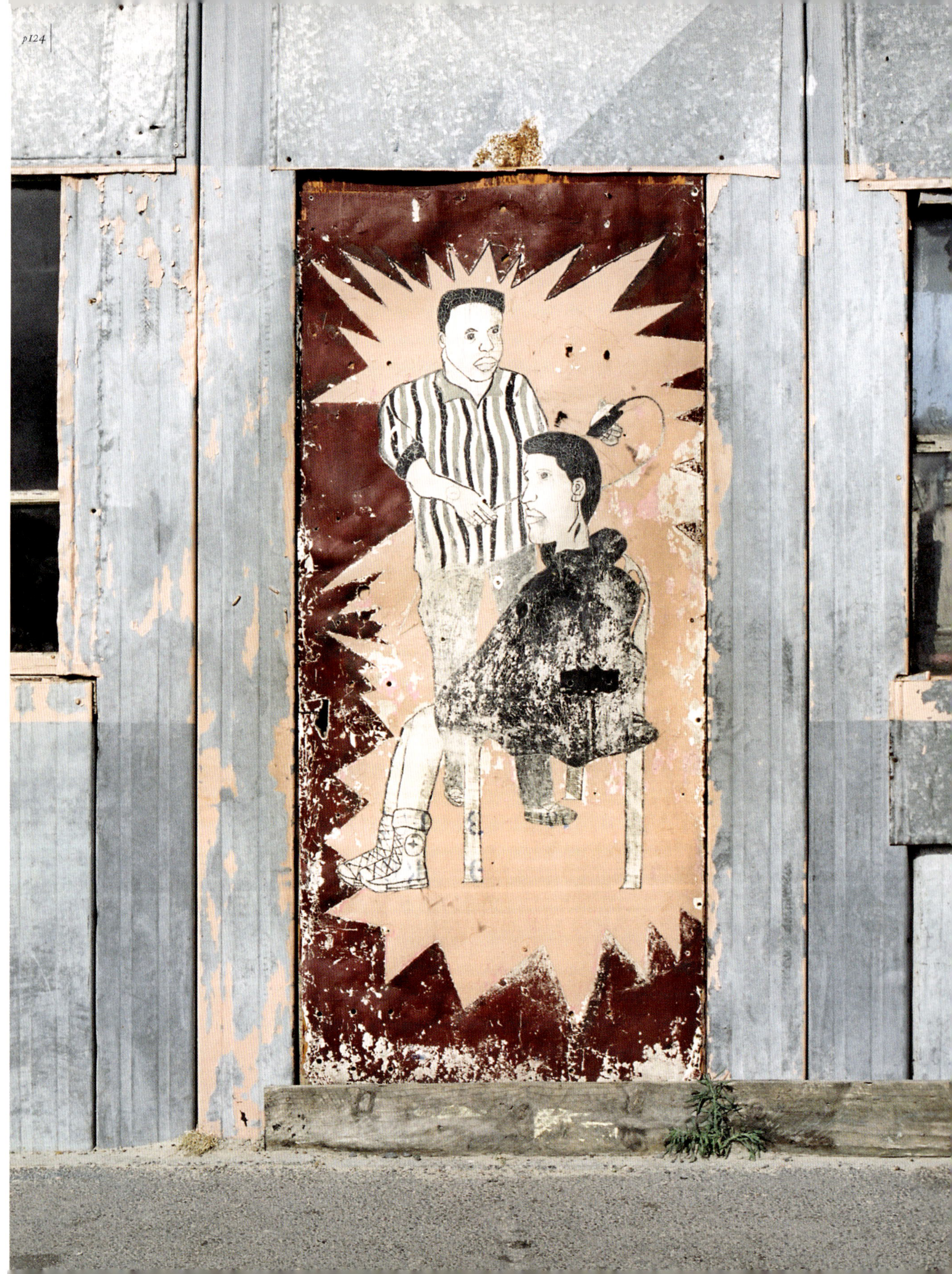

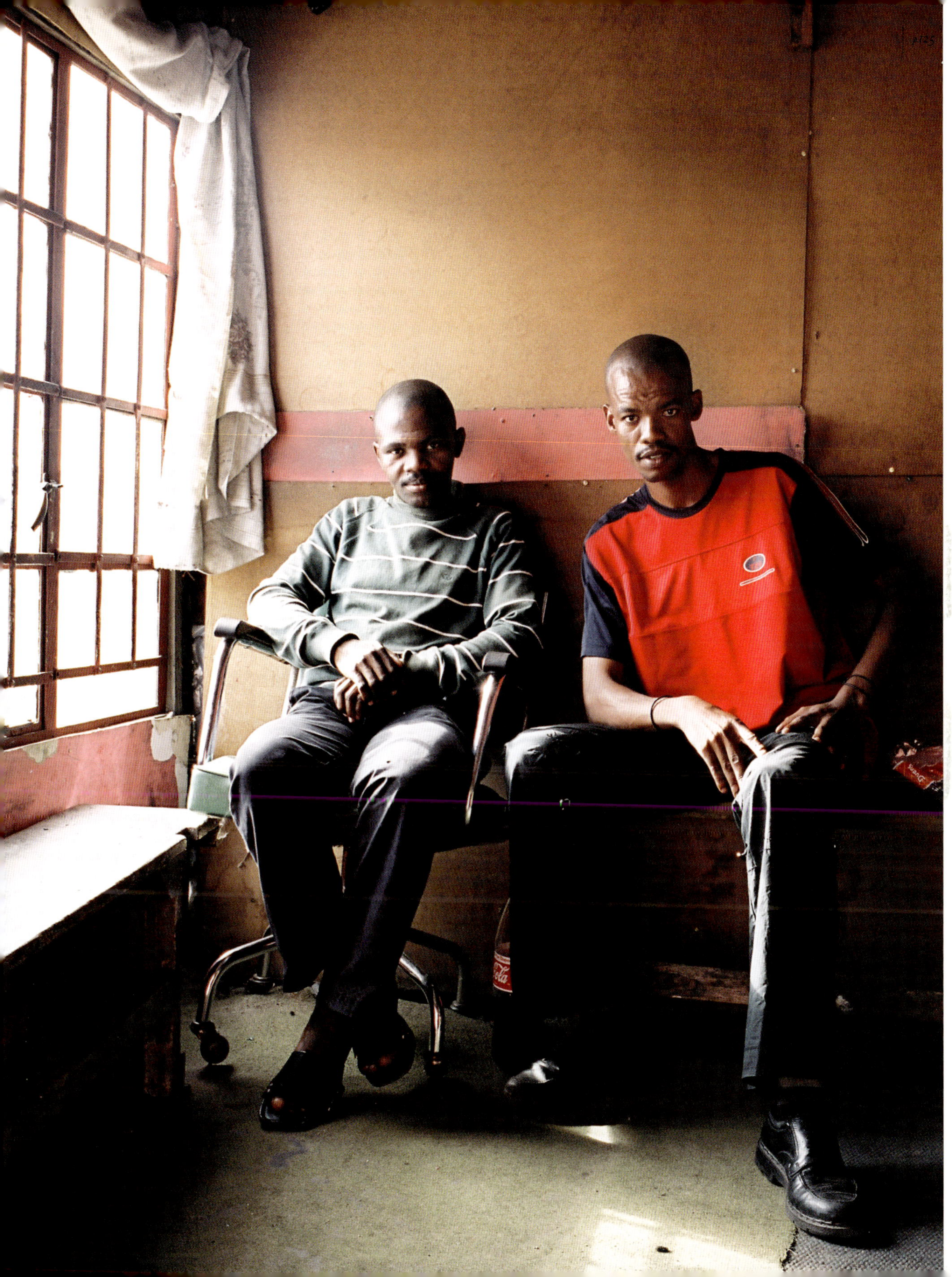

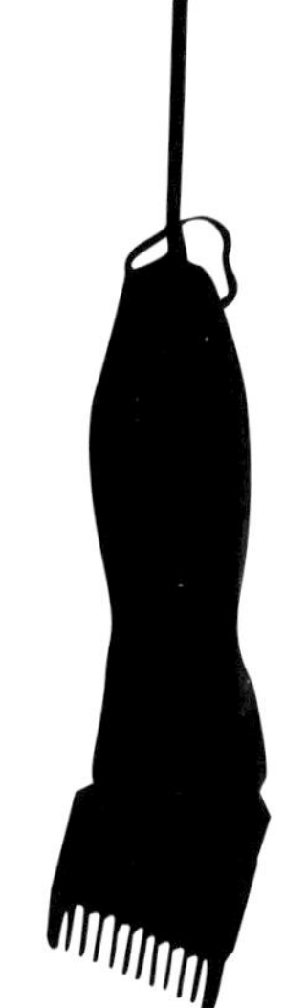

ACKNOWLEDGEMENTS –

To my family and friends too numerous to mention for their love, support and guidance over the years.

To Jo Shephard and Karim Rehmani-White who led me to MBP.

To Buzz Poole, Christopher D Salyers, Dejana Pupovac and all at MBP for their vision, which made this project a reality.

To Rudi and Sarah Jeggle for countless airport pick-ups and drop-offs, for housing me, feeding me and for opening my eyes to South Africa.

To Garth Walker for sharing his passion and knowledge of South African design.

To Mark Attwood at Art Prints SA for his great interview and help.

To the owners, staff and clients of the township barbershops and hair salons who welcomed me as a friend, not a stranger.

To my guides who helped me navigate their neighborhoods safely: Edwin "Dr Phil" Mkhonza (Tembisa), Treasure Sishi (Tembisa), Sello Matlala (Tembisa), Silindokuhle "Zama" Nongawuza (Soweto), Lungi Madi (Soweto), Kopano Kumalo (Alexandra), Vusi Ramothibe (Alexandra), Dennis Kgafane (Alexandra), Donald Moluleka (Soshanguve), Bongani Thabede (Umlazi), Abongile Gwabeni (Langa), Victor Yekiso (Khayelitsha).

To the township artists and sign writers who gave me insight into their craft: Chris Masekela (Soshanguve), Sipho "Smoky" Radebe (Soweto), Espoir Kennedy (Durban) Moses Magambo (Gugulethu), Anathi Tyawa (Khayelitsha), Simphiwe "Magic" Mxutu (Khayelitsha) and to the many more unknown artists whose work features in this book.

To Ross, Gavin and all Alyd Air, Cape Town International Airport.

To Mario and Michelle van Niekirk and the community of Heideveld.

To all at Lebo's Soweto Backpackers, Johannesburg.

To Dallas Oberholzer and everyone on the stoep at Musgrave Road.

To Toni Shina, Lee Harris, Brendan Tinsley, Sam Anderson and all the staff at The Backpack and Africa Travel Centre, Cape Town, for giving me a home away from home while I was in the city.

To all at eKasie Backpackers, Khayelitsha.

To Adrian Day, JJ Harris and everyone at Familia Skateboards, SA.

To Henry and all the staff at the film processing dept. at Orms Photograpic, Cape Town.

And finally, thank you to David Japhta for first taking me to Mzoli's in Gugulethu and introducing me to township life.

AUTHOR BIOGRAPHY –

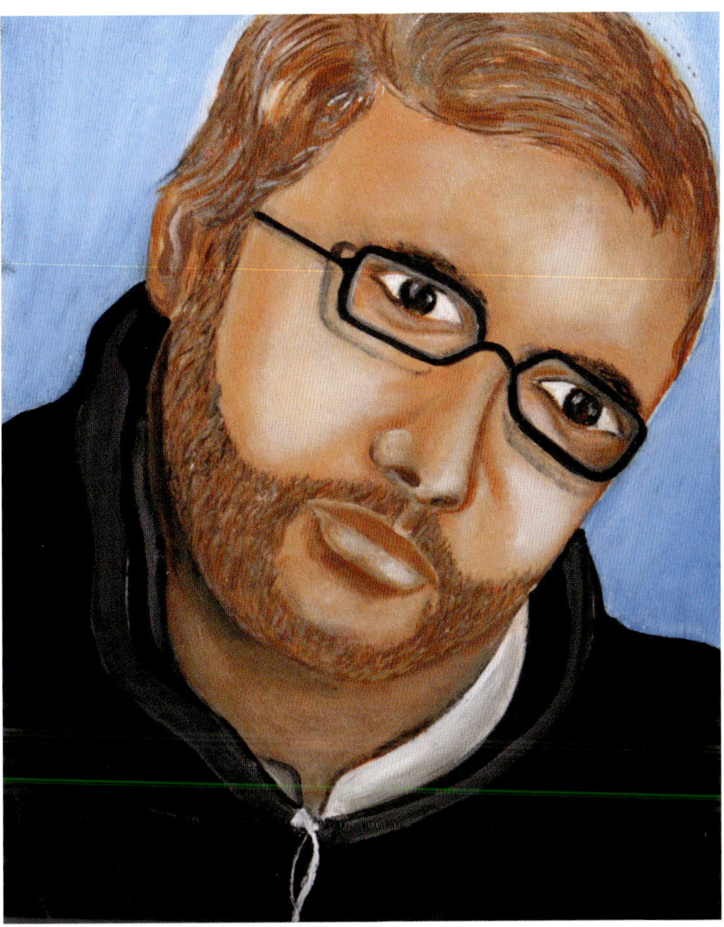

★
author portrait
by Moses Magambo
Gugulethu

Simon Weller graduated with a degree in graphic design from Staffordshire University. He worked as a cover designer in London for publishers Penguin Books and Harper Collins before becoming a freelance photographer in 2001.

His clients include Airstream, Channel 4 Television, EMI Records, Tate Gallery, Toyota and *Wired*. Simon's photographs are represented by Getty Images and Corbis. In the last decade he has photographed in China, India, Japan, Mongolia, Southeast Asia, Russia and the United States.

www.simonweller.com

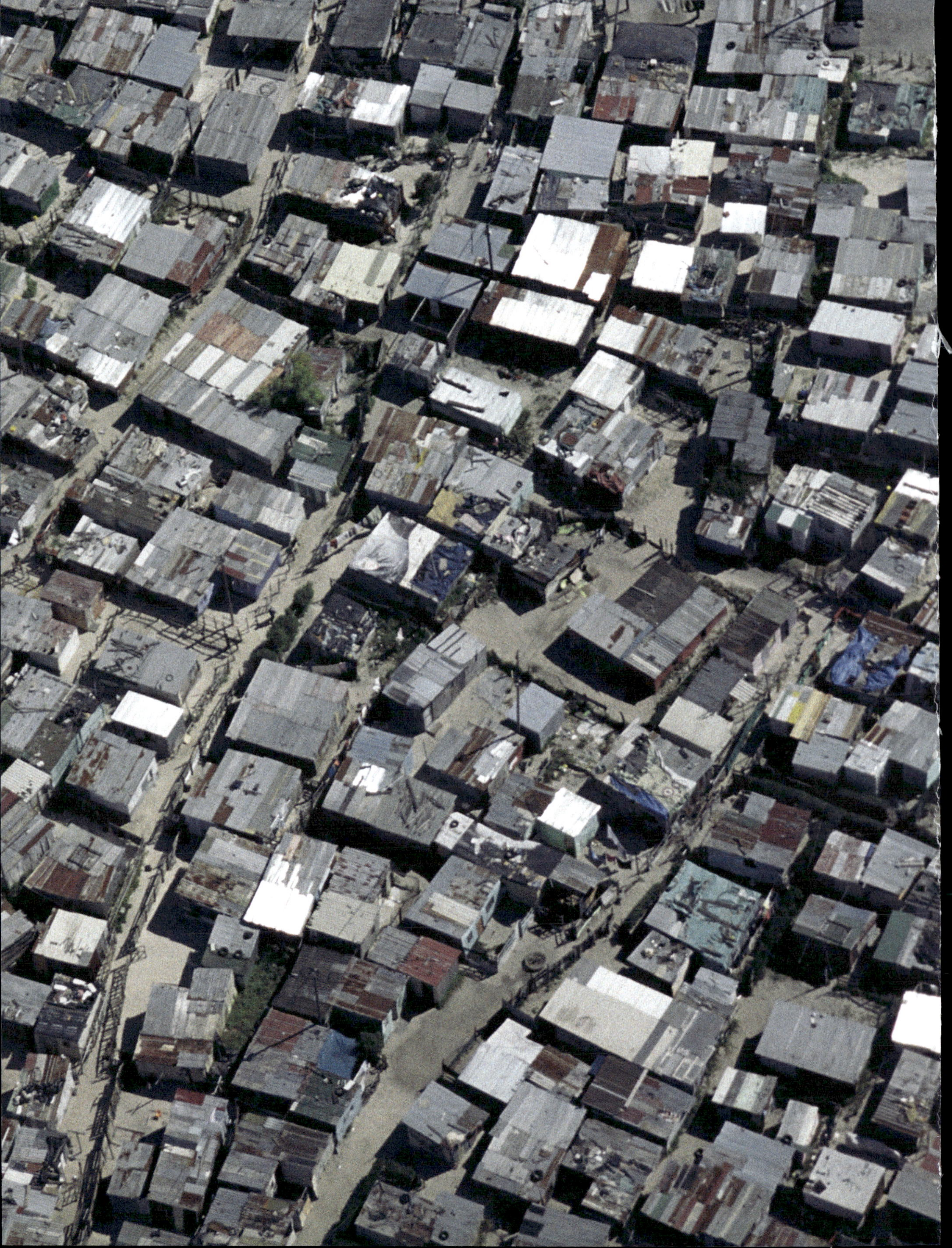